Hannah Arendt

Hannah Arendt is one of the great outsiders of twentieth-century political philosophy. After reporting on the trial of Nazi war criminal Adolf Eichmann, Arendt embarked on a series of reflections about how to make judgments and exercise responsibility without recourse to existing law, especially when existing law is judged as immoral. This book uses Hannah Arendt's text *Eichmann in Jerusalem* to examine major themes in legal theory, including the nature of law, legal authority, the duty of citizens, the nexus between morality and law and political action.

Peter Burdon is Associate Professor and Reader at Adelaide Law School, The University of Adelaide, Australia.

Nomikoi: Critical Legal Thinkers

Nomikoi: Critical Legal Thinkers presents analyses of key critical theorists whose thinking on law has contributed significantly to the development of the new interdisciplinary legal studies. Addressing those who have most influenced legal thought and thought about law, the aim of the series is to bring legal scholarship, the social sciences and the humanities into closer dialogue.

Other titles in the Series

Judith Butler: Ethics, Law, Politics
Elena Loizidou

Evgeny Pashukanis: A Critical Appraisal
Michael Head

Giorgio Agamben: Power, Law and the Uses of Criticism
Thanos Zartaloudis

Niklas Luhmann Law, Justice, Society
Andreas Philippopoulos-Mihalopoulos

Henri Lefebvre: Spatial Politics, Everyday Life and the Right to the City
Chris Butler

Carl Schmitt: Law as Politics, Ideology and Strategic Myth
Michael Salter

Althusser and Law
Edited by Laurent de Sutter

Deleuze & Guattari: Emergent Law
Jamie Murray

Bruno Latour: The Normativity of Networks
Kyle McGee

Zizek and Law
Edited by Laurent de Sutter

Roberto Esposito: Law, Community and the Political
Peter Langford

Jacques Derrida: Law as Absolute Hospitality
Jacques de Ville

Hannah Arendt: Legal Theory and the Eichmann Trial
Peter Burdon

Hannah Arendt

Legal Theory and the Eichmann Trial

Peter Burdon

Routledge
Taylor & Francis Group
LONDON AND NEW YORK

First published 2018 by Routledge

2 Park Square, Milton Park, Abingdon, Oxfordshire OX14 4RN
52 Vanderbilt Avenue, New York, NY 10017

Routledge is an imprint of the Taylor & Francis Group, an informa business

First issued in paperback 2019

British Library Cataloguing in Publication Data
A catalogue record for this book is available from the British Library

Library of Congress Cataloging in Publication Data
Names: Burdon, Peter, author.
Title: Hannah Arendt : legal theory and the Eichmann trial / By Peter D. Burdon.
Description: New York : Routledge, 2017. | Series: Nomikoi critical legal thinkers | Includes bibliographical references and index.
Identifiers: LCCN 2017018365 | ISBN 9781138193604 (hbk) | ISBN 9781315639277 (ebk)
Subjects: LCSH: Eichmann, Adolf, 1906-1962--Trials, litigation, etc. | Arendt, Hannah, 1906-1975. Eichmann in Jerusalem. | Law--Political aspects. | Holocaust, Jewish (1939-1945)--Historiography. | Trials (Genocide)--Jerusalem. | Collective memory--Political aspects.
Classification: LCC KMK44.E33 B87 2017 | DDC 340/.1--dc23
LC record available at https://lccn.loc.gov/2017018365

ISBN: 978-1-138-19360-4 (hbk)
ISBN: 978-0-367-23226-9 (pbk)

Typeset in Baskerville
by Taylor & Francis Books

And you have come, our precious enemy,
Forsaken creature, man ringed by death.
What can you say now, before our assembly?

– Primo Levi, 'For Adolf Eichmann' 1960

Contents

Acknowledgements

This book began as a reading group I initiated with friends and colleagues at the Adelaide Law School. Over the course of 2013 we met once a month to share food and discuss Arendt's report on the Eichmann trial. Unlike so much of academic life, the reading group was simply an opportunity to share each other's company and discuss ideas. So enjoyable was this experience that in 2015 I decided to teach legal theory using *Eichmann and Jerusalem* as the primary text. I have taught that course four times now (in Australia and Canada) and continue to be struck by the way the text brings people together and sparks debate. I am incredibly grateful to my friends and students who have shared this text with me and embodied Arendt's example of *humanitas*.

Because this book covers many professional areas I have benefited greatly from readers who generously gave their time to review chapters. In particular, I am thankful to Shani Burdon, Alex Reilly, Rebecca LaForgia, Joe McIntyre, Klaus Bosselmann, Gabrielle Appleby, James Martel and Ron Engel. Thank you also to David M. Seymour and Peter Goodrich, editors of the *Nomikoi Critical Legal Thinkers* series and Colin Perrin at Routledge. David provided invaluable comments and recommendations which helped pull this project together and link it more broadly to Arendt's other works. It was a pleasure working with an editor with such skill and patience.

Shani, thank you for your love, support, cutting intelligence, and for your counsel at several critical junctures of this book. Freya and Arlo thank you for encouraging me out of the study with games, adventures and cuddles.

This book is dedicated to my friend, Ron Engel. In my life Ron is a constant model of integrity. If Arendt had Jaspers as a mentor and correspondent, I have Ron.

Chapter 1

Introduction

The Eichmann fires

On 11 April 1961 the Israeli Government put Adolf Eichmann, a Nazi SS-Obersturmbannführer (lieutenant colonel), on trial in Jerusalem. Eichmann was responsible for transporting millions of Jews to extermination camps. The trial was set-up by the Israeli prosecution to be not just a trial of Eichmann but also a 'bearing witness' of the Holocaust. The prosecution called over 100 witnesses to testify, many of whom were survivors of the camps. For fourteen weeks the trial made international headlines. One of the trial's most famous observers was the political theorist Hannah Arendt. Arendt is one of the great outsiders of twentieth-century political philosophy: strikingly original and disturbingly unorthodox. At her request, Arendt reported her observations of the Eichmann trial for the *New Yorker*. These essays were then collated and published in her 1963 book *Eichmann in Jerusalem: A Report on the Banality of Evil.*

More than a half-century after its publication, Arendt's Eichmann book still manages to get under people's skin. In 2011 Arendt's biographer, Elisabeth Young-Bruehl (2011), was forced to defend old accusations that Arendt was not present at the trial to hear Eichmann testify.[1] More recently, the political theorist Seyla Benhabib (2014a) and the intellectual historian Richard Wolin (2014) engaged in a heated debate over Bettina Stangneth's (2015) biography of Eichmann and the extent to which Eichmann's motives could be characterised as banal.[2] During this exchange Wolin provided a partial explanation as to why the Eichmann fires continue to smoulder: 'Since Arendt's thesis has proved to be one of the most influential frameworks for understanding both the Holocaust and subsequent genocides, the interpretive stakes could not be higher.'

One reason Arendt's book continues to incite controversy is because it has eclipsed the trial itself. 'The book' writes political theorist Corey Robin (2015),

1 A close reading of Arendt's correspondence to her friends (Arendt and McCarthy 1995 and Arendt and Jaspers 1992) and husband (Arendt and Blucher 2000) suggest that she did see Eichmann testify. See further Robin (2014) and Benhabib (2014b).

2 Stangneth's book is the latest in a series arguing that Eichmann was more of an anti-Semite than Arendt had realised. See further Cesarani (2006), Safrian (2009) and Lipstadt (2011).

'has become the event.'[3] This is exceedingly rare, but one finds analogies in other books about trials. Consider Plato's (2002) rendering of the defence of Socrates; the portrait of child killer Mary Bell detailed by Gitta Sereny (1999); or Helen Garner's (2015) patient struggle to understand filicide in the trial of Robert Farquharson. As these examples illustrate, skilled authors have managed to get beyond the technical, arcane and at times boring event of a trial and produce a narrative that is compelling and provides insight beyond the narrow bounds of legal procedure. The author can ask questions or consider context that is considered immaterial or perhaps prejudicial in a criminal trial.

But this is only part of the story. Other controversial books are challenged and debated. Arendt's Eichmann book is different: '[i]ts errors and flaws, real and imagined, have not consigned it to the dustbin of history; they are perennially retrieved and held up as evidence of the book's viciousness and its author's vice' (Robin 2015). Arendt's critics regard her as a criminal in the dock. A subject to be judged and found wanting for the very crime she accuses Eichmann – a thoughtless disregard for the Jewish people. This judgment was primarily levelled at her comments on the role of the Jewish Councils (Judenräte) and Jewish collaborators in the Shoah.[4] In response, Arendt was accused of blaming the victims or as Deborah Lipstadt (2011: 173) argued – for seeing a 'symmetry between the Nazis and their victims where there was none'.[5]

Like other historical controversies, the conflict over *Eichmann in Jerusalem* reveals as much about our current political moment as it does about either Arendt or Eichmann. What then is it about our current preoccupations and political challenges that makes Arendt's book pertinent for a contemporary reader? Answering that question will occupy most of this book. For now, I wish to highlight the way Arendt's argument in *Eichmann* threatens attempts to position the Holocaust as a touchstone upon which political life is constructed.

One of the earliest attempts to position the Holocaust as a foundation or touchstone for morality was conducted by Robert Wuthnow, a sociologist from Princeton University. Wuthnow (1987) described the mass viewing of NBC's 1978 *Holocaust* television series as a 'public ritual' which dramatised the moral chaos and breakdown that many Americans feared and offered reassurance that good and evil could be clearly differentiated (Novick 2000: 233). The programme aired

3 See also Stangneth (2015: xxii): 'Ever since *Eichmann in Jerusalem: A Report on the Banality of Evil* was published in 1963, every essay on Adolf Eichmann has also been in a dialogue with Hannah Arendt.'

4 See for example Arendt (2006a: 123). As a counter to Arendt, Bauer (2002) argues that Jews were slaughtered often with greater speed when there was no cooperation with Jewish leadership. Consider for example the slaughter carried out by the Einsatzgruppen following the German invasion of the Soviet Union. See further Rabinovici (2011).

5 See also Wolin (2014) 'Arendt made it seem as though it was the Jews themselves, rather than their Nazi persecutors, who were responsible for their own destruction.' This is an old charge and could only be rendered from the most uncharitable and selective reading of Arendt's study of the Eichmann trial.

amidst a series of great moral challenges in American political life – including the Vietnam War, racial violence and the Watergate scandal. Many Americans thought the country had 'gotten on the wrong track' (Novick 1999: 233) and Wuthnow's research found a strong correlation between individuals' search for a moral order and the Holocaust. Wuthnow (quoted in Novick 1999: 234; 1987: 130; Robin 2015) described his findings as follows:

> Whether someone was politically liberal, moderate, or conservative, that person was more likely to be interested in the Holocaust if he or she perceived serious problems in the moral order … It was the Holocaust as symbol of ever present evil rather than the Holocaust as historical event that was of interest to persons troubled about the moral fabric.

While Wuthnow's study was restricted to one television series, Peter Novick (1999: 234) provides convincing evidence that the Holocaust came to represent a symbol for 'anxiety about moral chaos and social disarray and a yearning for firmer moorings'. He quotes for example leaders of the Washington Holocaust Museum who described the Shoah as providing a 'moral compass' for the nation. A reporter from the *Boston Globe* explained the success of the museum as follows:

> In an era of moral relativity, the Holocaust museum serves as a lodestone. Here there is no rationalization … Here is an absolute. And in that absolute of Evil, maybe, the prospect of an absolute Good … We live amid the ruins of 'the modern' – the era in which Western man discarded age-old standards and creeds and placed his faith in science … [Americans] flocking to the Holocaust museum are searching for answers – in the form of moral certainties … The Holocaust museum offers a basic moral foundation on which to build: a negative surety from which to begin (Novick 1999: 234; Robin 2015).

Arendt's thesis on the *banality of evil* is so controversial because she rejects attempts to characterise the Holocaust in demonic terms or as the personification of evil.[6] Rather, for Arendt the Holocaust was strictly a historical event, carried out by thousands of individuals with discrete biographies and motivations. Arendt elaborated on this point in an oft-quoted letter to Gershom Scholem: 'It is indeed my opinion that evil is never "radical", that it is only extreme, and that it possesses neither depth nor any demonic dimension' (Young-Bruehl 2004: 369). Arendt has endured decades of criticism and slander for demystifying evil and giving it a human face. Wolin (2014) captures perfectly a contemporary example of that criticism:

6 In constructing her description of the banality of evil Arendt was influenced by Gray (1998). I am indebted to Ron Engel for this insight.

> [I]f Eichmann was 'banal', then the Holocaust itself was banal. There is no avoiding the fact that these two claims are inextricably intertwined.

Is Wolin correct? There does not appear to be any necessary connection between the two propositions he cites. However, if we can inhabit his train of thought for a moment several fundamental questions arise: if the Holocaust is banal, on what foundation can we build a moral and juridical order? Moreover, if the Holocaust is displaced as a lodestone for political action, what does this mean for the founding narrative and legitimating discourse for the State of Israel (Butler 2014: 25, 132; Finkelstein 2015)? As Robin (2015) notes: 'if it can be shown that anti-Semitism was not present in the nadir of Jewish history [a claim that Arendt did not make[7]], what justification can there be for a Jewish-state today'?

This is really where the rubber hits the road and connects to Arendt's long and complicated history with Zionism. Very few (least of all, Arendt) would deny that Jewish victims of the Second World War required refuge and a sanctuary for protection. But as Arendt's (2008) early writings illustrate there was a robust debate about where the Jewish refugees wanted to go and what political aspirations they had.[8] This should not be surprising but as Idith Zertal (2005) illustrates, alternative narratives have been subsumed to the point that most people now believe that the Shoah naturally resulted in the creation of the State of Israel and that the State depended on those principles of Jewish sovereignty and political Zionism expressed by David Ben-Gurion. To complicate matters further, Judith Butler (2014: 25) contends that 'many now assume that any criticism of Israel contributes to the delegitimation of the state and so seeks to reverse that historical casualty and to open the Jewish people to a new destruction, figured as the Nazi genocide time and again.'

These issues are what motivate current debates about Arendt's report on the Eichmann trial. And it is not surprising – particularly as Israel continues to cite the Holocaust in justification of policies ranging from militarised settler colonialism, settlement expansion into the Palestinian territories and proposed amendment to Israel's basic laws to insist Israel is 'the nation state of one people only – the Jewish people – and of no other people' (Ravid *et al.* 2014). We do not need to look far to see what Arendt would have to say about these developments (Arendt 2008). Her work continues to provide tools for those seeking to 'locate sites of contingent emergence' and think outside the 'narrative lockdown' imposed by the dominant historical, political and legal discourse (Butler 2014: 25).

7 Writing just after the Eichmann trial Arendt (2005b: 43) stated: 'These mass murderers acted consistency with a racist or anti-Semitic, or at any rate a demographic ideology.'

8 See also Grodzinsky (2004).

Direction

The primary purpose of this book is to introduce law students, university academics and organic intellectuals to Arendt's book on the Eichmann trial and, through that book, to her broader oeuvre. While virtually all of Arendt's writing deals with some aspect of the law, there is a striking gap in the secondary literature regarding her treatment of law and legal theory (Bernstein 2013: vi). Indeed, Christian Volk (2010: 759) recently observed that while the question 'what is politics?' has been explored exhaustively from an Arendtian perspective, the question 'what is law?' has been neglected. To date, the only sustained and focused treatment of Arendt and the law was published in a remarkable volume edited by Goldoni and McCorkindale (2013a).[9]

My direction in this book is unique. I use the structure of *Eichmann in Jerusalem,* as a platform to examine major themes in contemporary legal theory. Specifically, Chapters 2–10 will mirror the chapter outline constructed by Arendt. In most instances, I have collapsed two or more of Arendt's chapters and extracted key themes for my investigation. Chapters 11 and 12 depart from the Eichmann report and consider the contemporary relevance of *Eichmann in Jerusalem* with respect to the corporatisation of democratic institutions (inverted totalitarianism), the Israeli-Palestinian conflict and the role of forgiveness in the aftermath of mass violence. In this sense, this book is both a companion to *Eichmann in Jerusalem* and an independent work of legal theory. Major theoretical themes examined include the nature of legal authority and civil disobedience, justice, criminal procedure, the validity of retroactive law, the act of judgment and the nexus between morality and law. These are all topics that one would find in a standard course or book on legal theory. However, despite common references to Antigone (Sophocles 2005) to discuss natural law or Hercules (Dworkin 1986) on legal interpretation, legal theory is frequently presented in an abstract way with little connection to historical or mythological examples.

Standard approaches to legal theory, which favour the abstract and analytical over the concrete, is one of the reasons why legal theory has become so dull and closed off to alternative conversations (Hershovitz 2015). Why should students or lawyers care about a stale conversation regarding the theoretical underpinnings of natural law and legal positivism? Rather, as the legal realist Karl Llewellyn (2008: 4) observed as early as 1929: 'We have learned that the concrete instance, the heaping up of concrete instances, the present, vital memory of a multitude of concrete instances, is necessary in order to make any general proposition, be it rule of law or any other, mean anything at all.' Following Llewellyn, I seek to ground my discussion of legal theory in concrete historical facts such as the juridical order of the Weimer Republic, the Holocaust and the trial of Adolf Eichmann. Where relevant, I will also draw connections between these historical events and

9 There have also been ad hoc articles by influential legal scholars. See for example Klabbers (2007), Seymour (2007) and Waldron (2000). See also Burdon (2014, 2015).

contemporary political and legal problems. Here I take seriously Arendt's (1970) injunction to draw upon the history of ideas as a resource for thinking in our own times and engaging with the world as it represents itself to us.

There are at least two ways to grasp Arendt's importance to, and distinctiveness within, legal-philosophical thought. The first of these approaches is to read Arendt alongside a range of thinkers who thought about law, politics and philosophy in a similar way. This includes those who influenced Arendt, such as Martin Heidegger and Karl Jaspers (Arendt 1970); current writers who reacted to her work, such as Judith Butler (2014, 2015), Giorgio Agamben (1998, 2000, 2002, 2005) and John Doris (2005); and others who have criticised, challenged or rejected her analysis such as Deborah Lipstadt (2011). My intention is to situate Arendt in a political theoretical tradition that critically engages with law, showing how her thought was shaped and how it impacted others. This is one way to avoid reading Arendt in conceptual isolation and it will tell a richer story about the development of her thought and its continued relevance.

The second way of grasping the importance of Arendt is historical. There is a burgeoning biographical and cinematic literature on Eichmann (Sivan 1999; Safrian 2009; Stangneth 2015), his capture in Argentina (Bascomb 2010), interrogation in Jerusalem (Young 2008 and Lang 2009) and trial (Lipstadt 2011 and von Trotta 2012). To this list should be added new analysis of the trials against Jewish collaborators (Ben-Naftali and Tuval 2006; Jockusch and Finder 2015), renewed interest in the Nuremberg trials (Tusa and Tusa 2010) and issues of law, justice and the nature of evil as revealed in more recent genocides such as Rwanda (Hatzfeld 2006). While the present book is not a work of history, it is important to locate Arendt's report on the Eichmann trial historically and consider what aspects of her analysis stand-up, change or take on new meaning in light of more recent scholarship.[10] Moreover, because Arendt was not writing for a legal audience, parts of her analysis related to the trial and legal theory need to be developed and expanded to achieve my purpose.

Reading Arendt

Further to my primary goal of introducing lawyers to Arendt's report on the Eichmann trial, a secondary goal of this book is to encourage readers to read the book on Arendt's own terms. This might sound ridiculous because many readers will be encountering Arendt for the first time and may not have any knowledge of her biography or cultural milieu.[11] But one of her terms is that you read – not just this text but as broadly as possible and across disciplines. 'Real learning' argues David Harvey (2011: vii) 'always entails a struggle to understand the unknown.'

10 For consistency I will refer to *Eichmann in Jerusalem* as a report. See Arendt (2006a: 280).
11 The definitive biography of Arendt remains Young-Bruehl (2004).

To read Arendt, one must first understand that she was an independent thinker. She did not align herself exclusively with any school of thought or identify with a dominant political philosophy (Bernstein 2013: v). Throughout the 1930s and 1940s Arendt set about critiquing and reconceptualising settled political categories such as differences between Zionism and assimilation, the nation state and the rights of man and even the polar positions of left and right in political discussion. The fruits of this work were captured in an exchange Arendt (1979: 333) had with Hans Morgenthau toward the end of her life at a conference dedicated to her legacy:

> Morgenthau: What are you? Are you a conservative? Are you a liberal? Where is your position within contemporary possibilities?
>
> Arendt: You know the left think that I am conservative and the conservatives think I am left or I am a maverick or God knows what. And I must say that I couldn't care less. I don't think the real questions of this century get any kind of illumination by this kind of thing.

Arendt (1979: 314) railed against simple ideological 'bannisters' as impediments to judgment and argued that they were a method people used to avoid encountering the singularity of the event. This is clearly observable in politics today where many individuals respond to policy not with reference to the substance of a proposal, but where they sit on the political spectrum.

Arendt's independence of thought should not be interpreted to mean that she presented herself as neutral or objective in making political judgments. Rather, Arendt is an exemplar of an intellectual who was not afraid to respond to the most pressing political issues of her time. To paraphrase Edward Said (1996: 12), Arendt understood her responsibility to raise difficult questions, to confront orthodoxy and express strong views on controversial questions. One of Arendt's favourite phrases was 'thinking without bannisters' and much of her writing can be understood as an expression of this ideal (Bernstein 2013: v).

In writing *Eichmann in Jerusalem* Arendt drew explicitly on a variety of disciplines and intellectual traditions. In no particular order they are law; philosophy, including the ancient Greeks and Immanuel Kant; and what she purposively called 'Jewishness'. I will introduce each in turn for further development over the course of this book.

With respect to law, Arendt is frequently described as someone without specific education or training in law (Goldoni and McCorkindale 2013b: 1; Luban 2011: 621). It is difficult to see why this matters or how this argument could have been made at an earlier point in history.[12] Indeed, Robert Jackson, the lead American prosecutor during the Nuremberg trials and Associate to the US Supreme Court, did not graduate from law school. Yet, Jackson's lack of formal training is often considered a virtue not a shortcoming (Jarrow 2008: 27). Further, most authors

12 John Marshall, the fourth Chief Justice of the Supreme Court between 1801 and 1835, received no formal legal training.

neglect to mention that between 1936 and 1938 Arendt worked for the International League against Racism and Anti-Semitism and provided legal assistance to several high profile clients including David Frankfurter who was accused of murdering a Nazi party leader in Davos, Switzerland (Young-Bruehl 2004: 144). She was also involved in preparations for the trial of Herbert Grynszpan, a young Polish-Jew whose assassination of Nazi diplomat Ernst vom Rath, provided the pretext for the *Kristallnacht* or 'night of broken glass'. While brief, these intense encounters with 'legal procedures and practices' gave Arendt the 'foundation for considering the complex legal questions involved' in the trial of Adolf Eichmann (Young-Bruehl 2004: 145).

The second resource that Arendt drew on was philosophy – a discipline that she regarded with some suspicion. In her last interview, conducted with the German journalist Günter Gaus on the 28 October 1964, Arendt rejected Gaus's introductory description of her as a philosopher:

> I am afraid I have to protest. I do not belong to the circle of philosophers. My profession, if one can speak of it at all, is political theory. I neither feel like a philosopher, nor do I believe that I have been accepted in the circle of philosophers, as you kindly suppose (Arendt 2013: 1).

This reaction reflects Arendt's understanding of philosophy as a set of abstract principles or platonic ideals that stand outside of the world and seek to instruct humans on how the world ought to be. In contrast, Arendt engaged philosophy as a tool that could help her think about and engage with the public realm. She did not see herself as standing outside or above the world or as being distant from human affairs as a number of influential German philosophers had done during the rise of National Socialism in Germany. Instead, Arendt thought that every human being was called upon to take responsibility for the world and that this public engagement was the highest form of action that people could undertake (Arendt 2005a).

In her description of Eichmann, Arendt drew on a philosophical tradition that included the Greeks and Immanuel Kant.[13] The Greeks were important for Arendt (2006a: 287) and supported her controversial assertion that 'Except for an extraordinary diligence in looking out for his personal advancement, [Eichmann] had no motives at all.' This description finds corollary in Greek literature where, as Robin (2015) argues, there is a 'cold, almost cruel, accent on the disproportion between actors and actions, intensions and consequences'. For example, it is not Achilles' evil that leads to the death of Patroclus but his arrogance. In her 1958 book *The Human Condition*, Arendt resurrected the Greek emphasis on action – an activity which expresses the person like 'no other human activity' (Arendt 2013: 37).

13 To this list could be added Martin Heidegger and Karl Jaspers. The intellectual relationship between Arendt and Heidegger has been most fully explored by Wolin (2001) and Dana Villa (1995). With respect to Arendt and Jaspers see the rich correspondence between Arendt and Jaspers (1992).

Once action is restored to its primary place in human activity, all of Eichmann's private reasons and motivations (his *mens rea*) are of secondary importance. As Susan Neiman (2015: 262) suggests: 'What counts is not what your road is paved with, but whether it leads to hell.' For his victims, Eichmann's roads were 'quite literally the end of the world' (Arendt 2006a: 151). His action caused a fundamental fracture in human plurality and it is on this basis that Arendt performatively sentences Eichmann to death at the conclusion of her report

Arendt began her lifelong study of Kant at the age of 14 (Arendt 2013: 15). Kant is also one of the few philosophers that Arendt expressly draws upon when grappling with the nature of Nazi evil – from her adoption of his term 'radical evil' in *The Origins of Totalitarianism* to her phrase the 'banality of evil' in *Eichmann in Jerusalem*. Despite Richard Wolin's (2014) claim that a Kantian reading of *Eichmann* is 'unsustainable'[14], scholars such as Seyla Benhabib (2003: 189–190) and Patchen Markell (2014: 62) have convincingly demonstrated Arendt's debt to Kant's *Critique of Judgement* (1987).[15] Consider, for example, Arendt's (2006a: 279) final judgment of Eichmann: 'And just as you supported and carried out a policy of not wanting to share the earth with the Jewish people … we find that no one, that is no member of the human race, can be expected to want to share the earth with you.' As Robin (2015) suggests, it is difficult to read this argument and not think about Kant's writing on taste and aesthetic judgment. For example, in 'The Crisis of Culture' (2006b: 204) Arendt wrote that an individual expression of taste not only discloses 'what kind of person' we are, but also enables us to construct a community of fellow appreciators. Moreover, Arendt (2006b: 204) claimed: 'Taste decides not only how the world is to look, but who belongs together in it.'

Further to these philosophical ideas it must also be noted that Arendt was fundamentally influenced by her own experience of being a Jewish refugee from the Second World War (Butler 2015: 116) and Jewishness as a cultural, historical and political category that is not necessarily connected to religious Judaism or the nation state (Arendt 2008 and 1973a: 66).[16] A lot has been written about Arendt's

14 Wolin (2014) notes: 'Arendt's reliance on Kant's theory of judgment – the idea that we broaden our mental horizons by virtue of our ability to reason from the standpoint of other persons – is limited to one meager passage' (*Eichmann in Jerusalem*, p. 48). Moreover, in the passage in question, Kant's name is not even mentioned. Casual allusions along these lines hardly qualify as systematic or serious employment. As most Arendt scholars are aware, Arendt only developed these Kantian precepts in earnest circa 1970, in the course of her *Lectures on Kant's Political Philosophy* and in the complementary essay 'Thinking and Moral Considerations'.

15 Arendt reflected on the influence of Kant during an interview with Joachim Fest: 'This inability, as Kant says … to think in the place of every other person … this kind of stupidity, it's like talking to a brick wall … such a person [is] infinitely worse [and] incomparably more fearsome type of person than any ordinary murderer, since he no longer has any relationship to the victim at all … he kills people as if they were flies (Arendt 2013: 49, 60).'

16 See further Arendt (1973b): 'I am by birth a Jew, and as far as religion goes I do not belong to any church, or to any synagogue, or to any denomination.'

Jewishness and her relationship to Jewish intellectual traditions (Arendt 2008; Bernstein 1996; Botstein 2009: 161–220; Bar 1997: 285–346; and Butler 2007 and 2012). Within this literature, Arendt has been described variously as someone who lacks 'love for the Jewish people' (Gershom Scholem quoted in Young-Bruehl 2004: 332) and a 'non-Jewish Jew' (Wolin 2001: 1). However, I find myself in agreement with Jerome Kohn (2008: xxvii) who argued that 'her experience as a Jew is literally the foundation of her thought'. Put another way, Arendt was influenced not only by her biography as a Jewish refugee but also by the Jewish intellectual tradition and some religious sources.

Starting with biography Arendt suffered directly at the hands of National Socialism and was active in resistance work until her emigration to the United States in 1941. Elizabeth Young-Bruehl (2004: 98) argues that Arendt saw early the darkening cloud of anti-Semitism and its political consequences inside of Germany. After the Reichstag fire in 1933 Arendt stated that she could 'no longer be an observer' (quoted in Young-Bruehl 2004: 98) and worked with an underground railroad that was helping political figures to flee Germany. At the same time, Arendt worked for the German Zionist Organisation collecting documents at the Prussian State Library to demonstrate the extent of anti-Semitic activity. This research was highly illegal and Arendt was arrested and spent eight days in prison before convincing the guard to release her (Young-Bruehl 2004: 105–106). Arendt continued to resist National Socialism after she moved to Paris. In 1937 she became the director of the Paris Branch of Youth Aliyah where she worked with emigrant children on the psychological impact of anti-Semitism and took a group to Palestine (Young-Bruehl 2004: 143). Arendt also engaged vigorously with debates in the Jewish community – particularly against the 'return to the ghetto' movement; worked at a Jewish Agency that assisted Austrian and Czechoslovakian refugees in Paris; and spent several months interned in a camp at Gurs which had formerly housed refugees from Spain and members of the International Brigade (Young-Bruehl 2004: 148–153).

Thus, when Arendt made judgments – either against Eichmann or against anyone who failed in their moral responsibility to resist dictatorship – she was not speaking as an abstract philosopher. Rather, Arendt judged from the standpoint of someone who made sacrifices and put herself in danger to resist National Socialism. Moreover, Arendt's judgment was a social act, performed in solidarity and drawing upon others who had also acted with ethical integrity. This included her friend and mentor Karl Jaspers who resisted National Socialism from inside Germany and Feldwebel (sergeant) Anton Schmid[17] who was executed for supplying the Jewish undergrounds with trucks and forged papers (Arendt 2006a: 230–231).

Further to this, Arendt's book on Eichmann was influenced by what she described as 'Jewishness' – a cultural, political and historical category that is distinct from religious Judaism (Arendt 2008: xiii). In Arendt's *Jewish Writings* (2008) we can see her

17 Misspelt 'Schmidt' in *Eichmann* (Horsman 2010: 31).

grappling with what it means to be a secular Jew whose life is organised outside of a religious context or community. What emerges from these writings is a perspective that inhabits several distinct identities and communicates the fact that there is no unitary definition of what it means to be Jewish (Butler 2014: 14). Jewishness was part of Arendt's natality or beginning and a continuous source of insight throughout her intellectual life. As she wrote to Gershom Scholem: 'I have always regarded my Jewishness as one of the indisputable factual data of my life, and I have never had the wish to change or disclaim facts of this kind' (quoted in Zertal 2005: 150).

Further to these points, Robin (2015) describes *Eichmann in Jerusalem* as a 'very Jewish text by a very Jewish author'. He goes on to contend: 'Jerusalem ... not the Athens of the Greeks or the Konigsberg of Kant ... may be not only the site but also the spirit of Arendt's text.' What then is Jewish about Arendt's book? The clearest example is the way Arendt draws deeply on the Jewish intellectual and religious traditions to formulate political principles (Butler 2014: 122; Botstein 2009: 167). While hidden or obscured in the text, Arendt told a German correspondent that her Eichmann text was more than simply a report on a trial – it was 'the groundwork for creating new political morals' (Arendt quoted in Robin 2015).

This is most obvious with respect to Arendt's reflections on thoughtlessness. For Arendt (2013: 58), political morality begins when a person 'reflects' on what they are doing. She expressed this point in a letter responding to questions submitted by the journalist Samuel Grafton: 'We resist evil by not being swept away by the surface of things, by stopping ourselves and beginning to think – that is, by reaching another dimension than the horizon of everyday life' (Arendt 2008: 279). In offering these reflections, Young-Bruehl (2009: 208–209) argues that Arendt was connected to the 'Axial Age prophetic tradition' which, among other things, prioritised the ability to 'think your way into the viewpoint, the position, the experience, or other people, past and present (perhaps future too)'. This capacity engages our imagination and by enlarging our experience, challenges us to appreciate the plurality of people with whom we share political space.

Robin (2015) argues further that the capacity for thoughtfulness is at the centre of Judaism which, he argues, is 'so dedicated to the extraction of the sacred from the profane, of locating the sacred within the profane, that it encircles human action with 613 commandments, lest any moment or gesture of a Jew's life be without thought of God'.[18] Arendt focuses on the smallest moments of the Holocaust

18 See further Arnold (1932: 129 and 131). On the importance of small events in the construction of great evil see Mayer (2012: viii): 'In the wake of Treblinka and Auschwitz it is difficult not to scorn Fernand Braudel's characterisation of short-term events as mere "dust." Braudel went so far as to imply that short-term events were not worth studying since, unlike long- and medium-range events, they "traverse history as flashes of light" destined instantly to "turn to darkness, often to oblivion." Pace Braudel and his epigones, I have tried not only to contemplate the circumstances in which millions of Jews – along with millions of non-Jews – were reduced to "dust" in seconds of historical time but also to recapture the evanescent "light" of their torment to illuminate the historical landscape in which it occurred.'

and highlights instances when Eichmann had the freedom to make a choice. The devil is in small, banal details. Susan Neiman (2015: 288) supports this reading, noting:

> Arendt was convinced that evil could be overcome only if we acknowledge that it overwhelms us in ways that are minute. Great temptations are easier to recognize and thus to resist, for resistance comes in heroic terms. Contemporary dangers begin with trivial and insidious steps. Once these are taken, they lead to consequences so vast they could hardly be foreseen. The claim that evil is banal is a claim not about magnitude but about proportions: if crimes that great can result from causes that small, there may be hope for overcoming them.

Arendt offers us an ethic of everyday life – thoughtfulness is a tool for preventing the reoccurrence of evil in the future. While this is not unique to Judaism, it is noteworthy that Arendt's prescription for avoiding the reoccurrence of evil and totalitarian regimes in the future centres on a practice directed at every impulse and action. Whether or not her prescription is sufficient is something to which I will return and critique throughout this book.

Chapter 2

The House of Judgment

The trial is pre-eminently a theatrical form (Sontag 2001: 118).

Arendt opens her report on the Eichmann trial with action – a moment of natality and creation. The words '*Beth Hamishpath*' are shouted by the court usher as part of a ritual that announces the arrival of the three German-Jewish judges whose presence is intended to transform the theatre at Beth Ha'am[1] into a sacred house of law.

Arendt translates Beth Hamishpath as 'The House of Justice' however other scholars, including Giorgio Agamben (Agamben and Butler 2009), contend that the correct translation is 'The House of Judgment' or the 'house where judgment is done.' A lawyer might contend that the words 'justice' and 'judgment' are synonymous or that they exist in necessary relationship to one another – justice is achieved through the act of legal judgment. There is some evidence that Arendt supports this view. For example, she writes (2006a: 5): 'Justice demands that the accused be prosecuted, defended and judged.' Moreover, Arendt (2006a: 6) writes that justice 'demands seclusion, it permits sorrow rather than anger, and it prescribes the most careful abstention from all of the nice pleasures of putting oneself in the limelight.'[2] And yet Arendt draws a distinction between judicial judgment and moral judgment: 'Legal and moral issues are by no means the same' (2005a: 22). While Arendt advocates for just legal procedure and the importance of locating the individual subject and their deeds, her ultimate fidelity is to moral judgment which she places above positive law. For someone who witnessed the corrupt law of National Socialism and placed primary importance on thoughtfulness, it could hardly be otherwise.

This chapter begins with concerns that Arendt raised about the relationship between trials and theatre. I also unpack key concepts such as the difference between theatre and drama and what it means for lawyers to behave theatrically. Following this I consider whether there might be some legitimate end that a

1 The auditorium is now called the Gerard Behar Center and it is a home to theatre, music and dance productions.
2 See also Breen (2013).

theatrical trial might serve, such as educating a population or national reconstruction. Against these arguments Arendt sought to defend a strict or legalistic conception of the trial which is focused on the accused and their deeds. In the next section, I consider whether or not the Eichmann trial was a show trial. This argument is distinct from concerns that the trial did not meet the minimum level of justice required of a liberal trial (discussed in Chapter 8). While there is evidence to support the conclusion that the Eichmann trial was a show trial, I argue that Arendt did not reach this conclusion. Central to her thinking on this point was the independence of the judges and their integrity in keeping most of the proceedings focused on Eichmann.

Law and theatre

The first image Arendt presents readers is the way courtroom proceedings mirror a theatrical production.[3] She highlights this view in a key passage at the beginning of the book: 'Whoever planned this auditorium in the newly built Beth Ha'am … had a theatre in mind, complete with orchestra and gallery, with proscenium and stage, and with side doors for the actor's entrance' (2006a: 4). This is followed later in the chapter when Arendt (2006a: 9) notes: 'A trial resembles a play in that both begin and end with the doer, not with the victim.' Such impressions are common to many who witness a criminal trial and are struck not only by the architecture of the courtroom but by the role playing, scripted lines, costumes and the gravitas projected by the parties.

To properly understand Arendt's meaning we need to draw a distinction between theatre and drama and between theatre and something performed theatrically. According to Bachmann (2010: 96) a drama has 'generic expectations' and may also be thought of as a text that exists independently from its theoretical performance. For example, we might call the text for Bertolt Brecht's play *The Decision* a drama. In contrast, the concept of theatre incorporates broader forms of spectacle that might exist independent from the text. An example is performance art where the presence of the actors takes precedence over the text (Bachmann 2010: 96 and Fischer-Lichte 2008). Finally, the concept 'theatricality' is a mode of perception. An event like a trial becomes theatrical if those who witness the trial (either in person or via an external medium) perceive it that way (Bachmann 2010: 96–97 and Burns 1972).

To describe an event 'theatrically' is not necessarily to degrade it. As Bachmann (2010: 99) notes: 'As long as trials follow their generic expectations (and are dramatic, in this sense), their theatricality is "good" because it vanishes insofar as it does not have any value in itself but only serves something other (the "making" of justice).' With this point in mind Arendt invokes the positive meaning of theatre when the prosecution called their final witness, Mr Aharon Hoter-Yishai. Arendt,

3 On the theoretical dimensions of the Eichmann trial see further Bilsky (1996); Felman (2001); and Flessas (2005).

who hitherto had been critical of evidence unconnected to Eichmann, lowered her guard and commented 'every once in a long while one was glad that Judge Landau had lost his battle' to control proceedings (2006a: 227). In contrast, the negative meaning of 'theatrically' refers to a perception that proceedings are staged as a spectacle and removed from the dramatic function of justice. Arendt (2006a: 4–5) hits on this latter point during her descriptions of the Israeli prosecutor, Gideon Hausner, whom she describes as a showman who sullies proceedings by giving 'press-conferences and interviews for television during the trial'.[4]

Tatiana Flessas (2005: 218) and Yasco Horsman (2010: 25) suggest that Arendt's criticism of the trial has its foundation in a disagreement over the theatrical genre the trial was modelled on and what type of spectator the trial required. As Flessas notes: 'Trials are not plays' and legal processes 'must be in service of something which itself cannot be displayed on a stage' – namely, justice. Arendt (2006a: 5) is very clear on this point. She notes for example:

> Justice demands that the accused be prosecuted, defended and judged and that all other questions of seemingly greater import – of 'How could it happen?' and 'Why did it happen?', or 'Why the Jews?' and 'Why the Germans', of 'What was the role of other nations?' and What was the extent of co-responsibility on the side of the Allies?', of 'How could the Jews through their own leaders cooperate in their own destruction?' and 'Why did they go to their death like lambs to the slaughter?' – be left in abeyance. Justice insists on the importance of Adolf Eichmann … On trial are his deeds, not the sufferings of the Jews, not the German people or mankind, not even anti-Semitism and racism.

Flessas (2005: 216) seeks to read Arendt's report as an attempt to elevate the trial to its proper home – the house of justice. This shift does not seek to remove every theatrical element but it is a deliberate rebalancing away from what Arendt (2006a: 19) calls 'bad history and cheap rhetoric' and toward a judgment of Eichmann's deeds.[5]

Oddly, Arendt never interrogated whether there might be some legitimate purpose that a theatrical trial might serve. She is not alone and indeed many lawyers would defend vigorously the idea of a neutral justice system which strives to apply the law in an objective manner. It was this commitment that led some lawyers to express concern that the Nuremberg tribunal would be perceived as 'victor's justice' (Tusa and Tusa 2010: 140). Scholars have also argued that the court is not the appropriate venue to establish a historical record. Worse still, a

4 In his memoir Gideon Hausner (1966: 292) emphasises the 'extra-legal' effect of the trial and 'correctional and educational aspect' for young people in Israel. Hausner writes that in 'any criminal proceedings the proof of guilt and the imposition of a penalty … are not the exclusive objects.'

5 See also Rogat (2011: 20).

trial with theatrical aims might degrade historical evidence and exploit the victims. On this point, Ian Buruma (2015: 140) writes:

> Just as belief belongs in church, surely history education belongs in school. When the court of law is used for history lessons, then the risk of show trials cannot be far off. It may be that show trials can be good politics … but good politics don't necessarily serve the truth.

Michael Marrus (quoted in Eviatar 2002) agrees: 'Legal procedures are not designed to tell a historical narrative, but to facilitate a fair judgment … [i]f you want history written, turn to historians, not to lawyers.' Released from the rigour of the procedural system, lawyers could slide into 'the realm of fiction' and the role of the judiciary drops away (Minow 1999: 45–46).

In contrast, some scholars claim that significant trials, such as a war crimes proceedings, should always have a pronounced theatrical element. For Judith Shklar, international trials are always political because they seek to render judgment of other countries' political leaders. Still, Shklar (1964: 145) argues that they may serve the cause of fairness: '[i]t is not the political trial itself but the situation in which it takes place and the ends that it serves which matter.' In agreement, Lawrence Douglas (2005: 2) claims that Arendt was wrong to view the Eichmann trial in narrow terms – focusing on the accused and his deeds. Instead, Douglas claims that a post-genocide trial should offer a stage for victims to be heard and create an official historical record.

Mark Osiel has most forcefully expressed the view that trials can assist in the re-construction of a nation and its relation to the past. Osiel (1999: 2) describes criminal proceedings for war crimes as a 'social drama' and argues that they are a 'transformative opportunity in the lives of individuals and societies'. Osiel (1999: 6) suggests further that trials can help nations consolidate memories and engage in 'secular rituals of commemoration' that 'problematize the very distinction between true and false representations of reality'. Most lawyers would find this extreme but for Osiel the end justifies the means. A theatrical trial creates a controlled space for the public to collectively explore trauma and political violence.[6] However, Osiel (1999: 6) contends that this end may only be achieved if the underlying goal is hidden from the public. In this sense, the trial acts like a kind of placebo – revealing an orchestrated plan to shape the psychology of subjects would spoil the fantasy and erode public confidence in the legal system.

What greater purpose did David Ben-Gurion, who Arendt (2006a: 5) describes as 'the invisible stage manager of the proceedings', have in mind in bringing Eichmann

6 Horsman (2010: 3) argues that this exploration of trauma may not happen through awareness raising: 'The paradox is that as information about the past accumulates, there emerges ever stronger forms of resistance against accepting this information and its implications … What Germany needed was an altogether different project of public education, one that would use different strategies and require a different type of intellectual work.'

to trial? Here we do not need to speculate because the Government's intentions were not hidden. The first purpose was a display of power to Israel's neighbours and their tormentors further abroad.[7] Lipstadt (2011: xii) articulates this point: 'The State of Israel, which was then entering its Bar Mitzvah year, exemplified the victims' emergence from the very powerlessness that had helped make the Final Solution possible.' After enduring so much, a Jewish State could strike back and deliver justice to victims. *Yedioth Ahronoth* (quoted in Zertal 2005: 96), the Israeli daily newspaper noted at the time: 'Jewish blood will never be defenseless again ... However powerful all the pogromchiks under the sun may be – they will be caught by us and judged by a Jewish tribunal.' *Ma'arvivs*, the Israeli evening newspaper, made an even stronger statement:

> From the mounds of the ashes of the burned, from all the anonymous, nameless buried, rose the silent cry that shattered Israel: The greatest nations on earth could not catch him. The young men of Israel – did ... And justice will be done now. Justice befitting a lawful country and a Jewish state, millions of whose potential builders and soldiers were butchered on Eichmann's orders (quoted in Zertal 2005: 96).

The Eichmann case – from capture to execution – became a vehicle through which Israel could project its sovereignty and power.[8] The Holocaust would not be remembered for itself. Instead, it became entangled in a greater political project which advocated that only the state of Israel and political Zionism could guarantee the protection of the Jewish people (Arendt 2006a: 8). This, as Susan Sontag (1964: 123) notes, is memory in the service of politics. Control of this memory became critical and Ben-Gurion was strident, even macho in defence of Israel's display of strength. In an opinion piece for the *New York Times* Ben-Gurion (1960: 7) argued: '[o]nly a Jew with an inferiority complex could say' that Israel should not try Eichmann. Moreover, in answer to the charge that Eichmann should be tried before an international court, Ben-Gurion argued that only 'anti-Semites or Jews

7 David Ben-Gurion (1960: 7) is explicit on this point: 'It may be that Eichmann's trial will help to ferret out other Nazis – for example, the connection between Nazis and some Arab rulers. From what we hear on the Egyptian radio, some Egyptian propaganda is conducted on purely Nazi lines. The Egyptians charge that Jews ... dominate the United States, Jews dominate England, Jews dominate France, and they must be fought. I have no doubt that the Egyptian dictatorship is being instructed by the large number of Nazis who are there.' See also Lipstadt (2011: xxvii) who writes about the former Iranian president Mahmoud Ahmadinejad: 'a Holocaust-denying president of a large country ... poised to have nuclear weapons' to 'threaten the existence of the Jewish state'.

8 Arendt (2006a: 271) acknowledged this point: 'For Israel the only unprecedented feature of the trial was that, for the first time (since the year 70, when Jerusalem was destroyed by the Romans), Jews were able to sit in judgment on crimes committed against their own people, that, for the first time, they did not need to appeal to others for protection and justice.'

with an inferiority complex' could suggest that Israel needs the protection of an international court.

Connected to this display of strength, Ben-Gurion also wanted the Eichmann trial to educate Israel's youth, many of whom were the children of survivors, about the Holocaust. Once again, Ben-Gurion (1960: 7) was explicit about this objective:

> It is necessary that our youth remember what happened to the Jewish people. We want them to know the most tragic facts in our history, the most tragic facts in world history. I don't care whether they want to know them; they ought to know them. They should be taught the lesson that Jews are not sheep to be slaughtered but a people who can hit back – as Jews did in the War of Independence.

To help facilitate this objective, the government submitted a bill to the Knesset to amend the *Courts (Offenses Punishable by Death) Law*. Under Israeli criminal procedure, once a defendant pleads guilty they are convicted and the judges only need to pass an appropriate sentence. Ben-Gurion was concerned that this procedure would enable Eichmann to enter a quick plea to bring proceedings to a dramatic close. In response, a new law (unofficially called the *Eichmann Law*) stated: '[I]n case the accused pleads guilty as charged, the court may continue the proceedings as if the accused had not pleaded guilty' (Zertal 2007: 1140). The bill was passed swiftly but removed from the law books a few years after the Eichmann trial (Zertal 2005: 107).

Despite Ben-Gurion's efforts, the auditorium at Beth Hamishpath did not attract Israel's youth. Arendt (2006a: 8) reports that after the journalists had departed the court 'there were hardly any young people ... it was filled with "survivors" with middle-aged and elderly people ... who know by heart all that there was to know and ... certainly did not need this trial to draw their own conclusions.' While young people did not attend the trial in person, they could not have missed the daily newspaper coverage, television clips and rolling coverage provided by *Kol Yisrael* (Voice of Israel) radio station. Indeed, Israeli historian Idith Zertal (2005: 95 and 93) argues that Ben-Gurion's 'grand national pedagogy' was largely successful and that the trial 'changed the face of Israel, psychologically binding the pastless young Israelis with their recent history and revolutionizing their self-perception.'[9]

How did the trial accomplish this? The key was witness testimony. Unlike the Nuremberg tribunal, which relied principally on documentary evidence, the Eichmann trial was driven by the sworn testimony of survivors. Over sixty-two sessions 'horror was piled upon horror' and the audience 'listened in public to stories they would hardly have been able to endure in private' (Arendt 2006a: 8).

9 For the extensive literature on the impact of the Eichmann trial on Israel's self-perception, see Segev (2000).

The line between evidence and some kind of public 'bearing witness' was crossed and blurred time and again. In total, 23 sessions were dedicated to 'background witnesses' (Arendt 2006a: 207, 225) and numerous other sessions were designed to 'paint a picture' of the Holocaust without necessarily connecting that evidence to Eichmann. This was powerful and Segev (2000: 340) suggests that a significant part of the trial's historical impact was in its providing a forum for survivors to publicly share their story to an international audience. Annette Wieviorka (2006: 96) argues further that the Eichmann trial is characterised as the 'coming into being of the witness'.[10]

Arendt wanted to resist attempts to use the courtroom for these purposes. She stands virtually alone amongst those reporting on the Eichmann trial and has been labelled unsympathetic, conservative, legalistic and over dogmatic (Douglas 2005: 2ff and Felman 2002: 120, 122 and 183; Douglas 2005: 111–113). Those who castigate Arendt often assume that the trial required a compassionate observer – someone who would foster feelings of compassion for the victims and the Israeli state. However, instead of the sympathetic audience of the theatre, Arendt suggested that a legal trial required a rational observer who engaged with proceedings with detachment and who was prepared to render their own individual judgment (Horsman 2010: 24). Arendt takes this position to the trial, not because she is cold or heartless but because she believes in a notion of legal justice and is generally suspicious of sentiment or pity in the public sphere (Nelson 2004: 219–244).

With respect to the latter point, it should be noted that *Eichmann in Jerusalem* was written at the same time as Arendt's previous book, *On Revolution* was being prepared for publication. In *On Revolution* Arendt (2006d: 86) argues that pity constitutes a threat to the political sphere: 'Because compassion abolishes the distance, the worldly space between men where political matters, the whole of human affairs, are located, it remains, politically speaking, irrelevant and without consequence.' A revolutionary politics that is grounded in pity threatens the political realm as a separate sphere for human action. We may extrapolate that a legal trial must similarly guard against becoming rooted in sympathy and compassion. 'Moreover' Horsman (2010: 25) argues 'because the Eichmann trial was organised in the wake of the massive onslaught on the public realm by the Nazis its contribution to a process of overcoming the past may need to rely on a judgmental coldness rather than on empathy.' Arendt would certainly agree with this point and stated in a letter to Gershom Scholem: 'I believe we shall only come to terms with this past if we begin to judge and to be frank about it' (Arendt 1978a: 248).

Show trial

Lurking in the background to this discussion is the suggestion that the proceedings in Jerusalem are not just theatrical but a 'show trial' and thus a complete

10 See also Felman (2002).

corruption of legal process. In a show trial, the goal is to present the accused and the pre-determined verdict to the public as a warning to other would-be dissidents. Moreover, as evidenced during Stalin's purges, show trials lack independence between the prosecution and judiciary and the accused are convicted of each charge brought against them (Hodos 1987: 3).

While Arendt ultimately refused to label the Eichmann trial a 'show trial' it was clearly on her mind and motivated aspects of her analysis.[11] She also understood, for example, that regardless of the outcome of the trial, Eichmann would never leave Israeli custody. And she notes provocatively that the trial venue is 'not a bad place for the show trial David Ben-Gurion … had in mind when he decided to have Eichmann kidnaped in Argentina' (Arendt 2006a: 4). Prominent news outlets in the United States initially shared this concern. Deborah Lipstadt (2011: 24) provides the following examples:

> In the space of a month, *The Washington Post* ran two vituperative editorials condemning Israel's 'jungle law' and predicting that an Israeli trial would be 'tainted with lawlessness,' 'wreck vengeance,' and 'debase the law.' The proceedings would be 'divorced from justice.' An Indiana paper branded Israel 'a little upstart foreign state.' *Time* condemned Israel's 'high handed disregard of international law.' *The New York Post* predicted that this would be a 'show trial' which should rightfully be held in Germany. *The Christian Science Monitor*, taking an even more extreme stance, argued that Israel's claim to have the authority to adjudicate crimes against Jews committed outside of Israel was identical to the Nazis' claim on 'the loyalty of persons of German birth or descent' wherever they lived.

In rejecting the idea that proceedings against Eichmann amounted to a show trial, Arendt constructs a conflict between two sets of actors, each equipped with irreconcilable commitments. On the one side are David Ben-Gurion and Gideon Hausner who represent political Zionism and claim to speak on behalf of the Jewish people.[12] On the other side are the three judges and their commitment to legal integrity. Arendt is gushing in praise of the judges and the institution they represent.[13] She introduces the judges in the following passage:

11 It is common for writers to misread Arendt as concluding that the Eichmann trial was a show trial. See Douglas (2005: 111): '… it was the alleged failure of the prosecution scrupulously to respect these tenets that led Arendt to describe the Eichmann proceedings precisely as a "show trial" produced and choreographed by the "invisible stage manager of the proceedings," Prime Minister Ben-Gurion.'

12 See Lipstadt (2011: xxii): 'Ben-Gurion justified holding the trial in Israel because he believed that Israel, as the Jewish state, had the right to speak in the name of those who had been killed as Jews. Hausner had begun his opening statement by asserting that standing by his side were six million victims.'

13 Arendt (2005a: 21–22) expresses a romantic or idealistic perspective of law: '… it is fortunate that there exists still one institution in society in which it is well-nigh impossible to evade issues of personal responsibility, where all justifications of a nonspecific,

> At no time is there anything theatrical in the conduct of the judges. Their walk is unstudied, their sober and intense attention visibly stiffening under the impact of grief as they listen to the tales of suffering, is natural; their impatience with the prosecutor's attempt to drag out these hearings forever is spontaneous and refreshing, their attitude to the defence perhaps a shade over-polite ... their manner toward the accused always beyond reproach. They are so obviously three good, honest men that one is not surprised that none of them yields to the greatest temptation to playact in this setting (Arendt 2006a: 4).

Anyone who has read Arendt's letters or the portraits she wrote of friends and mentors will be struck by the unqualified nature of these observations. Yet, while Arendt praises all three judges, it is clear that she has particular respect for Moshe Landau: 'There is no doubt from the very beginning that it is Judge Landau who sets the tone and that he is doing his best, his very best, to prevent this trial from becoming a show trial under the influence of the prosecutor's love of showmanship' (Arendt 2006a: 4). Thus, if the Eichmann trial did not degenerate to a show trial it was not for lack of trying. Rather, it was prevented by the judges who were independent from the State, had control of the proceedings and were determined to uphold some measure of procedural justice to the accused (Arendt 2006a: 9). Whether or not these judges managed to accord Eichmann the minimum level of justice expected in a liberal trial is the question that I discuss in Chapter 8.

abstract nature – from the Zeitgeist down to the Oedipus complex – break down, where not systems or trends or original sin are judged, but men of flesh and blood like you and me, whose deeds are of course still human deeds but who appear before a tribunal because they have broken some law whose maintenance we regard as essential for the integrity of our common humanity.'

Chapter 3

The gray zone

Kapo trials

After setting the scene for the trial Arendt (2006a: 21) turns to consider the charges against Eichmann under the *Nazis and Nazi Collaborators (Punishment) Law* (1950) (NNCL). Eichmann was charged with four counts for crimes against the Jewish people; seven counts for crimes against humanity; one count for war crimes; and three counts for being a member of and holding a post of an enemy organisation. Recognition of crimes against the Jewish people is unique to the NNCL and represents an attempt by the Knesset to recognise the unprecedented nature of the mass exterminations and elevate that offence above crimes against humanity (Segev 2000: 335; Bazyler and Tuerkheimer 2014: 207).[1] Indeed, a person could be convicted of crimes against the Jewish people for less serious acts than for crimes against humanity. Moreover, while every instance of crimes against the Jewish people is simultaneously a crime against humanity, the opposite is not true.[2] A relevant extract from the NNCL is extracted below (for the full text, see Appendix).[3]

1. a) A person who has committed one of the following offences:

    1 done, during the period of the Nazi regime in an enemy country, an act constituting a crime against the Jewish people;

1 As I will discuss, unprecedentedness includes unpacking accepted notions of subjectivity and personal responsibility.

2 The relationship between crimes against the Jewish people and crimes against humanity mirrors the debate between genocide and crimes against humanity at Nuremberg. See Sands (2016: 4, 6 and 11). See also Sands' (2016: 365) reflection on the tension between crimes against humanity and genocide which is equally applicable in the current context: '[O]n the one hand, people are killed because they happen to be members of a certain group; on the other, the recognition of that fact by the law tends to make more likely the possibility of conflict between groups, by reinforcing the sense of group identity. Perhaps Leopold Kohr got it right, in the strong but private letter he wrote to his friend Lemkin, that the crime of genocide will end up giving rise to the very conditions it seeks to ameliorate.'

3 For a detailed study of the *Nazis and Nazi Collaborators (Punishment) Law* (1950) see Ben-Naftali and Tuval (2006).

2 done, during the period of the Nazi regime, in an enemy country, an act constituting a crime against humanity;
3 done, during the period of the Second World War, in an enemy country, an act constituting a war crime.

is liable to the death penalty.

3. (a) A person who, during the period of the Nazi regime, in an enemy country, was a member of, or held any post or exercised any function in, an enemy organisation is liable to imprisonment for a term not exceeding seven years.

Sections 10 and 11 of the Act provided the circumstances under which an accused person might be released from criminal responsibility. Importantly, the NNCL does not reference criminal intent and it is sufficient to prove that the act itself was committed (Segev 2000: 335). The NNCL notes:

1 If a persecuted person has done or omitted to do any act, such act or omission constituting an offence under this Law, the Court shall release him from criminal responsibility –

   a if he did or omitted to do the act in order to save himself from the danger of immediate death threatening him and the court is satisfied that he did his best to avert the consequences of the act or omission; or
   b if he did or omitted to do the act with intent to avert consequences more serious than those which resulted from the act or omission, and actually averted them;

2 however, these provisions shall not apply to an act or omission, constituting an offence under section 1 or 2(f).
3 In determining the punishment of a person convicted of an offence under the Law, the court may take into account, as grounds for mitigating the punishment, the following circumstances:

   a that the person committed the offence under conditions which, but for section 8, would have exempted him from criminal responsibility or constituted a reason for pardoning the offence, and that he did his best to reduce the gravity of the consequences of the offence;
   b that the offence was committed with the intent to avert, and was indeed calculated to avert, consequences more serious than those which resulted from the offence;

4 however, in the case of an offence under section 1, the court shall not impose on the offender a lighter punishment than imprisonment for a term of ten years.

A close reading of these extracts reveals that the NNCL was not written with Nazi war criminals in mind. It is difficult, for example, to see how sections 10 and 11 could apply to collaborators like Eichmann. Arendt (2006a: 91) picks up on this point, noting that the NNCL was designed to punish Jews who had collaborated with the Nazis. This included 'Jewish *Sonderkommandos* (special units)' who had been involved in 'the actual killing process' and 'Jewish Councils and Elders' who cooperated with administrative and logistical matters.[4] Deborah Lipstadt (2011: 195) notes further that the Israeli law 'under which Eichmann had been tried, the 1950 Nazis and Their Collaborators Law, was instituted in response to grassroots pressure from survivors, not to punish Nazis, but to punish Jews.' Lipstadt (2011: 195) adds:

> The Knesset did not adopt the law in anticipation of the arrival of Nazi war criminals in Israel. The intent of the law was to ensure that Jewish survivors who had 'collaborated' with the Nazis by serving as Kapos or the like were punished.

It was not necessary for Arendt, concerned as she was with the proceedings before her, to provide further context to the law under which Eichmann was charged. However, the legislative history and application of the NNCL represents a rich and understudied aspect of the Eichmann trial and contains many lessons for lawyers and theorists alike. Collaborators assumed many different roles and so this chapter will start with a discussion of Kapos and the context within which they made decisions in death camps. Following this I consider the informal trials which took place inside displaced persons' camps at the end of the war and finally the trials of Jewish collaborators which were conducted in Israel between 1951 and 1964.

Kapo: function and role

The word Kapo is derived from Italian and literally means 'chief' or 'head' (Trunk 1996: 551; Bazyler and Tuerkheimer 2014: 195). The term was used in Nazi war and concentration camps for inmates appointed by the SS to head work commandos or assist in camp administration. The number and influence of Kapos increased dramatically during the war as the ratio between SS and prisoners became more acute.[5]

Kapos were usually political, criminal or Jewish inmates of different nationalities who had little in common as a group except for their position of power in the camp. In exchange for their obedience, Kapos received improved conditions – better food,

4 Trunk (1996: 562) notes that in Israel, 'no trials were held against former council members.' In contrast Ben-Naftali and Tuval (2006: 152) note that 'one of the individuals charged under … the Law was a member of the *Judenräte* and served as the Chief of the Jewish Police in Benedin, Poland.' See also Rabinovici (2011: 4). For further analysis see also Arendt (2006a: 117–119).

5 Wachsmann (2015: 513) notes that the ratio between SS and prisoners fell from below 1:2 in the late 1930s to around 1:15 by mid-1943.

clothing and more comfortable sleeping quarters. Put simply, the terms of the Faustian pact were unfaltering obedience for a significantly increased chance of survival. Nikolaus Wachsmann (2015: 513) argues that in Ebensee, 'prisoner functionaries were almost ten times more likely to survive than ordinary inmates'. And yet, the logic and organisation of the camps demanded that Kapos lived in a precarious state of security. For example, if Kapos refused to obey orders they could be killed or put back in the general population (Rabinovici 2011: 4). This was just one of the many features of 'prisoner self-administration' which was used by the SS to 'divide and rule' the camps and 'minimize resistance' (Wolf 2007: 618). Heinrich Himmler, Reichsführer-SS, commented directly on this point in a letter to the generals of the Wehrmacht camp in 1944:

> Okay, so one man is the responsible supervisor, I mean to say chief, with power over 30, 40, over 100 other prisoners. Once he becomes Kapo, he no longer sleeps together with them. It's his responsibility to see that they reach the performance target, that there are no acts of sabotage, that the men are clean, and their beds made according to regulations … A fresh recruit in a military barracks can't be any neater and more thorough than what is expected here. And the Kapo has responsibility for this. So he has to push his men. The moment we're not satisfied with him, he's no longer a Kapo, and he goes back to sleep with his men. But he knows full well that he'll be murdered by them the first night (quoted in Sofsky 1993: 314, n. 19).

The role of Kapos differed from camp to camp but their precarious status made them deadly instruments through which the SS could maintain a constant regime of terror over the general population. Moreover, Jewish Kapos found themselves in an impossible position – as both victim and oppressor.[6] The Italian writer and Auschwitz survivor, Primo Levi, called this sphere 'the gray zone'. Levi (1996: 91) tries to explain the basic social conflict inherent in the role of the Kapo. He wrote:

> if one offers a position of privilege to a few individuals in a state of slavery, exacting in exchange the betrayal of a natural solidarity with their comrades, there will certainly be someone who will accept. He will be withdrawn from the common law and will become untouchable; the more power that he is given, the more he will be consequently hateful and hated. When he is given the command of a group of unfortunates, with the right of life or death over them, he will be cruel and tyrannical, because he will understand that if he is not sufficiently so, someone else, judged more suitable, will take over his post. Moreover, his capacity for hatred, unfulfilled in the direction of the oppressors, will double back, beyond all reason, on the oppressed; and he will only be satisfied when he has unloaded onto his underlings the injury received from above.

6 On the dialectic between the persecutor and the persecuted see Césaire (2000).

Levi's words illustrate the pressure, frustration and emotional toll experienced by Kapos. Yet, as the war stretched on, the Kapos' duties were focused increasingly on coercion and terror. This took many forms from regular beatings to selecting inmates for execution, escorting inmates to execution sites or killing them directly. Wachsmann (2015: 514) argues further that it 'was not uncommon for Kapos to receive open or thinly veiled instructions to murder certain inmates…and Kapos murdered on their own initiative, too, acting far more brutally than before the war.'

Liberation and community honour courts

For those Kapos who survived the war, the days immediately following liberation did not necessarily mean freedom. As the camp social order collapsed, the Kapos were toppled from their position of power and existed in a new state of precariousness. On the one hand they were finally released from Nazi oppression. But, they were also in danger of being beaten or killed by former prisoners seeking revenge (Bazyler and Tuerkheimer 2014: 199). In one case, Lisa Yavnai (2006) notes that a group of 31 inmates decided to hold a brief trial for five Kapos whom they judged to be murderers. The Kapos were sentenced to death in absentia and one was beaten to death while another hung himself before being captured (the remaining Kapos escaped unharmed). In the days of liberation an eye for an eye became a common form of reckoning. Indeed, Yavnai (2008: 63) notes that inmates killed in excess of 50 Kapos in Ebensee concentration camp alone.

Benjamin Ferencz, the chief prosecutor of the *Einsatzgruppen* trial at Nuremberg, was able to see the helplessness of the law when, as a young war crimes investigator he visited the newly liberated Flossenbürg concentration camp. In a letter dated 29 April 1945, Ferencz captures an essential dilemma facing war crimes investigators in post-war Europe:

> Many of the prisoner guards had been recruited from the prisoners themselves, these 'trustees' have been even more brutal than the SS men. What was to be done about them? At first I thought we would handle them the same way we would war criminals … The first one was accused, by several witnesses, of beating a sick Frenchman to death with a rubber hose. I called in the perpetrator and confronted him with the facts I had gathered. The man had been a prisoner there for six years. He had sought to curry favour and perhaps a few privileges from the Nazis by his mistreatment of his fellow prisoners. He denied everything but was obviously lying. What punishment does that man deserve? It was established against another prisoner that, while he was a hospital orderly, he had killed a few patients by beating them and then putting a rubber hose in their mouths and turning the water on full pressure. Brutal you say? That perpetrator had been in prison there for four years … Elsewhere in the world these things would undoubtedly have been charged with murder … but in a context where murder is as common as eating, how

> responsible is a persecuted victim who does only what he sees being done day in day out? Can we apply the values and standards of a civilized world to people who have been subjected to a murder camp for four or six years? (Ferencz quoted in Bazyler and Tuerkheimer 2014: 217).

The Allied Forces in Germany were the first to charge Kapos for war crimes, murder and mistreatment of concentration camp inmates. From June 1945 through to December 1947, American and British occupation forces prosecuted close to 3,000 Nazi concentration camp personnel, including Jews, for violation of the laws of war (Yavnai 2006). Shortly after the allied war crimes tribunals began in Germany, national courts across Europe began their own proceedings. For those countries that had suffered under Nazi occupation, such as Belgium, France, the Netherlands, Hungary and Poland, part of the national healing and rebuilding process involved the prosecution of individuals suspected of collaboration with the enemy.

But what of the Jewish survivors who found themselves stateless at the end of the war? While waiting transfer in the displaced person camps (DPC) that had sprung up over Europe, heated debates began over the culpability of Jews and others accused of collaboration with the Nazis, including members of the Judenräte and the Jewish Ghetto police. Some groups, particularly in Germany and Italy,[7] also began to think about legal process and even established 'courts of honour' to hear accusations from survivors (Trunk 1996: 548). Proceedings against Kapos were brought by survivors[8] and committees to which they belonged (for example the Central Committee of Liberated Jews). And in some cases the accused themselves initiated proceedings in order to clear their names (Trunk 1996: 548).

For the most part, the judges in the courts of honour were survivors. While questions can be asked about impartiality (a charge that was levelled at the three German-Jewish judges who presided over the Eichmann trial) court procedure was based on orthodox legal principles. For example, cases were to be judged on their individual merits with supporting evidence for each charge (Trunk 1996: 549). For example, on 17 May 1948, the Rehabilitation Commission of the Central Committee in Munich issued the following decision in the case of Kaunas Ghetto policeman Beinish Tkach:

> The ghetto inmates considered the police no good in general. However, to generalize this opinion and extend it to all policemen without exception, without an individual approach to each case, may lead to harmful injustice (quoted in Trunk 1996: 549–550).

7 Trunk (1996: 549) notes that courts of honour were established where displaced persons were concentrated, in particular, Bergen-Belsen, Munich and Rome.

8 Trunk (1996: 551) notes that, as a procedural matter 'an accusation by a single person was not enough to open an investigation, unless it was confirmed by other witnesses'.

If an honour court found a defendant guilty, it could impose three kinds of social punishment (Trunk 1996: 551; Bazyler and Tuerkheimer 2014: 200). First, ban the defendant from holding any position in the organisation and institutions of the DPC or remove them from any position that they held. Second, ban the defendant from receiving any material assistance or immigration assistance from a relief organisation. Finally, the most severe sentence was to label the defendant a 'traitor to the Jewish people' which involved banishment from the Jewish community or perhaps even transfer to an allied military court (Trunk 1996: 551). The sentences of the honour court were binding and accepted by the displaced person's community. Similar proceedings also took place in Jewish communities outside of the DPCs.

Trials in Israel

> … the Israeli political and cultural establishment tried to establish a new, revolutionary-messianic profile of Israel and 'Israeli-ness' by erasing or making selective use of the previous historical Jewish background and recent past (Zertal 2005: 59).

Following a brief period in the displaced person's camps, almost 400,000 survivors (almost one-quarter of the population) made their way to Palestine. Against the myth that everybody in the Yishuv (the organised Jewish community in Palestine before 1948) sympathised with the dispirited refugees in displaced-persons camps, the welcome was less than compassionate. 'After the war', contends Segev (2000: 11), 'a great silence surrounded the destruction of the Jews.' This silence was compounded by the 'guilt' consciousness of Holocaust survivors (Rabinovici 2011: 1–10; Yablonka 2003: 10). Guilt consciousness had two primary expressions; first a belief that victims had been killed 'like sheep to the slaughter' suggested that victims did not measure up to the strength and honour of the '1948 generation' (Weitz 1996: 158). Second, survivors felt shame about what they were required to do in the camps to survive. Levi (1996: 9) captures this feeling: 'Those who were "saved" in the camps were not the best of us' rather they were 'the worst; the egotists, the violent, the insensitive, the collaborators … the best all died.'[9]

Those who had acted as Kapos tried to lead anonymous lives but found it impossible in the small state, which was home to thousands of survivors. Survivors encountered Kapos in everyday situations such as going to the theatre, walking in a park or eating at a café. And yet, despite the crushing anxiety that those encounters produced, there was no obvious legal recourse that they could pursue.

9 See also Frankl (2006: 19): 'On the average, only those prisoners could keep alive who, after years of trekking from camp to camp, had lost all scruples in their fight for existence; they were prepared to use every means, honest and otherwise, even brutal force, theft, and betrayal of their friends, in order to save themselves. We who have come back, by the aid of many lucky chances or miracles – whatever one may choose to call them – we know: the best of us did not return.'

Segev (2000: 260, n. 15) explains: '[T]he police were powerless – there was no law that covered this situation or allowed them to arrest the suspects.'[10] In fact, the absence of such a law was the reason Nazi collaborators, like Slovakian priest Baniek, sought refuge in Israel (Ben-Naftali and Tuval 2006: 129, n. 5).

In response, the Ministry of Justice drafted legislation called the *Act Against Jewish War Criminals* in 1949 but did not seek to enact the law immediately (Bazyler and Scheppach 2012: 421). After ten months, the legislation was reintroduced as the NNCL and won Knesset approval on 1 August 1950 (Bazyler and Scheppach 2012: 421). Pinchas Rosan, Israel's first Minister of Justice, was a major proponent of the NNCL. On 27 March 1950 Rosen spoke before the Knesset and clearly articulated the primary purpose of the legislation to parliamentarians:

> While other nations legislated laws immediately following the war, and some of them even beforehand, concerning bringing the Nazi and their collaborators to justice, the Jewish people, the people whose grievance against the Nazi is the most severe, was deprived until the creation of the state of the authority to bring the Nazi criminals and their collaborators to justice … This will be changed now … finally, let me add a word on the practical significance of the law. It is assumed that Nazi criminals, who could be charged on the basis of the crimes included in the Law, would not dare come to Israel. But the Law applies also to Nazi collaborators, and, unfortunately, we cannot be certain that such people would not be found in our camp, even if their numbers are probably not many … The proposed Law may also contribute to the cleansing of the atmosphere amongst the survivors who immigrated to the land of Israel. Whoever knows their problems, knows how painfully embedded in them is the question of suspicions and reciprocal accusations … the police could not, given the absence of the proposed Law, commence an investigation … let our camp be pure (quote in Ben-Naftali and Tuval 2006: 143).

Rosen's closing words – *let our camp be pure* – seek to deny the existence of the gray zone and assume that a clear dichotomy between good and evil can be maintained. Idith Zertal (2005: 60) argues further that the NNCL was one of several legal documents the state used to begin history anew: 'By deleting the shame of their mothers and fathers, the shame of Jews, the disgrace of the Jewish Diaspora, they believed they were inaugurating a new era, and reinventing themselves into a new world … The deletion project evolved eventually into a purge.'

10 Zertal (2005: 62) questions whether complaints from survivors motivated the law: 'The police were under some pressure from survivors – a few dozen all in all – who demanded justice and action against "collaborators." According to this quasi-official narrative, the "predicament" of the survivors is therefore what expedited the legislative process. The Justice and Police Ministries joined forces to draft an appropriate law based on the complaints of a handful (out of more than a quarter of a million) of survivors against other survivors.'

To this end, between 30 and 40 Kapo trials were conducted.[11] Most collaborators were charged with using excessive violence in carrying out camp discipline. It is also revealing that no Jew was ever charged under the NNCL for committing crimes against the Jewish people. The reason, as expressed by the Israeli Supreme Court, was that the offence required 'the intent to destroy the collectivity against which the crimes are committed' (quoted in Ben-Naftali and Tuval 2006: 153). Unfortunately, the courts did not explore this point in depth or ask the obvious question: 'Is it normatively possible for a persecuted person to harm the persecuted collectivity of which s/he is a member?' (Ben-Naftali & Tuval 2006: 157). Instead, the courts approached the issue of intent in a way that drew no distinction between the Nazis and their collaborators.

Law projects certainty through its use of binary categories of right/wrong or good/evil. The 'gray zone' challenged this dichotomy and exposed the limits law. As Giorgio Agamben (1998: 170) contends, with respect to the camps: 'every question concerning the legality of illegality of what happened there simply makes no sense'. Levi (1996: 44) agrees noting that 'I know of no human tribunal to which one could delegate judgment.' Levi (1996: 87) enriches this claim with an example concerning the economics of survival in Auschwitz:

> [T]heft in Buna (the factory outside the camp), punished by the civil direction, is authorized and encouraged by the SS; theft in camp, severely repressed by the SS, is considered by the civilian as a normal exchange operation; theft among Häftlinge is generally punished, but the punishment strikes the thief and the victim with equal gravity. We now invite the reader to contemplate the possible meaning in the Lager of the words 'good' and 'evil', 'just' and 'unjust'; let everyone judge, on the basis of this picture we have outlined … how much of our ordinary moral world could survive on this side of the barbed wire.

None of the participants in the Kapo trials – from the judges down to the witnesses – were able to meet Levi's challenge or initiate a sustained discussion about how to judge human conduct amidst moral collapse. According to Ben-Naftali and Tuval (2006: 171), only two cases attempt to grapple with the complexity confronting Kapos. In *Goldstein*,[12] the court posed for itself the following problem:

11 Most of the judgments are not publically available. Yablonka (2004: 146) is the only author that gives a specific number: 'During the 1950's there were 33 trials. I have obtained twenty-one of them: thirteen ended in conviction and imprisonment and eight in acquittal.' See also Bazyler and Tuerkheimer (2014: 196) and Jockusch and Finder (2015).

12 *Attorney General v. Friedman*; Cr. C 93/52, In that case, the defendant, a Kapo in a forced-labour camp was accused of having caused bodily harm to a persecuted person in a bathhouse.

> Let me conclude with a general comment: from a moral perspective, convictions under the Nazi and Nazi Collaborators Law can stain a person more than regular convictions. Therefore, I find it necessary to write for the sake of memory that I have no reason to doubt that up to the Nazi Holocaust the defendant was a decent, fair tempered person, and a good Jew throughout his life. I also believe that this nature did not change due to the horror of the Nazi Holocaust … So, what happened?
>
> First, it is impossible to sustain a human community without installing order, and a place of confinement is no exception. As of necessity, the Jewish policemen were also investigators, judges and executioners for the purpose of sustaining this order, and had no means of execution other than blows. According to the evidence presented to me, and I have nothing more than what my eyes could see, the general routine of the Jewish police in these places of confinement did not deviate from what had seemed to it to be reasonable for the maintenance of good order. Second, the concentration of investigative, judicial and execution powers in the hands of one person may put a man to a test few men would not fail to one degree or another. I assume that the defendant had even reached, at least to some extent, the point where resorting to blows was a means of first, rather than last resort. But I did not find in his behavior the vice of sadism, and in his case, one may say publicly 'do not judge your fellow-man until you have walked in his shoes' … I am convinced that the defendant did not behave any differently than any other ordinary person would have behaved once the rings comprising the social chain have melted … I cannot get rid of the thought that had the representative of the Attorney General anticipated my pronouncements, he would not have charged the defendant under the Nazi and Nazi Collaborators Law (quoted in Ben-Naftali and Tuval 2006: 171–172).

The judge's response to this question is revealing and provides insight into the limits of law and legal judgment. Similarly, in the *Barnblatt* decision, the court noted: 'It will be presumptuous and self-righteous on our part, us who never walked in the shoes of those … and of those who managed to escape from there, like the witnesses for the prosecution, to be critical of these "small people" who were incapable of transcending in to an ultimate level of morality, at the time when they had been persecuted severely by a regime the primary purpose of which was to wipe out their humanity' (quoted in Ben-Naftali and Tuval 2006: 173).[13] This statement of judicial empathy is based on the presumption that the legislator would not set a standard for human behaviour that was impossible to meet. And

13 See further Levi (1996: 44–45): '[I]t is necessary to declare the imprudence of issuing hasty moral judgments on such human cases … It is a judgment that we would like to entrust only to those who found themselves in similar circumstances and had the opportunity to test for themselves what it means to act in a state of coercion … The condition … does not exclude culpability, but I know of no human tribunals to which one could delegate the judgment.'

yet, by constructing a dichotomy between 'heroes' and 'villains' that is precisely what the NNCL did. Kapos, far from becoming assimilated back into the Jewish community would be exiled to the ranks of the villains.

Before concluding this chapter, it is worth turning briefly to Arendt's position on judgment in hard cases. As noted, during the Kapo trials, most judges felt uneasy about rendering judgment in circumstances where one could not conceive of the circumstances or walk in the shoes of the accused. In *Barnblatt,* the court went so far as to note: 'maybe one can talk about a good *Judenrat* and a bad *Judenrat* because the very existence of this institution … should be rejected … but this is a question for history and not for the courts' (quoted in Ben-Naftali and Tuval 2006: 174). Arendt's humanistic impulse would give her sympathy with this view. As would her contention that the death camps were spaces of lawlessness which dissolved the juridical person and turned inmates into 'living corpses' (Arendt 1973a: 447). When Arendt wrote *The Origins of Totalitarianism* she describes a degraded and damaged humanity. Inmates were not human beings, they were 'bundles of reactions' who responded only to harsh words of threats to their body (1973a: 456). The inmates were rendered singular and their actions became predictable, lacking that human capacity 'to begin something new out of [one's] resources, something that cannot be explained on the basis of reactions to environment and events' (1973a: 455). After bearing witness to such violence, threats and intimidation, Arendt (1973a: 455) argued that nothing remained 'but ghastly marionettes with human faces, which all behave like the dog in Pavlov's experiments, which all react with perfect reliability even when going to their own death, and which do nothing but react.'

From what vantage point might one judge this unprecedented space of lawlessness? Reading *The Origins of Totalitarianism,* one could reasonably contend that Arendt judged actions that took place within the camp as outside of ordinary moral judgment. Yet, as Arendt was preparing the manuscript for her Eichmann book she expressed increasingly strong views on the political importance of judgment – even in hard cases: 'If you say to yourself in such matters: who am I to judge? – you are already lost' (quoted in Young-Bruehl 2004: 339).[14] Thus, whatever anxiety one might feel about rendering judgment the alternative, for Arendt, was unthinkable and had vast political consequences. This perspective on judgment was strengthened by Arendt's (2005a: 21) growing appreciation of the court as one of the few institutions in society where we could set aside our anxiety of judgment and where 'it is well-nigh impossible' for the accused to evade personal responsibility or hide behind notions of collective guilt.[15] A court may consider

14 Arendt's judgment of Eichmann makes it clear individual guilt can still be found in the context of general criminality. Consider, for example, her rejection of the statement 'where all, or most are guilty, nobody is' (2006a: 278) and the way she evokes the biblical story of Sodom and Gomorrah in which both cities were destroyed because all of the inhabitants were guilty.

15 On Arendt's attitude toward the Supreme Court see Goldoni and McCorkindale (2013b).

any mitigating circumstances, but ultimately, it has a profound duty to judge the choices made by flesh and blood human beings (Arendt 2005a: 21–22; Arendt 2013: 57). And as Frankl (2006: 75) reminds us – 'there were always choices to make'.[16] Compounding this perspective, many Israelis felt it was intolerable to forego judgment against those who had collaborated in the murder of their countrymen.

It is not necessary to attempt to reconcile these perspectives and arrive at a final synthesis. However, to enrich the discussion further it should be noted that Arendt did not limit judgment to a courtroom or hold that a court was always the most appropriate venue to evaluate past behaviour. In *Eichmann in Jerusalem*, she frequently criticised the narrowness of legal inquiry and her report is an example of performance of moral judgment. While Arendt did live to see the emergence of alternative justice mechanisms or the Truth and Reconciliation, she did view forgiveness as an essential component of human politics and a method for reversing certain kinds of action. Whether Arendt would have considered alternative justice mechanisms as a more flexible and appropriate venue for judging unpreceded crimes is something we cannot know. However, I return to the topics of forgiveness and alternative justice in Chapter 12 in the context of contemporary trials Nazi war criminals.

16 Arendt (2005a: 44) does uphold a moral code which recommends death over committed inhuman action: 'they asked themselves to what extent they would still be able to live in peace with themselves after having committed certain deeds; and they decided that it would be better to do nothing, not because the world would then be charged for the better, but because only on this condition could they go on living with themselves.'

Chapter 4

The accused

While the NNCL was not realistically directed at Nazi war criminals, its drafters left open the aspiration of bringing Nazis to trial in Israel. To facilitate this, the NNCL created a new legal category without precedent in international law – crimes against the Jewish people.[1] As mentioned, in the previous chapter, no Jewish collaborator was charged with this offence. Moreover, the rationale provided by the Israeli Supreme Court (that crimes against the Jewish people required the intention to destroy the collectivity) virtually foreclosed this possibility. Eichmann was charged with crimes against the Jewish people but the NNCL defined this term in a fashion consistent with the definition of genocide in the *Convention on the Prevention and Punishment of the Crime of Genocid*e (1951). Arendt did not agree with this approach because she felt that the Holocaust concerned all of humanity. She argued: '[T]he physical extermination of the Jewish people was a crime against humanity, perpetrated upon the body of the Jewish people' (Arendt 2006a: 268–269).[2]

In response to the 15 counts against him (including four charges of crimes against the Jewish people), the court transcript records that Eichmann pleaded: 'In the sense of the indictment, no' (Nizkor 1991). This wording was not unique and constituted the basis of defence for several of Eichmann's colleagues at Nuremberg. For example, Hermann Goering, Joachim von Ribbentrop, Alfred Rosenberg and Baldur von Schirach each pleaded: 'I declare myself in the sense of the Indictment not guilty' (Avalon 2008). Moreover, Fritz Sauckel, whom Eichmann's lawyer Dr Robert Servatius represented in Nuremberg, pleaded: 'I

1 Article 1 (a)(1) and (b) of the NNCL defines seven acts, which, if committed during the Nazi regime in an enemy country, would constitute a crime against the Jewish people: 1) Killing Jews; 2) Causing serious bodily or mental harm to Jews; 3) Placing Jews in living conditions calculated to bring about their physical destruction; 4) Imposing measures intended to prevent births among Jews; 5) Forcibly transferring Jewish children to another national or religious group; 6) Destroying or desecrating Jewish religious or cultural assets or values; and 7) Inciting hatred of Jews. The wording of these acts follows the definition of genocide in Article II of the Genocide Convention (1948).

2 A similar debate concerning crimes against humanity and genocide occurred before the Nuremberg trials. See Sands (2016: 4, 6, 11) and Luban (2011: 631).

declare myself in the sense of the Indictment, before God and the world and particularly before my people, not guilty' (Avalon 2008). In response, to Eichmann's plea Arendt (2006a: 21) noted:

> In what sense did he think he was guilty? In the long cross-examination of the accused ... neither the defense nor the prosecution, nor finally, any of the three judges ever bothered to ask him this obvious question.

Servatius attempted to clarify Eichmann's plea by telling the Israeli press: 'Eichmann feels guilty before God, not before the law' (Arendt 2006a: 21). In other words, Eichmann's actions, while morally wrong and contrary to the laws of God, were not illegal and nobody who committed those crimes would have been charged with a criminal offence. A court of law has no jurisdiction to enforce morality and cannot create a crime in retrospect – its function is to interpret and apply the law.

Eichmann's plea gives Arendt permission to inquire into his biography and motivation for collaborating in genocide. With respect to criminal intention (*mens rea*) Arendt concluded that Eichmann was not motivated 'by an insane hatred of the Jews' and that 'he would have had a bad conscience only if he had not done what he had been ordered to do' (Arendt 2006a: 26). This is supported with reference to Eichmann's psychiatric evaluation[3] and Arendt's own portrayal of Eichmann as a banal bureaucrat whose primary motivation was to progress his career and social status. Arendt (2006a: 32) argues further Eichmann was a 'joiner' who found security and meaning inside hierarchical organisations. This focus on careerism is at odds with Arendt's analysis in *The Origins of Totalitarianism* (1973a: 409) where jobholding is dismissed and Arendt argues that few Nazis had any 'genuine interest in specific jobs'. In fact, Corey Robin (2004: 116) argues that '*Eichmann in Jerusalem* is our sole sustained enquiry into the relationship between careerism and rule by fear.'

Eichmann's need for orders also meant that he did not develop the capacity to think for himself. Instead, he relied on direction from his superiors and fell back on officialese, stock phrases and self-invented clichés to navigate the world around him. Arendt (2006a: 49) presented a preliminary assessment of Eichmann's toward the end of chapter 3:

> The longer one listened to him, the more obvious it became that his inability to speak was closely connected with an inability to *think*, namely, to think from the standpoint of somebody else. No communication was possible with him, not because he lied but because he was surrounded by the most reliable of all safeguards against the words and the presence of others, and hence against reality as such.

3 Arendt (2006a: 25): 'Half a dozen psychiatrists had certified him as "normal" – "More normal, at any rate, than I am after having examined him," one of them was said to have exclaimed. See further Brunner (2000).

The court, like subsequent biographers (Cesarani 2006; Stangneth 2015), did not believe Eichmann's evidence. However, by adopting a positivist outlook and not pressing Eichmann on the meaning of his plea, Arendt argues that the court missed the most important moral and legal issue in the case. Arendt (2006a: 26) explains:

> [The prosecution's] case rested on the assumption that the defendant, like all 'normal persons' must have been aware of the criminal nature of his acts, and Eichmann was indeed normal insofar as he was 'no exception within the Nazi regime.' However, under the conditions of the Third Reich only 'exceptions' could be expected to react 'normally.' This simple truth of the matter created a dilemma for the judges which they could neither resolve nor escape.[4]

Here Arendt is pointing to the limits of law and the impoverishment of a purely positivistic approach to legal inquiry. The court had the power to judge Eichmann, but it did not have the tools or inclination to ask more fundamental question about the defendant or the nature of 'choice' under the Third Reich (a limitation we saw in the Kapo trials).[5] This begs the question – what defences or lines of inquiry were open to Eichmann and his lawyer? Eichmann's defence strategy was composed of several strands. This included:

- The ability of the State of Israel to exercise jurisdiction over the alleged crimes given that it was not a state at the time the crimes were committed and the actions were not committed on its territory or against its citizens;
- The retroactive application of the NNCL;
- The impossibility for the three German-Jewish judges, to ensure a fair trial;[6]
- Eichmann's illegal detention and transport into the custody of Israel in violation of basic principles of public international law;
- Whether or not Eichmann's conduct should be considered as acts of state; and
- Irrespective of issues surrounding the legality of the proceedings, at a fundamental level Eichmann should be found not guilty on the charges as in all aspects of his conduct he had been merely faithfully and patriotically carrying out the orders of his superiors.

With the exception of Eichmann's claim that Israel did not have the right to punish Nazi crimes and the circumstances under which he arrived in Israel, each of these arguments had been raised (unsuccessfully) at the Nuremberg and

4 See further Arendt (2006a: 263 and 2013: 43) and de Wall (2012: 133–134).

5 As discussed in Chapter 10, Arendt ultimately falls back on liberal notions of law in judging the crimes of Eichmann.

6 Lipstadt (2011: 40) also notes that Judge Halevi had previously compared Eichmann to the devil.

other post-war legal proceedings across Europe (Arendt 2006a: 93). In this chapter, I will consider the two novel claims raised by Eichmann and consider Arendt's comments on the retroactivity of the Israeli law and the acts of state defence.

Jurisdiction

After the presiding judge had read the charges against Eichmann, Servatius rose to challenge proceedings. This objection was anticipated. Indeed, Servatius had described the Nuremberg tribunal as a 'regression to barbarism' (quoted in Lipstadt 2011: 58) and prior to arriving in Israel he told a gathering of the Catholic Academy in Bavaria: '[T]he only legitimate criminal problem of the Eichmann trial lies in pronouncing judgment against his Israeli captors, which so far has not been done' (Arendt 2006a: 22).[7] With respect to the issue of jurisdiction, Servatius made the following argument:

> The law for punishing Nazis and their collaborators of 10 August 1950 seeks to provide punishment in regard to persons and acts before the existence of the State of Israel, outside the present boundaries of the State, which wronged persons who were not residents of the State of Israel ... The dispensing of justice to a foreign subject, as is being claimed here, would not be recognized by the territorial principle, nor the protective principle or the personal principle, nor the principle of international justice (Nizkor 1991).

According to international law, the state does not have unlimited power to institute its own right to punish violations committed abroad. To do this it needs a 'linking point' between the state and the persons who committed the act (Luban 2011: 629–630). As Servatius suggests, this connection might arise because the deed was committed on a country's territory (territoriality principle); because the person who commits the act is one of its citizens (personal principle); or because the act is harmful to a country's legal system or its citizens (international justice). These are, according to Servatius, fundamental principles of international law which must be upheld because they 'constitute a guarantee for international living as a community' (Nizkor 1991).

Despite his advocacy, Servatius must have known that Israel was going to claim jurisdiction to prosecute Eichmann (Lipstadt 2011: 58). The rationale for the court's decision was based on Israeli domestic law and international legal principles. First, the court argued that their jurisdiction to hear the case 'is based on the Nazis and Nazi Collaborators (Punishment) Law, the provisions of which are perfectly unequivocal' (Nizkor 1991). Moreover, the court highlighted the universal nature of Eichmann's crimes and the fact that the NNCL concerned offences

7 Arendt (2006a: 22) notes that Servatius adopted a different view of the trial once he had arrived in Israel and described proceedings as 'a great spiritual achievement'.

which have been recognised as crimes against humanity.[8] While an international tribunal should normally sit in judgment of Eichmann, one did not currently exist and there was little prospect of resurrecting the Nuremberg tribunal during the Cold War (Lipstadt 2011: 5).[9] Moreover, Arendt (2006a: 15) noted that courts in post-war Germany showed great reluctance to prosecute war crimes and passed down 'fantastically lenient sentences' to the accused. In these circumstances, the court reasoned that international law invests the legislative and judicial organs of each state with the power to punish war criminals.

The District Court also responded at length to the claim that Israel lacked a 'linking point' to Eichmann's crimes. At the time of judgment there was significant debate about what actually constituted this bond. However, sweeping aside this ambiguity the court posed for itself the following question:

> The question is: What is the special connection between the State of Israel and the offences attributed to the accused, and whether this connection is sufficiently close to form a foundation of Israel's right of punishment as against the accused. This is no merely technical question but a wide and universal one; for the principles of international law are wide and universal principles and not articles in an express code (Nizkor 1991).

In response, the court ruled that the 'crime against the Jewish people', as defined under the NNCL, was the main link between Israel and the defendant. Integral to this link was view that while the Holocaust was directed at a range of ethnic groups the Jewish people were its primary target. Arendt (1973a: 7) supports this point, noting that anti-Semitism constituted the central element within Nazism: 'The point for the historian is that the Jews, before becoming the main victims of terror, were the centre of Nazi ideology' (Arendt 1979: 3, 7). Lipstadt (2011: 9) elaborates: 'Killing all Jews – irrespective of age, location, education, profession, religious orientation, political outlook, or ethnic self-identification – was the priority in the race war that Nazi Germany conducted.' This crime concerned Israel directly because the land has historical importance for the Jewish people[10] and because the State was formed in direct response to the Holocaust. David Ben-Gurion summarised these points in a long letter to Konrad Adenauer, the Chancellor of West Germany from 1949 to 1963:

> The Jewish state (which is called Israel) is the heir of the six million who were murdered, the only heir for these millions … regarding themselves as sons of

8 The idea of submitting crimes against humanity to universal jurisdiction was supported by a number of legal theorists. See Hyde (1947: 804) and Cowles (1945: 177).

9 Lipstadt (2011: 22) notes that the Soviet Union threatened to reconvene the Nuremberg tribunals after Argentina approached the Security Council in response to Israel's abduction of Eichmann.

10 In support of this link, the court quoted from the proclamation of the State of Israel, which begins: 'In the land of Israel there arose the Jewish people'.

> the Jewish people and only as sons of the Jewish people. If they had lived, the great majority of them would have come to Israel. The only historic prosecuting attorney for these millions is Israel, and for reasons of historic justice, it is the duty of the Israeli government, as the government of the Jewish state … to try their murderers (Segev 2000: 330–331).

Against the judgment of many of her friends and confidants, Arendt (Arendt and Jaspers 1992: 47) agreed with Israel's right to speak on behalf of the victims because 'the larger majority of them (300,000) are living in Israel now as citizens', and the trial will take place 'in a country in which the injured parties and those who happened to survive are'.[11] Further to this, Arendt affirmed Israel's right because 'Eichmann was responsible for Jews and Jews only, regardless of their nationality' and also for want of a better alternative. With respect to this last point Arendt (Arendt and Jaspers 1992: 415) stated: 'Israel is the only political entity we have … I don't like it but then there's not much I can do about that.' Further to these points, Arendt (2006a: 262–263) also provided a creative argument to justify Israel's claim to territorial jurisdiction:

> Israel could easily have claimed territorial jurisdiction if she had only explained that 'territory', as the law understands it, is a political and a legal concept, and not merely a geographical term. It relates not so much, and not primarily, to a piece of land as to the space between individuals in a group whose members are bound to, and at the same time separated and protected from, each other by all kinds of relationships, based on a common language, religion, a common history, customs and laws.

This approach, which regards territorial jurisdiction as a legal fact, is arguably unnecessary (Luban 2011: 630). However, there are precedents for a geographical test – the most obvious being a ship whose territorial jurisdiction is determined by its flag state. Another example is Arendt's advocacy for a federated Israeli state which might exist without a geographical territory.[12] From this perspective, the Jewish people had 'created and maintained its own specific in-between space through the long centuries of dispersion' and this is what enabled the state to claim jurisdiction upon its founding (Arendt 2006a: 263). While perhaps insensitive to the wishes and diverse aspirations of Holocaust survivors (Grodzinsky 2004; Zertal 2005), the District Court used exactly this argument to justify its jurisdiction according to the protective principle (Luban 2011: 630). Curiously,

11 Jaspers, for example, disagreed and proposed a truth commission: 'It would be wonderful to do without the trial altogether and make it instead a process of examination and clarification. The goal would be the best possible objectification of the historical facts. The end result would not be the judges' sentence, but certainty about the facts, to the extent such certainty can be attained' (Arendt and Jaspers 1992: 413).

12 See further Chapter 11.

Arendt does not reference the protective principle in her report and instead turned her attention to the circumstances surrounding Eichmann's abduction.

The abduction of the defendant

Arendt's (2006a: 238–242) first consideration of Eichmann's abduction occurs late in her report. The basic facts are well known (Bascomb 2010; Malkin and Stein 1990; Lipstadt 2011: 15–20 and Stangneth 2015: 311–360) and can be summarised briefly. On 11 May 1960, Eichmann was kidnapped from Argentina where he had lived for 11 years under the name Ricardo Klement. After arriving at a safe house, Eichmann is alleged to have confessed his identity and stated: 'I do not wish this but am prepared to stand trial in Argentina or in Germany' (quoted in Hausner 1966: 275). After several hours Eichmann, buckled and agreed to travel to Israel for trial. He signed a declaration to that effect which read:

> I, the undersigned, Adolf Eichmann, declare of my own free will that, since my true identify has been discovered, I realize that it is futile for me to attempt to go on evading justice. I state that I am prepared to travel to Israel to stand trial in that country before a competent court. I understand that I shall receive legal aid, and I shall endeavour to give a straightforward account of the facts of my last years of service in Germany so that a true picture of the facts may be passed on to future generations. I make this declaration of my own free will. I have been promised nothing, nor have any threats been made against me. I wish at last to achieve inner peace. As I am unable to remember all the details and may be confused about certain facts, I ask to be granted assistance in my endeavours to establish the truth by giving access to documents and evidence.
>
> Buenos Aires, May 1960 (Signed) Adolf Eichmann

It is curious that Eichmann's kidnappers, who were engaged in an illegal activity on foreign soil, were concerned with formalities like getting a signed statement from Eichmann. Gideon Hausner (1966: 275) wrote in his memoir that Eichmann was 'obviously afraid of being liquidated on the spot'. Servatius argued further: 'A man who hid himself for fifteen years, in order that he should not appear before a Court, does not suddenly ask nor is he willing to appear before a Court … [particularly in a country where] he would be exceedingly afraid' (Nizkor 1991).

Declarations made under duress are inadmissible in court and have limited political value for the simple reason that they are utterly unconvincing.[13] But this mattered little. A moral judgment had been pronounced against Argentina for

13 In the opening session, Servatius sought to produce witnesses to prove that Eichmann's declaration had been signed under pressure and threats. The court denied this request.

harbouring 'numerous Nazis' with no intention of bringing them to trial (Lipstadt 2011: 21). Moreover, possession is nine-tenths of the law and Israel had the physical power to force Eichmann onto a plane and fly him to Lod airport (now Ben-Gurion airport) via Dakar, Senegal. Appeals from Argentina before the UN Security Council to make Israel pay reparations for violating their sovereignty were squashed after US Ambassador Henry Lodge declared that an apology from Israel's foreign minister, Golda Meir, was sufficient. Other members of the Security Council agreed and that was the end of the matter (Lipstadt 2011: 22–23).

The issue of Eichmann's kidnapping was raised by Servatius in the opening session of the trial. Characterising the kidnapping as an 'act of violence' he argued that the defendant had been brought to Israel as the result of a breach of international law, which was accomplished by persons carrying out the instructions of the Israeli Government. Moreover, Servatius argued that a court cannot base its jurisdiction on an illegal act of state and so the District Court did not have legitimate grounds to try Eichmann. In response Hausner, with whom the court agreed, presented a long list of precedents from the United States and Europe to demonstrate that the circumstances of the arrest have no bearing on a person being brought to trial (Gordon 2012: 590–591). This is true, Hausner argued, whether the circumstances surrounding the arrest involved conduct that was illegal according to local law or international law. Servatius responded, arguing that international precedents 'are not to be relied on' because in each of those cases the judges simply 'closed their eyes and disregard the actual kidnapping of the Accused' (Nizkor 1991). The court did not accept this argument and held that the right to plead violation of sovereignty was the sole prerogative of states. Thus, the individual defendant has no authority to assert this right and courts likewise have no power to decide upon the matter.

The retrospectivity of Israeli law

The acts for which Eichmann was charged in Israel were made punishable at least five years after they had been committed. They were not illegal crimes but 'acts of state' and Eichmann had sworn an oath to obey superior orders. Arendt (2006a: 24) summarises this position: 'What he had done was a crime only in retrospect, and he had always been a law-abiding citizen because Hitler's orders, which he had certainly executed to the best of his ability, had possessed "the force of law" in the Third Reich.' This raises many questions, including whether or not the NNCL contravened the principle against retroactive punishment and the demand for closure if an act was legal at the time it was committed.

The rule against retroactive punishment is a fundamental postulate of justice and a pillar of the rule of law. The rule states that punishable acts should be defined in law before criminal proceedings can commence so that citizens feel secure and know which of their actions and omissions are illegal. This is related to the idea of legal guilt. A person does not bring guilt upon themselves if they can reasonably conclude that their behaviour was not punishable at the time (Schlink

2009: 58). With reference to the Third Reich, people in Eichmann's position could rationally conclude that their actions would never be prosecuted or punished by the Nazi regime.[14] Schlink (2009: 59) provides an example: 'when soldiers had murdered Jews without command to do so and were called into account for their actions before the law, it was for failing to follow the military code and expressly not because of killing Jews'.

In post-war Germany, the Allies asserted sovereignty over Germany and prevented those few legislative bodies that remained from enacting retrospective legislation. Instead, the Allies enacted their own retrospective laws for the punishment of war criminals, such as the London Agreement (1945) and Law No. 10 of the Allied Control Council (Tusa and Tusa 2010: 71). This approach was justified on several grounds; first the Allies did not trust the Federal Republic of Germany to deal appropriately with the devastation committed so recently by their countrymen (Arendt 2006a: 15). Second, the Allies referenced principles expressed in provisions such as Article 15 II of the International Covenant on Civil and Political Rights which contains an apparent exception to the principle against retroactive legislation by permitting the trial and punishment of people charged with violating the general principles of international law (Joseph and Castan 2014: 529). Finally, over time, courts in West Germany justified their actions with reference to the 'Radbruch formula' – named after the pre-war Social Democratic Justice Minister Gustav Radbruch. While cloaked in conceptual theory, the Radbruch formula is really a tool for judicial decision-making (Bix 2011: 49). It has two different elaborations:

> 1 The positive law, secured by legislation and power, takes precedence even when its content is unjust and fails to benefit the people, unless the conflict between statute and justice reaches such an intolerable degree that the statute, as 'flawed law,' must yield to justice.[15]
>
> 2 Where there is not even an attempt at justice, where equality, the core of justice, is deliberately betrayed in the issuance of positive law, then the statute is not merely 'flawed law,' it lacks completely the very nature of law. For law, including positive law, cannot be otherwise defined than as a system and an institution whose very meaning is to serve justice (Radbruch 2006: 7).[16]

14 In Germany, a constitutional prohibition of retrospective criminal laws ('punishability') appeared in Art. 116 of the Weimar Constitution (1919). While never formally repealed, the provision became a façade under the Third Reich. For instance, after the Reichstag fire of March 1933, the death penalty was retrospectively reintroduced for arson, high treason and other offences. The law was enacted on 29 March 1933 with retrospective effect to 31 January 1933.

15 This is a version of what Murphy (2006: 10) calls 'strong natural law theory'.

16 Hans Frank, Hitler's personal lawyer, justified the numerous retrospective laws enacted under the Nazi regime in a similar way: 'How often have we heard that it is a grave injustice to punish an act under a law that was not in force when the act was committed. What, even if the act was prohibited when it was done, as it contravened the demands of social ethics? Was it not precisely the most essential prohibitions

Given the likely problem of trying to understand the subjective intention of legislators, judges have tended to use the first formulation. Courts punished the killing of Jews and other offences in accordance with the criminal laws valid during the Third Reich, but by applying the Radbruch formula, they stripped the laws of those justifications and exemptions that would have prevented the perpetrators from being punished.[17] These developments gave rise to the famous 1958 debate between H. L. A. Hart and Lon Fuller (The Hart-Fuller debate).[18] Briefly, Hart (1958: 616) read Radbruch as encouraging the judiciary to regard immoral laws as 'not law'. Hart rejected this approach and argued that courts should clearly separate questions concerning whether a norm is a law from the secondary question about whether the law should be applied. If Nazis were to be punished, Hart (1958: 620) argued, it should be done under frankly 'retrospective criminal legislation'. Fuller, by contrast, viewed Radbruch's position as a pragmatic response and one that provided a deep insight into the nature of law. For example, Fuller argued that Nazi laws that were secretive or retroactive were 'contrary to the very nature of law itself'.[19]

For Radbruch and Fuller, the positivist tradition could too easily become unhinged from moral principles and comply with the notion that might is right (Paulson 1994). In fact, Radbruch argued that the experience of National Socialism should turn everyone into advocates of natural law.[20] To prevent this, he argued that 'we must thoroughly overcome the positivistic legal philosophy that rendered impotent every possible defense against the abuses of the National Socialist Legislation' (quoted in Fuller 1954: 485). The Federal Constitutional Court in

("Thou shalt not kill") that were once brought into force without the threat of punishment attached?' (Frank 1935: 1322).

17 For an overview of cases see Radbruch (2006).

18 Arendt dismisses the notion that Nazism is a form of natural law or positivist law and thus undercuts the orthodox debate between Hart and Fuller. Arendt (1973a: 463) argues that Nazi law 'has nothing in common with the *lumen naturale* or the voice of conscience, by which Nature or Divinity as the sources of authority for the *ius naturale* or the historically revealed comments of God are supposed to announce their authority. This never made man a walking embodiment of the law, but on the contrary remained distinct from him as the source of authority that demanded consent and obedience. Nature and Divinity as the source of authority for positive laws were thought of as permanent and eternal; positive laws were changing and changeable according to circumstances, but they possessed a relative permanence as compared with the much more rapidly changing actions of men; and they derived this permanence from the eternal presence of their source of authority. Positive laws, therefore, are primarily designed to function as stabilizing factors for the ever-changing movements of men.'

19 This became the focus of Fuller's (1969) procedural natural law theory. Subsequent writers, Dworkin above all, have argued that legality itself embodies certain distinct moral principles.

20 For a contrasting interpretation see Paulson (1995: 489, 493). Moreover, Nazi jurisprudence, which appealed ultimately to the will of the Führer shared some structural similarities with natural law (Caldwell 1994–1995: 411).

Germany confirmed that this use of natural law was consistent with the Constitution (basic law) although not every Nazi law is sufficiently unjust to enable courts to invalidate it as 'illegal law'. The test to be used is 'the nature and possible contents of law' and the 'Radbruch formula' (Taylor 2000: 215).

This debate was beyond the scope of the District Court in Jerusalem. The three judges did not need to engage with jurisprudence or high theory. Ultimately they could fall back on the precedent set by the Nuremberg trials and other post-war trials to justify the validity of the NNCL and their sitting in judgment of Eichmann. This point was openly acknowledged by the Israeli Supreme Court when hearing the appeal from the District Court:

> If we are to regard customary international law as a developing progressive system, the criticism becomes devoid of value … for ever since the International Military Tribunal at Nuremberg decided this question, that very decision must be seen as a judicial act which establishes a 'precedent' defining the rule of international law. In any event it would be unseemly for any other court to disregard such a rule and not to follow it (Nizkor 1991).

In arriving at this conclusion, the Israeli courts played down any argument that Nuremberg constituted a victor's court. Rather, in almost metaphysical terms, they concluded that the outcome at Nuremberg and the principles upon which it was based constituted a moral conquest by humanity which could not be ignored. Moreover, coming from a juridical organ rendering international justice, this affirmation reinforced the conviction, already widespread in Israel, that courts of law were an appropriate venue for bringing Nazi functionaries to justice.

While dissent continued, large parts of the international press reported satisfaction with the legitimacy of Eichmann's trial. Lipstadt (2011: 60) provides examples such as London's *Sunday Times* which wrote that 'The Israeli Government … is resolved that the case against Eichmann shall rest … on the established theory and practice of civilized states.' Reporters from the *New York Herald Tribune* declared: 'We hear American voices speaking to the tribunal through Mr. Hausner with such weight that if there is lingering doubt about the properties of the trial then our quarrel is without own lawgivers.' Finally, the *Washington Post,* which had been critical of the trial reported that their legal objections had 'fallen by the wayside under the driving, painstaking mountainously documented argumentation of the prosecutor Hausner.' With preliminary matters settled, the court could turn their attention to Eichmann's deeds, embedded within the history, drama and narrative of the Final Solution.

Chapter 5

From expulsion to extermination

> The Nazi destruction process did not come out of a void; it was the culmination of a cyclical trend ... The missionaries of Christianity had said in effect: you have no right to live among us as Jews. The secular rulers who followed had proclaimed: you have no right to live among us. The Nazis at last decreed: You have no right to live (Hilberg 1985a: 8).

The German-Jewish historian George Mosse once proposed a hypothetical scenario: 'If someone had predicted in 1900 that within fifty years the Jews of Europe would be murdered, one possible response would have been: "well, I suppose that is possible. Those French or Russians are capable of anything"' (quoted in Browning 2015). Fresh in Mosse's memory was the wave of pogroms that swept over Russia during the 1880s (Berk 1985) and the Dreyfus Affair in France in 1894 (Arendt 1973a: 89–122).[1] By contrast, while blocked from the higher civil service and the military, Jews living in Germany experienced a significantly greater degree of assimilation and career prospects than in other European countries. Moreover, while Catholics had been persecuted during the 1870s (Gross 2005) and socialists were repressed in the 1880s (Lidtke 1966), anti-Semitic parties had failed to gain political traction and had little popular support in Germany.

So what happened? Or to paraphrase from Götz Aly (2015: 1), why the Germans and why the Jews? Arendt offers several provocative perspectives on this question in *The Origins of Totalitarianism*.[2] Her starting point is to reject explanations that perpetuate the 'scapegoat explanation' of 'eternal antisemitism' – the idea that 'Jew hatred is a normal and natural reaction to which history gives only more or less opportunity' (1973a: 7). This way of addressing the Holocaust, she argued, distorted the character of modern anti-Semitism, provided anti-Semites with an alibi for violence and failed to engage with the specific reasons Jews were targeted for mass extermination. Outside of a general theory for anti-Semitism, Arendt developed a perspective which recognised the Jews as 'one group of people

1 See also Seymour (2007: 116–117).

2 For a sustained critique of Arendt's analysis of anti-Semitism see Staudenmaier (2012).

among other groups, all of whom are involved in the business of this world' (1973a: 6). In positioning Jews in the public realm and recognising their agency for political action, Arendt also highlighted Jewish responsibility for anti-Semitism.[3] The critical point here is that Jews were not 'objects of history' but 'purposeful and responsible subjects' (Seymour 2007: 113).[4]

With this background in place, Arendt focused on material explanations for anti-Semitism, located in the political and social history of Jewish emancipation. Briefly, Arendt (1973a: 267) argued that modern anti-Semitism developed as the national state was in decline and an increasing number of people found themselves excluded from state structures and protections (Arendt 1973a: 267–290 and Seymour 2007: 97–112 and 121). Prior to the twentieth century, the Jewish people had never been fully integrated into the class-structure of the body-politic but rather maintained an 'autonomous' existence and provided much needed resources for the state. This arrangement, Arendt argued, served not only the interests of the state, but also the most influential strata of the Jewish community (such as the Rothschild family). However, over time, the unique role that the Jews filled was supplanted by an imperialist bourgeoisie and many Jews endured a dramatic decline in social standing as a result. Drawing on Tocqueville analysis of the decline of the French aristocracy, Arendt (1973a: 4) argued that a group is most vulnerable when they suffer a 'rapid loss of real power not accompanied by any considerable decline in their fortunes'.[5] When emancipation and assimilation were granted to European Jews, they were thrust into an increasingly anti-Semitic environment and rendered more vulnerable to hostility and violence.[6]

Rather than viewing Nazism as radical nationalism, Arendt argued that it was an unprecedented form of political organisation which sought the destruction of modern political forms and notions of law. Chapters 4–6 of *Eichmann in Jerusalem* pick up on this thread and describe the stages of the Final Solution and the legal apparatus that was constructed, first to deprive the Jews of legal rights and finally to make German controlled areas Judenrein ('clean of Jews'). Her treatment of

3 In her Eichmann report Arendt (2006a: 123) pointed to the role of Jewish Councils (Judenräte) and Jewish collaborators in the Holocaust. As noted in the introduction, while other scholars had reached similar conclusions, it was Arendt's tone and style that generated controversy.

4 See for example Arendt (1973a: 83): 'If it is true that "Jewishness" could not have been perverted into an interesting vice without a prejudice which considered it a crime, it is also true that such perversion was made possible by those Jews who considered it an innate virtue.'

5 See further Arendt (1973a: 4): 'Neither oppression nor exploitation as such is ever the main cause for resentment; wealth without visible function is much more intolerable because nobody can understand why it should be tolerated.' See also Seymour (2007: 113–114).

6 For a discussion of why the institution of legal rights failed to protect the Jews see Arendt (1973a: 290–304). As Arendt (1973a: 296–297) notes, before one could claim human rights, one first needed to possess a 'right to have rights' – a 'right to belong to some kind of organised community'.

these topics is cursory and structured with reference to the narrative presented by Gideon Hausner and his attempt to use witness testimony and official documents to present a general history of the Holocaust. One striking feature of this section of Arendt's book is just how reliant the Nazis were on law and legal process in formalising anti-Semitism and carrying out the extermination process. As Robert Miller notes, the Nazis were 'fastidious about following legal requirements' and bureaucrats, lawyers, and judges all followed formal procedures as authorised and interpreted Hitler's commands (Miller 1995: 1). In fact, the sheer volume of authorised documents was the principal evidence used against defendants at Nuremberg (Salter 2007: 399) and essential to the backgrounding and prosecution of Eichmann (Hausner 1966: 404–406).

This chapter begins with a description of Nazi juridical process and considers how the Party reimagined its governance structures so that it legalised and promoted total terror (Arendt 1973a: 44). I also discuss measures directed at boycotting Jewish business and the Nuremberg laws of 1935. Following this, the chapter looks at the importance of language rules and doublespeak in Nazi law and communication. These tools gave members of the Nazi elite (and German society more generally) an objective and non-descriptive language which they could use to disguise from themselves the true nature of their activities. Finally, the chapter concludes with a brief note on German resistance to the Nazi regime and highlights the importance of reviving instances when people disobeyed the law and demonstrated moral courage.

The rise of Nazism

> No constitution on earth had so easily legalized a coup d'état as did the Weimer Constitution (Schmitt 1995: 25 quoted in Agamben 2005: 15).

One reason anti-Semitism erupted the way that it did in Germany was because of the nature of Nazism and the processes it established to remake political forms and notions of law (Schoenbaum 1997: 193–233). For Arendt, the rise of the Nazi government was not lawless, but it did establish a kind of special or unique legality based on the law of movement and the dissolution of the juridical person (Arendt 1973a: 461–462 and 577; Goldoni and McCorkindale 2013b: 7; Canovan 2000: 28).[7] From the outset it was clear that Hitler and the protest voters who supported him did not simply want to outfit the Weimar system with a new executive – they wanted to create a new kind of state. While details were

7 Arendt (1973a: 463) argues that for totalitarianism, 'all laws have become laws of movement'. See also Seymour (2010: 211): 'Despite the reference here to the concepts of "law", it is important to note that her definition of its meaning and place within totalitarianism is distinct from that within liberalism. For Arendt, totalitarian law and its components of ideology and terror mark the demise of subjectivity upon which liberal legal responsibility is premised.' This perspective underpins Arendt's reservation about the Eichmann trial.

vague, Hitler articulated this ambition as a witness at a 1930 trial of three Nazis who were changed with subversion: 'In this constitutional [i.e. through legal means] way we shall try to gain decisive majorities in the legislative bodies so that the moment we succeed we can give the state the form that corresponds to our ideas' (Noakes and Pridham 1984: 90).

Following his appointment as Chancellor in 1933, Hitler consolidated his power and imposed a 'rule of terror' against opposition political parties (Caldwell 1994–1995: 406). Most significantly, in response to the Reichstag fire, on 28 February 1933, the Nazi government issued a Decree for the Protection for the People and of the State, which suspended those articles of the Weimar Constitution related to basic rights and civil liberties.[8] The decree also restricted rights to speech and assembly and removed restraints on the ability of the police to detain individuals and conduct investigations. Because this decree was never repealed Agamben (2005: 2) argues that the 'entire Third Reich can be considered a "state of exception"[9] that lasted twelve years'. Agamben (2005: 2) notes further that 'modern totalitarianism' may be defined as 'the establishment, by means of the state of exception, or a legal civil war that allows for the physical elimination not only of political adversaries but of entire categories of citizens who for some reason cannot be integrated into the political system'.[10]

Once inside the 'state of exception' the Nazi party prepared an Enabling Law which granted the government emergency powers and transfered executive and legislative power to the government under Hitler's direction. The Enabling Law also eradicated any controls or limits that might be exercised by an independent or elected body.[11] Under the coercion of paramilitary guards from the SA (*Sturmabteilung*) two-thirds of the Reichstag passed the Enabling Law and secured an amendment to the Weimar Constitution (Bracher 1970: 199–211). The significance of this new law was not lost on German jurists. For example, Carl Schmitt wrote a commentary for the journal *Deutsche Juristen-Zeitung* which described the Decree as 'a turning point of constitutional significance' and a 'national

8 Hitler's rise to absolute power was facilitated, in part, by Article 48 of the Weimar Constitution. The text of Article 48 reads: 'If public security and order are seriously disturbed or endangered within the German Reich, the President of the Reich may take measures necessary for their restoration, intervening if need be with the assistance of the armed forces. For this purpose, he may suspend for a while, in whole or in part, the fundamental rights provided in Articles 114, 115, 117, 118, 123, 124 and 153.' Article 48 added that a law would specify in detail the conditions and limitation under which presidential power could be exercised; however, such a law was never passed.

9 A state of exception occurs when ordinary laws and legal procedures are put aside and sovereign power resides in a person or group of people (Schmitt 2006: 5).

10 There is an important difference in the way Arendt and Agamben theorise totalitarianism. While Agamben argued that the 'state of exception' was common to most post-enlightenment nation-states, Arendt argued totalitarian rule and the Holocaust were unprecedented.

11 The only limit was that the elderly President von Hindenburg would remove Hitler from office and this was not a realistic possibility (Bendersky 1983: 198).

revolution' that cleared the way for a 'new construction of the state' that would retain the 'old German conservative heritage … in National Socialist countenance' (quoted in Caldwell 1994–1995: 407).

Schmitt was not alone in extolling the virtues of National Socialism. In fact, the two tenets of Nazi rule – the Führer principle (*Führerprinzip*) and the principle of essential unity became 'articles of faith' for many legal jurists (Caldwell 1994–1995: 410).[12] The Führer principle held that the Führer's word is more authoritative than the written law and must be obeyed by all branches of the state. By contrast, the unity principle called for unity of the species, type and race of the German *volk* or people (Schwab 1989: 111; Mosse 1966). For Otto Koellreutter, a constitutional lawyer, the two principles stood in organic relationship: 'Leadership … means ordering together a racially equal (*artgleich*) group of humans and holding off or if necessary, eradicating enemy forces, [two activities that are] mutually complementary' (quoted in Caldwell 1994–1995: 408). Koellreutter argued further: 'Authority from above as the result of leadership conscious of its responsibility, trust, and discipline from below: these qualities of what is, in the end, a soldierly mentality (*Geisteshaltung*) characterise the essence of today's Führer-state' (quoted in Caldwell 1994–1995: 409).

The Führer principle and the principle of unity provided National Socialism with the concepts and ideology it needed to radically transform the State. Moreover, it gave the Nazi system internal meaning and a legal order that borrowed the hierarchical structure of natural law (with the Führer rather than universal moral principles or God at the apex).[13] In drawing a distinction between Nazism and natural law and legal positivism, Arendt (1973a: 463) argues that totalitarian governments 'obey strictly and unequivocally those laws of Nature or of History from which all positive laws always have been supposed to spring'. Arendt (1973a: 462–463) argues further:

> It is the monstrous, yet seemingly unanswerable claim of totalitarian rule that, far from being 'lawless,' it goes to the sources of authority from which positive laws received their ultimate legitimation, that far from being arbitrary it is more obedient to these suprahuman forces than any government ever was before, and that far from wielding its power in the interest of one man, it is quite prepared to sacrifice everybody's vital immediate interests to the execution of what it assumes to be the law of History or the Law of Nature.

Cast in these terms, Nazi law was freed from the constraints of subjective reflection and positivist expression. As David M. Seymour (2007: 100) argues, the law of nature 'eschews every aspect of its human subject' and its 'judgements of nature

12 For a discussion of the courts and legal profession during the Weimar period and the Third Reich see Müller (1992), Stolleis (1998), Steinweis and Rachlin (2015).

13 Caldwell (1994–1995: 411) noted: 'all major Nazi theorists tended to reject positivism'.

are "always already" made'.[14] Rather than reflecting the laws of nature, Seymour (2007: 101) describes that Nazi law was a 'guise' or 'parody' of nature. Nazism was an inversion of the 'relationship between humanity, nature and the cosmos' that defined previous cultures and Nazi law also inverted the 'the relationship between the restless movement of nature and the stability of society' (Seymour 2007: 101).

Freed from the constraints of reflection and subjectivity, human institutions inside of Nazi Germany were cast as the executors of the natural or eternal will. As Arendt (1973a: 465) notes, the rulers 'do not apply laws, but execute a movement in accordance with its inherent law'.[15] This shift from law to terror served to justify any action or whim that Hitler or his agents wanted to undertake. Moreover, in structural terms, the Enabling Law meant that Hitler did not require higher approval and his actions were not subject to review by either a court or an elected assembly. This gave the Nazis free rein to define which groups of people were part of the national community and exclude those who they deemed inferior for 'racial' or eugenic reasons (Burleigh and Wippermann 1991: 44–74). The Nazi regime felt it could abolish the foundations of its legitimacy because it promised to 'release the fulfillment of law from all action and will of man; and it promises justice on earth because it claims to make mankind itself the embodiment of the law' (Arendt 1973a: 462). In other words totalitarian rule sought the 'identification of man and law' and 'to make mankind itself the embodiment of the law' (Arendt 1973a: 462).

This perspective on legality was the 'first essential step on the road to total domination' (Arendt 1973a: 447). After the Enabling Law was enacted, the circle of despotism was complete – 'the will of the Führer was the will of the *Volk*, the *Volk* was defined by the will of the Führer, and all elements foreign to the *Volk* were to be excised from the body of the *Volk*' (Caldwell 1994–1995: 410). Germany's constitutional forms were being eroded into an amorphous bonding of people, a racially defined *Volk*, which was fuelled by a popular subscription to something energetic – the Führer's will (Arendt 1973a: 3, 39–42 and Young-Bruehl 2002: 574). Some scholars saw clearly the direction the party was heading. For example, in 1934 the Jewish scholar Jacob R. Marcus wrote:

> The spectacle of this new weapon – the legal arm of the anti-Jewish legislation of the Third Reich – used against a whole people, crushing not heads and bones but souls and spirits, is a new one. This approach is more subtle; it

14 Arendt (1973a: 462) argues: 'Totalitarian lawfulness, defying legality and pretending to establish the direct reign of justice on earth, executes the law of History or of Nature without translating it into the standards of right and wrong for individual behaviour. It applies the law directly to mankind without bothering with the behaviour of men … Totalitarian policy claims to transform the human species into an active unfailing carrier of a law to which human beings would only passively and reluctantly be subjected.'

15 See also Seymour (2007: 101).

> is endowed more with the aspect of permanence; it can be challenged with much greater difficulty; it does not lend itself easily to vivid dramatization and is hence less potent than cracked skulls or torn beards in arousing the horrific sympathy of foreign nations.

Public lawyers in Germany delicately avoided stating that fact so explicitly (Caldwell 1994–1995: 413; Jacobson and Schlink 2002). Moreover, those that actively opposed the Nazi regime lacked the influence or power to do anything about it. The difficult work was done and the Nazi party, believing itself to be riding the wave of history, had no intention of voluntarily relinquishing its power.

With these foundations laid and power concentrated in the hands of a radical anti-Semite, mass destruction (if not genocide) was a probable outcome. Arendt captures the essence of totalitarian violence in her phrase 'total terror' which entails the disappearance or erasure of politics.[16] Totalitarianism attacks politics by erasing human agency for political action and attacking humanity itself: 'Total terror … is designed to translate into reality the law of movement of history or nature' (Arendt 1973a: 464). Anything which seeks to moderate the dynamism of totalitarianism must be removed to 'to make it possible for the force of nature or of history to race freely through mankind, unhindered by any spontaneous human action' (Arendt 1973a: 465). Human beings (even political leaders) must serve this movement, 'either riding atop their triumphant car or crushed under its wheels' (Arendt 2005e: 341). Individuality must also be diminished by 'the iron band of terror, which destroys the plurality of men and makes out of man the One who unfailingly will act as though he himself were part of the course of history or nature' (Arendt 1973a: 466).

Raul Hilberg, who Arendt draws on extensively in chapters 4–6[17] of her Eichmann report, outlined the process of destruction in his monumental work, *The Destruction of the European Jews*. See Figure 5.1 below.

During her report on the Eichmann trial Arendt comments on several critical aspects of the destruction process. For example, with respect to the second stage Arendt (2006a: 59) highlights 1 April 1933 when Hitler ordered a general boycott of Jewish businesses and offices (the boycott lasted three days). She also cites the Nuremberg laws which were passed at the annual Nuremberg Rally of the Nazi Party on 15 September 1935. The Nuremberg laws consisted of two pieces of legislation; first the *Law for the Protection of German Blood and German Honour* banned marriage and sexual relations between Jews[18] and Germans. It also prohibited German women under the age of 45 from gaining employment in Jewish

16 Shortly after the Second World War, Arendt (1950: 353) published an article where she noted that totalitarianism 'kills the roots' of a people's political, social and personal life.

17 Arendt (2006a: 71). See also Hilberg (2002: 133–142).

18 Note that Jews of mixed parentage or *Mischlinge* were permitted to marry Germans.

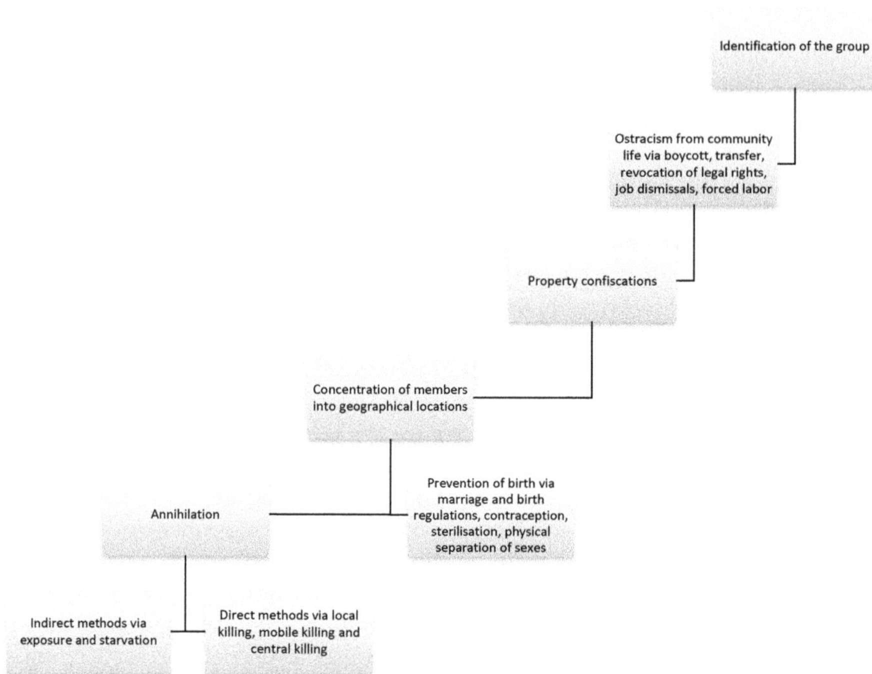

Figure 5.1 The destruction process[19]

households (consistent with the objectives of the legislation, this provision sought to prevent 'race defilement' or mixed children). Second, the *Reich Citizenship Law* defined Jews in racial terms[20] and held that Reich citizenship was limited to those with German blood. Under this legislation, the Jews were classified, not as citizens, but as subjects of the state (Arendt 2006a: 39).

Of these regulations, Arendt (2006a: 39) argues that only the ban on German workers in Jewish households was of practical significance: 'The others merely legalized a de facto situation.' Moreover, by recognising Jews as legal subjects and defining the boundaries of discrimination, the Nuremberg laws provided the Jewish community with certainty as to their second-class status. There was also a hope that the discriminatory provisions were conclusive and '[i]f they kept to themselves, as they had been forced to do anyhow, they would be able to live unmolested' (Arendt 2006a: 39–40). To further help us understand this perspective, Arendt (2006a: 40) quotes from Hans Lamm:

19 This diagram is adapted from Miller (1995: 3) and Hilberg (1985b: 1189).

20 The Nazi party rejected the traditional view of Jews as members of a religious or cultural community. They claimed instead that Jews were a race defined by birth and by blood.

> Life is possible under every law. However, in complete ignorance of what is permitted and what is not one cannot live.

Alongside these examples, Arendt (2006a: 56) spends time discussing three further attempts to find a legal solution to the Jewish question – the *Haavara* or transfer agreement (Arendt 2006a: 60), the Nisko plan (Arendt 2006a: 74–75) and the Madagascar project (Arendt 2006a: 76–77). In his testimony, Eichmann claimed that these initiatives were directed at 'putting firm soil under [the Jewish people's] feet' and that he 'cooperated in reaching such a solution, gladly and joyfully' (Arendt 2006a: 56). He also used these examples to impress upon the court the 'inner rapport' he felt with his early work and the attempts he made to save Jewish lives. Eichmann also stressed the close relationships he developed with members of the Zionist community and spoke about them as 'the decent Jews' because, like the Nazis, they also 'thought in "national terms" and opposed assimilation into the German state' (Arendt 2006a: 57, 59, 60).

Rather than engaging with the details of the transfer proposals, Arendt uses them as a platform to further her analysis of Eichmann's character and other facts pushed aside by the court (Arendt 2006a: 56). For example, commenting on Eichmann's selective memory, she notes that he only remembered those Jews 'who had been completely in his power' and that he 'underwent a genuine and lasting personality change' once he had been 'promoted to a position with executive power' (Arendt 2006a: 63–65). Against Eichmann's claims that he worked to support Zionist aims or that he had personally saved hundreds of thousands of Jews, Arendt argued that the principal objectives of the Nisko plan and Madagascar project was to extend the influence of the Security Service in the East (Arendt 2006a: 63, 74–75; Lipstadt 2011: 139). This objective was linked to Arendt's (2006a: 75) analysis of careerism and Eichmann's personal ambition to advance in rank:

> Eichmann's eagerness to acquire some territory for 'his' Jews is best understood in terms of his own career. The Nisko plan was 'born' during the time of his rapid advancement, and it is more than likely that he saw himself as the future Governor General, like Hans Frank in Poland, of the future Protector like Heydrich in Czechoslovakia, of a 'Jewish State'.

Finally, Arendt (2006a: 77) argues that the transfer projects were a cloak which disguised preparations that were underway to carry out the 'physical extermination' of Jews from Western Europe. The Nazis' lack of concern for conditions in the new territory was evident from Erich Rajakowitsch's description of the Nisko territory:

> There are no dwellings, there are no houses. If you build, there will be a roof over your heads. There is no water, the wells all around carry disease, there

is cholera, dysentery, and typhoid. If you bore and find water, you will have water (quoted in Arendt 2006a: 75).

When plans for Madagascar came to a standstill, the impact took on psychological significance: 'everybody was psychologically, or rather, logically, prepared for the next step: since there existed no territory to which one could "evacuate," the only "solution" was extermination' (Arendt 2006a: 77). It was at this time that letters and legal documents went into circulation that contained reference to a 'final aim' which Eichmann testified could only refer to 'physical extermination' and stated that 'this basic idea was already rooted in the minds of the higher leaders' (Arendt 2006a: 77–78).

Objective language and double speak

On 27 September 1939 Himmler created the Head Office for Reich Security (RSHA) by fusing the SS Security Service with the State security police. This organisational restructure fused the civil service with the most radical elements of the Nazi regime (Browder 1996: 11). In fact, Arendt (2006a: 68) declared that it was at this moment that the 'Nazi regime became openly totalitarian and openly criminal'. While legal under its own juridical processes, Arendt used the phrase 'openly criminal' to highlight the regime's *public* adoption of policies relating to concentration and mass murder – policies which were contrary to standards articulated in international law (Joseph and Castan 2014: 529). It is also important to note that Eichmann's organisation – the SS – was regarded as a criminal organisation under Articles 9 and 10 of the Nuremberg Charter[21] and section three of the NNCL.[22]

While the Nazi party were increasingly open about their treatment of Jews, they also understood the importance of objective language and doublespeak[23] to

21 Article 9 stated: 'At the trial of any individual or any group or organisation the tribunal may declare (in connection with any act of which the individual may be convicted) that the group or organisation of which the individual was a member was a criminal organisation.' Article 10 reinforced this provision by providing that once the tribunal declared an organisation criminal, this would be final and the 'competent national authority of any Signatory shall have the right to bring individuals to trial for membership'.

22 Section 3 of the NNCL uses the phrase 'Enemy Organisation' but this is defined in section 3(b) as a 'body of persons' which has been declared by the Nuremberg tribunal as a 'criminal organisation'. Eichmann's lawyer, Servatius, protested arguing that it mirrored laws implemented by Hitler to persecute the Jews. In response Lipstadt (2011: 139) noted: 'Servatius's comparison disregarded many essential facts, primary among them that one had to choose to be a member of the SS, Gestapo, or SD, whereas Jews did not choose to be Jews. Furthermore, membership in these organizations meant complicity in acts of violence against others.'

23 Herman (1992: 1) defines doublespeak as 'the misuse of words by implicit redefinition, selective application of "snarl" and "purr" words, and other forms of verbal manipulation'.

disguise the true nature of their activities. This is a common feature of legislation and policy documents. For example, in Australia legislation purporting to enforce animal welfare standards may also legitimate meat production by stating animals should be killed in a way that limits 'unnecessary pain';[24] and in refugee law, a 'fast track' applicant is a person with extremely limited review rights who can be removed quickly.[25] Objectivity and doublespeak are even more pervasive for military matters. Think for example of how the *Patriot Act US* (2001) eroded civil liberties or the death of innocent bystanders is rationalised by the term 'collateral damage'.

Eichmann was very proud of his fluency in doublespeak. He described concentration camps in terms of 'administration' and extermination camps using the language of 'economy' (Arendt 2006a: 48, 69). However, it was a comment from Eichmann's lawyer, Servatius, that revealed just how deep and entrenched the application of certain language rules had become in German society – even for those who had not joined the Nazi party. Arendt (2006a: 69) recalls a scene which occurred near the end of the trial when Servatius declared the accused innocent of all charges relating to 'the collection of skeletons, sterilizations, killings by gas, and *similar medical matters*'. The Israeli judge at this point interrupted him to suggest that he had made a slip of the tongue when he said that the killing of people using gas was a medical matter. But Servatius, undaunted replied: 'It was indeed a medical matter, since it was prepared by physicians; it was a matter of killing, and killing, too, is a medical matter.'

The true nature of the 'final solution of the Jewish question' was further disguised by the way information was controlled in the Nazi hierarchy. Those who had been officially told of the Führer's orders were promoted to 'bearers of secrets' (*Geheimnisträger*) and were required to take a special oath (Arendt 2006a: 85). All official correspondence between them was required to comply with strict language rules and this was one reason why Hausner had such a difficult time finding documents that explicitly described Eichmann's role in the extermination process. Arendt (2006a: 85) provides a helpful list of language rules: 'The prescribed code names for killing were "final solution," "evacuation" (*Aussiedlung*), and "special treatment" (*Sonderbehandlung*); deportation – unless it involved Jews directed to Theresienstadt, the "old people's ghetto" for privileged Jews, in which case it was called "change of residence" – received the names of "resettlement" (*Umsiedlung*) and "labor in the East" (*Arbeitseinsatz im Osten*).'

Only in private were the bearers of secrets allowed to talk explicitly about their work. However, the purpose of the rules was not just to disguise reality from the public – it was to disguise it from oneself. It was a psychological trick that worked more effectively once internalised.[26] Thus, it is unlikely the 'bearers of secrets'

24 Section 13, *Animal Welfare Act 1975* (SA) 1985.
25 Part 7AA, *Migration Act* (Cth) 1958.
26 See Orwell (2009: 183): 'In the end the Party would announce that two and two made five, and you would have to believe it. It was inevitable that they should make that claim sooner or later: the logic of their position demanded it.'

looked for opportunities to talk openly with their brethren. Arendt (2006a: 85) notes: 'For whatever other reasons the language rules may have been devised, they proved of enormous help in the maintenance of order and sanity in the various widely diversified services whose cooperation was essential in this matter.'

So consumed were the German elite in undertaking their 'historic mission' for the destiny of the German people that some were even able to turn their instincts around and direct pity on themselves. This was most perverse for Himmler who 'instead of saying: what horrible things I did to people!' was able to say: 'What horrible things I had to watch in the pursuance of my duties, how heavily the task weighed upon my shoulders' (Arendt 2006a: 106). Something similar can be noted in the way Eichmann presented his testimony as a hard luck story, evidently oblivious to the fact that few would have sympathy for his troubles (Arendt 2006a: 50).

Resistance to immoral law

Before concluding this chapter, it is necessary to comment briefly on resistance – an action which many legal and political theorists claim becomes a duty in the face of immoral law (Austin 1954: 186; Hart 1958: 598). Arendt affirms this perspective throughout her political writings but particularly in her 1972 book, *Crises of the Republic*. Here Arendt (1972: 88) argues that the tacit consent we give to laws and norms which govern our daily lives can only be truly voluntary if we have the power of dissent (the power of voice and exit). Dissent, in other words, implies consent to the Constitution (not necessarily individual laws) and keeps consent alive by giving back its actuality. By binding ourselves to the Constitution as a foundational settlement, we leave ourselves free to dissent from particular laws which are immoral or otherwise harmful to the sociality of which we are a part.

In her Eichmann report, Arendt (2006a: 103–104) offers many examples of ordinary Germans whose 'ability to tell right from wrong had remained intact' and who sacrificed and even lost their lives resisting Nazi law. She describes, for example, two peasant boys who were drafted into the SS toward the end of the war but refused to join the Nazi party. The boys were sentenced to death but before their execution they wrote to their families: 'We would rather die than burden our conscience with such terrible things' (Arendt 2006a: 104). There are also interesting examples from German lawyers like Hans Litten who represented opponents of the Nazi party between 1929 and 1932 and put Hitler on the witness stand (Hett 2008) and Josef Hartinger who sought to bring to justice those responsible for the first murders at the Dachau Concentration Camp (Ryback 2014).

That more Germans did not resist, was due not to their respect for the law or fear of reprisal,[27] but to factors ranging from obedience to authority, complicity, ambition, the elimination of alternative organisational structures and a sense that

27 See Browning (1994: 57)

they were individually powerless. These explanations are intimately human and represent key reasons why people struggle to resist immoral laws today. And yet, Arendt offers these brief glimpses of resistance, not to romanticise the past but to highlight the fact that the history of the Third Reich is a history 'not only of cruelty, but also of compassion, sacrifice, courage, kindness' (Zinn 2005: 11). For Arendt, this is more than symbolic – it is political. What we emphasise in history determines what future possibilities are open to us in the future as we confront new political challenges. Arendt (2006a: 231) underlines this point toward the end of her report: 'how utterly different everything would be today in this courtroom, in Israel, in Germany, in all of Europe, and perhaps in all the countries of the world, if only more such stories [of resistance] could have been told'.

Chapter 6

Wannsee

The enabling conference

> It was the first time in my life [that I] took part in such a conference in which ... senior officials participated, such as Secretaries of State – it was conducted very quietly and with much courtesy, with much friendliness – politely and nicely, there was not much speaking and it did not last a long time, the waiters served cognac, and in this way it ended (Eichmann Trial, Session 10, 19 April 1961).

In popular culture the visual images associated with the Wannsee conference have become iconographic. Movies portray a stately lakeside villa, set against a snowy landscape.[1] Nazi officials gather in a decadently furnished boardroom to calmly discuss what General Telford Taylor described as 'perhaps the most shameful document of modern history' (Roseman 2002: 2).

For decades, historians regarded the Wannsee conference as a central moment in the extermination of the Jews. Some historians even suggested that the final solution was decided at the meeting and that Eichmann was central to the decision-making process (Cesarani 2006: 107). For example, in his opening address, Gideon Hausner argued that Eichmann 'proposed that a meeting be called of the senior officials who might be considered suitable to carry out the plan of slaughter and Heydrich agreed' (Nizkor 1991). Hausner (1966: 94–98) scaled back this assessment in his biography and since the 1980s historians have sought to put the meeting in its proper context and most now recognise that genocide was being orchestrated well before Wannsee.[2] While disagreements remain about the purpose of the meeting, Arendt (2006a: 112–113) is close to the mark in noting that organised mass-murder required the 'active cooperation of all Ministries and the whole of the civil service' and that the 'aim of the conference was to coordinate all efforts toward the implementation of the Final Solution'.[3]

1 *The Wannsee Conference* (1984) and *Conspiracy* (2001).

2 Although Williams (2016) repeats the idea that genocide was decided at Wannsee.

3 Arendt's comments are consistent with the invitation letter which Eichmann drafted for participants. It stated that the objective of the meeting was to 'make all necessary organisational and technical preparations for a comprehensive solution of the Jewish question'.

Further to these aims, writers such as Saul Friedländer (1997: 283), Ian Kershaw (2000: 486) and David Cesarani (2006: 111, 2016: 454) have argued that the meeting provided Heydrich with a decisive way to establish his primacy and the dominance of the RHSA over Jews' affairs across the continent (including the General government in Poland and the Occupied Eastern Territories).[4] Heydrich also wanted to end arguments over the interpretation of anti-Jewish legislation and whether or not the RHSA or Ministry of Interior had jurisdiction over those of mixed parentage. Finally, he also wanted to make clear that the Final Solution was total and that no member of the Jewish people would survive. This objective was implicit in one of the most significant sections from the minutes of the meeting:

> In the course of the final solution and under appropriate leadership, the Jews should be put to work in the East. In large, single-sex labour columns, Jews fit to work will work their way eastwards constructing roads. Doubtless the large majority will be eliminated by natural causes. And doubtless any final remnant that survives will consist of the most resistant elements. They will have to be dealt with appropriately, because otherwise, by natural selection, they would form the germ cell of a new Jewish revival (quoted in Roseman 2002: 70).

For Arendt, the significance of the Wannsee conference pertains to her assessment of Eichmann's criminal guilt and circumstances under which ordinary people could become complicit in war crimes. The conference represented a key moment or cross road when Eichmann might have left his post or requested an alternative assignment. Instead, surrounded by some of the most powerful leaders in the Nazi regime, Eichmann pushed aside his doubts and described feeling free of guilt about the work ahead (Arendt 2006a: 114). Notwithstanding disagreements amongst scholars about Eichmann's purported psychological transition (Stangneth 2015; Lipstadt 2011; Cesarani 2006),[5] Arendt's comments on the Wannsee conference are of enduring relevance for criminal lawyers and criminologists seeking to comprehend the nature of intention and criminal responsibility. I consider this issue with reference to moral psychology and studies like the Milgram experiment which demonstrate that individual behaviour is more affected by situation and context then standard globalist conceptions of moral character acknowledge.

Following this, I examine the key agenda item at the Wannsee conference – the legal definition of 'Jew' and Nazi policy with respect to half-Jews and Jews from mixed marriage. In this discussion I highlight the flexibility of legal definitions, the

4 Arendt (2006a: 133) claims that 'Heydrich was half-Jewish'. See also Gerwarth (2012: 26).

5 It is difficult to reconcile Eichmann's testimony in Jerusalem with comments he made during a notorious farewell speech in Berlin: 'I will leap into my grave laughing because the feeling that I have five million human beings on my conscience is for me a source of extraordinary satisfaction' (Stangneth 2015: 297; Arendt 2006a: 46).

categories of exception that existed after the conference and the way 'prominent Jews' or those with political leverage could subvert anti-Jewish legislation. While exception categories saved numerous lives, they also implicitly acknowledged and validated laws aimed at the extermination of the Jewish people.

Pontius Pilate

We have learned that our personality is fragile (Levi 1996: 55).

During the course of her report on the Eichmann trial, Arendt sought to locate the chain of events that caused Eichmann to adopt a guilty mind and become complicit in mass murder. She writes: 'It is of great political interest to know how long it takes an average person to overcome his innate repugnance toward crime, and what exactly happens to him once he has reached that point' (Arendt 2006a: 93).[6] Over the course of 1941, Eichmann was ordered to report on the killing operations underway at Minsk, Lwów (Lemberg)[7] and Lublin. He presented vivid memories to the court, including witnessing columns of naked Jews that had been killed with cyanic acid and blood gushing from the ground like a fountain (Arendt 2006a: 89). Eichmann testified that he felt repelled by these scenes, however he was able to push these feeling aside and assume responsibility for transporting victims to those same death camps. In response to Judge Landau's question on whether Eichmann had a conscience, Arendt (2006a: 95) answered: 'yes, he had a conscience, and his conscience functioned in the expected way for about four weeks, whereupon it began to function the other way round'.

This shift in Eichmann's personality was cemented during the Wannsee conference. The invitees represented some of the most influential figures in the Nazi regime and the German political class. Most had university degrees and almost half bore the title Doctor of Law (Roseman 2002: 67). Surprisingly, given the complexity of discussion items and the distance some had travelled to attend, the formal meeting only lasted an hour and a half. Afterwards, Eichmann was invited to converse and enjoy a drink by the fire with Müller and Heydrich. This may sound like an incidental and unimportant fact, but Eichmann was a social climber and a careerist of the first order.[8] While he had trouble recalling important details about deportations or Jewish leaders he had met, Eichmann recalled this moment with uncharacteristic clarity: 'that was the first time I saw Heydrich smoke and drink … [they] enjoyed some rest after long hours of work' (Arendt 2006a: 114).

6 Fine (2001: 111) argues that this overcoming of repugnance 'was also due to the skilful use of moral imperatives to overcome the natural resistance of "ordinary men" of slaughtering entirely innocent human beings'.

7 See Sands (2016).

8 It was Hitler's ability to work his way up from the bottom that made him and his movement worthy of Eichmann's esteem (Arendt 2006a: 126).

The combination of these facts – the authority of those in attendance, the formal setting of the meeting and Eichmann's desire for political ascendance – provided the former vacuum salesman with the opportunity to hitch his ambition to a genocidal project (Robin 2004: 118). Moreover, Eichmann identifies this as the moment when he felt relieved of guilt about the task ahead. Arendt (2006a: 114) reports:

> Although he had been doing his best right along to help with the Final Solution, he had still harboured some doubts about 'such a bloody solution through violence,' and these doubts had now been dispelled. 'Here now, during this conference, the most prominent people had spoken, the Popes of the Third Reich.' Now he could see with his own eyes and hear with his own ears that not only Hitler, not only Heydrich of the 'sphinx' Müller, not just the S.S. or the Party, but the élite of the good old Civil Service were vying and fighting with each other for the honor of taking the lead in these 'bloody' matters. 'At that moment, I sensed a kind of Pontius Pilate feeling, for I felt free of all guilt.' *Who was he to judge?* Who was he 'to have [his] own thoughts in his matter'?

While recognising the shortcomings in Eichmann's testimony (Browning 2002: 4), I would like to take seriously his contention the Wannsee conference represented a seminal moment in his decision to participate in the Final Solution. In particular, I am interested in examining the extent to which the *Nazis and Nazi Collaborators (Punishment) Law* (1950) (NNCL) recognised context and obedience to authority in judging criminal responsibility. Moreover, I consider whether our understanding of criminal responsibility ought to shift in circumstances where murder is commonplace and 'only "exceptions" could be expected to behave "normally"' (Arendt 2006a: 26).

In common law systems (such as Australia, the United Kingdom and the United States) criminal law is sensitive to the context in which an act is committed. For example, arguments of self-defence, duress or necessity may constitute a formal defence and completely exonerate an accused person. On the other hand context can aggravate an offence, such as when assault is committed using a deadly weapon. Circumstances that are not caught by a formal defence, such as personal history or evidence of previous criminal activity, are relevant to sentencing and may aggravate or mitigate a punishment (Arenson *et al.* 2015).

This attention to context represents a gradual shift away from 'character' as a marker of criminal intention and responsibility.[9] Following John Doris (2005: 5),

9 See also Lacey (2013: 153–154) who argues that 'character-based patterns of attribution are enjoying a revival in contemporary English (and American) criminal responsibility … not only in mandatory sentencing laws applying to particular categories of "dangerous" offender, but also in the substantive law, particularly that dealing with terrorism, and in the operation of evidential presumptions, detention rules, practices of offender profiling, and the renewed admissibility of evidence of bad character'.

by character I refer to the globalist conception of an integrated association of robust traits, i.e. 'The brave person acts distinctively, with distinct motives, affects, and cognitions.' Criminal law's shift away from character is supported by research in social psychology which suggests that character is not a dependable reference point for understanding a person's behaviour or their motivations for acting in a particular way. Character, Doris (2005: 2) suggests, is extremely sensitive to variation:

> The experimental record suggests that situational factors are often better predictors of behaviour than personal factors ... in most situations it looks as though personality is less than robustly determinative of behaviour. To put things crudely, people typically lack character.

Arendt's reflections on German society during and after the Nazi regime are consistent with this argument. Commenting on the moral collapse of German society, Arendt lamented that ordinary men and women, indeed the vast majority of the German people, relieved themselves of their foundational moral beliefs as easily as they might repudiate the rule that one should not begin eating until everyone is served (Arendt 2005c: 54). Just as shocking for Arendt was that once the Nazis were defeated the mass of German citizens, apart from notable exceptions, could earnestly and enthusiastically adopt or return to the principles of enlightened morality and liberalism. Whatever was previously thought about the character of ordinary people, the moral order in Germany was revealed to have no greater substance than social mores – 'manners, customs, conventions to be changed at will' (Arendt 2005c: 54).

How could one make sense of these events? This question motivated intense research during the later half of the twentieth century. The most relevant for our purpose was the Milgram experiment conducted at Yale University between 1960 and 1963 (intersecting the period between Eichmann's kidnap and execution).[10] Milgram ran various permutations of his experiment which involved over 1,000 participants drawn from diverse socio-economic backgrounds.[11] Milgram's method of inquiry is well known but I will provide a brief summary here:[12]

The subject is met by an experimenter wearing a lab-coat. The experimenter introduces the subject to another ostensible volunteer who is actually a confederate and actor. The experimenter explains that the study concerns the effects of punishment on learning and rigs a process so that the subject is given the role of 'teacher' while the confederate is the 'learner'. The learner is strapped to a chair and an electrode is attached to his wrist. The experimenter assures participants that the shocks will cause no 'permanent tissue damage' and the teacher is not told that the

10 For other similar experiments see Doris (2005: 28–61).

11 The majority of Milgram's participants were men. However, experiment 8 involved all women and 65% were classified as obedient (Milgram 2009: 62–63). See also Miller *et al.* (1974). There is also little evidence that results vary with respect to age, Shanab and Yahya (1977).

12 For more detail see Milgram (2009: 13–26).

shocks are fake. The teacher is then taken to another room and seated in front of a sophisticated 'shock generator', which they are told, is connected to the learner in the other room. The teacher and learner can hear but not see each other. Next, the teacher administers the word-association test (i.e. blue/box, nice/day) and with each wrong answer they are prompted to administer a shock. The shock gradually increases in intensity and the learner cries out in pain, begging the teacher to stop and sometimes indicating that they have a bad heart. If the teacher expresses concern about the process (which most teachers did) the experimenter responds in sequence with the following prods: (1) Please continue, or, please go on; (2) The experiment requires that you continue; (3) It is absolutely essential that you continue; or (4) You have no other choice, you must go on. After the last protest at 330 volts, the learner is unresponsive. The teacher is told to treat no answer as a wrong answer and continue the experiment up to the maximum 450 volts.

While a substantial portion of subjects displayed disobedient behaviour, almost two-thirds continued the experiment to the end (Milgram 2009: 5).[13] Those that did resist typically went no further than passive noncompliance (Milgram 2009: 73–87; Ross 1988: 102; Zimbardo 1974: 567). Milgram's experiment revealed, not that the teachers were of low character, but the power of situation and context on how a person behaves. Strikingly, the majority of teachers were 'willing to torture another individual to what seemed the door of death without any more direct pressure than the polite insistence' from an authority figure (Doris 2005: 42). The teachers did not carry out their role with ease, but they persisted and managed to push down physical reactions such as sweating, groaning and biting lips (Milgram 1963: 375). One participant, who was observed to be 'approaching a point of nervous collapse' after 20 minutes, still managed to complete the experiment (Milgram 1963: 377).

Milgram understood clearly the importance of his study for understanding why individuals like Eichmann participated in genocide. Reflecting on his experiment, he commented:

> After witnessing hundreds of ordinary people submit to the authority of our own experiments, I must conclude that Arendt's conception of the *banality of evil* comes closer to the truth than one might dare imagine. The ordinary person who shocked the victim did so out of a sense of obligation – a conception of his duties as a subject – and not from any particularly aggressive tendencies (Milgram 2009: 6).

In making this point, Milgram was not saying that anyone could have behaved like Eichmann or that situation *determines* behaviour. There is no evidence for those conclusions and both Milgram and Arendt went to great lengths to highlight that individuals refused to conform and disobeyed orders. However, Milgram's experiments ought to give lawyers pause to consider the role that situation and context might play in criminal behaviour. Eichmann's character (including his

13 The Milgram experiment has been replicated numerous times in different countries. See Doris (2002: 45).

anti-Semitism) has far less explanatory power for those seeking to comprehend his actions than the situation that he, and thousands of other Germans, were in during the Second World War. A situation, which according to Eichmann, crystallised at the Wannsee conference.

With this in mind, it is important to note that the NNCL has very little to say about situation or context. As discussed in Chapter 2, the legislation embodies a dichotomy between good/evil and revives 'character' as determinative of criminal responsibility. Consider, for example, section 10 of the Act[14] which operates to release an accused from criminal responsibility in circumstances of extreme duress. Section 10 has no application with respect to crimes against the Jewish people, crimes against humanity, acts constituting war crimes or murder. Thus, even if Eichmann was able to support his fanciful claim that certain actions were undertaken to avert more serious consequences, that contention was immaterial for 12 of his 15 charges and Eichmann already had orders to 'avoid unnecessary hardships' in his dealings with prisoners (Arendt 2006a: 92, 94).

Moreover, while prosecutor Hausner was given leeway to put Eichmann's actions in a historical framework, Eichmann's personal history and the context of his choices were not legally relevant to the court's determination of his criminal responsibility. Constrained by the legislation, it was not necessary for the court to ask questions about obedience to authority or the murderous context within which Eichmann made decisions.

Ever since the Eichmann trial, scholars have focused on his character – was Eichmann a liar? A banal bureaucrat? A fanatical anti-Semite? While interesting, these questions avoid coming honestly to terms with what Arendt (2006a: 26) describes as the 'greatest moral and even legal challenge of the whole case' – namely how ordinary people could put aside their faculty of reason and become nothing more than a 'walking embodiment of the law' and complicit in mass murder (Arendt 1973a: 463).[15] In other words, Arendt questions how one can judge an individual for a specific act when the individual is operating in a context that has erased all notions of subjectivity (Seymour 2010: 2012). A focus on Eichmann's personality also distracts us from Arendt's rejection of attempts to define evil in terms of ultimate sinfulness and human corruption (Benhabib 2014a). Arendt invites us to recognise the humanness of men like Eichmann and to judge him with full awareness in the context of his actions. This ought to inspire humility, as Arendt (2005a: 19) notes: 'Even the judge who condemns a man for murder may still say, and there but for the grace of God go I!' (Arendt 2005a: 19).

Race laws

> The superfluousness of these decrees already spoke of the superfluousness of those it named (Seymour 2007: 103).

14 Sections 10 and 11 of the NNCL have been reproduced in Chapter 2. See also Appendix.
15 See also Arendt (2013: 43) and Culbert (2009: 147–148).

As discussed in Chapter 3, the Nazi regime was fastidious about cloaking their actions in legal form (Miller 1995: 1).[16] Words were important and their interpretation revealed striking differences within the Nazi regime. Arguably no word was more important or controversial than 'Jew'. The definition of this term varied with respect to the interpreter's subjective experience in an 'interpretative community' and the extent to which their interpretation was motivated by underlying political goals or emotional attachments (Fish 1982: 3).

Arendt provides several examples that illustrate the complexity involved in defining the term 'Jew'. For example, while the Nazi regime was committed to the extermination of Jews, some within the party viewed Zionists as 'decent' because 'they too thought in "national" terms' (Arendt 2006a: 60). Further, a distinction was drawn between Jews raised with the benefits of German culture and Jews from Eastern Europe. Eichmann, for example, baulked at the idea that German Jews were being murdered: 'I never denied that I knew that the *Einsatzgruppen* had orders to kill, but I did not know that Jews from the Reich, evacuated to the East were subject to the same treatment' (quoted in Arendt 2006a: 96). In agreement, Wilhem Kube, a Nazi stationed in Occupied Russia wrote in a letter: 'I am certainly tough and I am ready to help solve the Jewish question, but people who come from our own cultural milieu are certainly something else than the native animalized hordes' (quoted in Arendt 2006a: 96).

Alongside issues of politics and culture, the definitional question was further complicated by the pressure Jews felt to assimilate into European society, convert to Christianity or abandon religious identity all together (Gutman 1998: 291). Assimilation was also marked by a dramatic increase in intermarriage which increased from 200 between 1831 and 1840 to 15,288 between 1931 and 1940. In 1932 there were an additional 3,400 mixed marriages (Gutman 1998: 291). What was to be done with progeny of these marriages, whom the Nazis described as 'half- and quarter Jews' (Arendt 2006a: 113). Should they also be 'killed or only sterilized?' (Arendt 2006a: 113).

The Wannsee conference was tasked with resolving these issues and it looked directly at 'borderline' cases of assimilated Jews and children from mixed marriages.[17] The background to this discussion was the Nuremberg Laws of 1935 and a supplementary regulation which created a new legal category, the *Mischlinge*, defined with reference to a two part test reproduced below:[18]

Part One: Three categories

1 A person with either three or four Jewish grandparents is considered to be a Jew;

16 Recent scholarship contends that the American regime of racial oppression inspired Nazi legislation. See Whitman (2017).

17 A number of historians have shown that this discussion formed the real policy content of discussions. See for example Gutman (1998).

18 Categories adapted from Kershaw (2000: 551–570).

2 A person with exactly two Jewish grandparents is considered to be either a Jew or a Mischling of the first degree; or
3 A person with only one Jewish grandparent is considered to be a Mischling of the second degree.

Part Two: Persons with two Jewish, and two non-Jewish, grandparents

A person with exactly two Jewish grandparents was deemed a Jew if:

1 He is a member of the Jewish religious community on 14 November 1935 or later becomes a member; or
2 He is married to a Jew on 14 November 1935 or later marries a Jew; or
3 His parents were married on or after 17 September 1935, and one of his parents is Jewish; or
4 He is born out of wedlock after 31 July 1936, and one of his parents is Jewish.

If such a person is not classified as a Jew under any of these four subtests, then he is a Mischling of the first degree.

The absurdity of these provisions is clear. Consider the example of X who was born with two Jewish grandparents. X was raised in the Jewish religious tradition but converted to Christianity on 1 November 1935. According to the supplementary regulation, X would be classified a first degree Mischling. However, if X had waited two weeks, he would be classified a Jew. Under the Nuremberg Laws, a Mischling was able to marry other Germans but not other Mischlinge or Jews (Hilberg 1985b: 72). The intention, as documented in Eichmann's minutes of the meeting, was to 'prevent any offspring and to eliminate the problem of persons of mixed blood once and for all'.[19]

Heydrich had long been dissatisfied with the compromise established by the Nuremberg Laws. At Wannsee he launched a frontal assault and asked attendees to equate first degree Mischlinge with full Jews.[20] Only those who had provided exceptional service to the state or had children with a German parent, could hope for privileged status (meaning voluntary sterilisation). With respect to second degree Mischlinge Heydrich argued that they could be treated as Jews if the person looked racially unfavourable or had a criminal record (Roseman 2002: 82). However, a second degree Mischling with a criminal record would not be exterminated if they were married to a German partner. With respect to mixed

19 In 1939 there were 64,000 first degree and 43,000 second degree Mischlinge in Germany, Austria and the Sudeten area.
20 Roseman (2002: 82) notes that Eichmann called for a similar merging of categories on 21 August 1941, at a meeting involving the Party Chancellery, the Racial Policy Office and the RSHA.

marriages, Heydrich argued that all Jewish partners of German spouses could be murdered or sent to an old-age ghetto. Half-Jews who had married Germans could be saved from deportation if they had children but were required to undergo sterilisation (Roseman 2002: 82).[21]

Heydrich had little reason to expect opposition to these proposals and, as Eichmann stated, the meeting provided him the opportunity to press his will 'on the highest level' of government and the civil ministries (quoted in Roseman 2002: 85).[22] Yet, despite Heydrich's best attempt to lay down an authoritative definition of the term 'Jew' exceptions persisted – particularly for 'prominent' Jews or those with political connections. Whilst exceptions saved lives, they also enabled German society to maintain the rule in favour of extermination for the masses. This is a complex point, captured neatly by Arendt (2006a: 132) toward the end of chapter 7: 'What was morally so disastrous in the acceptance of these privileged categories was that everyone who demanded to have an "exception" made in his case implicitly recognized the rule.' This argument applied to Rezsö Kasztner, a Jewish-Hungarian lawyer who saved 1,684 'prominent Jews and was later charged under the same legislation as Eichmann for involuntary complicity in the final solution' (Arendt 2006a: 132; Kasztner 2014). Even Hitler, argued Arendt (2006a: 113), 'is said to have known three hundred and forty "first-rate Jews," whom he had either altogether assimilated to the status of Germans or granted the privileges of half-Jews'.

The persistence of these exceptions reveals something quite important about law in its relationship with power. Words are flexible and bend toward privilege. 'If', Arendt (2006a: 134) notes, 'interventions on behalf of "prominent Jews" came from "prominent" people, they often were quite successful.' Money, prestige and political influence opened doors, brought your case to the attention of the 'right people' and in some cases, saved your life. Arendt was keenly aware of the relationship between law and power. She does not argue against prominent people trying to save their lives. However, she wants to draw our attention to the way exceptions validated the extermination of those less fortunate. In making this point, Arendt communicating directly to Germany of the 1960s and against those who deplore that exceptional people like Einstein were forced to leave 'without realizing that it was a much greater crime to kill little Hans Cohn from around the corner, even though he was no genius' (2006a: 134). Masses of nameless people died so that some prominent people could escape. This was the flipside of exception categories and it must be acknowledged, even as we feel relief for those who escaped.

21 The minutes (protocol) of the meeting can be viewed online: http://avalon.law.yale.edu/imt/wannsee.asp.

22 Eichmann applied Heydrich's ideas during the deportation process. See Arendt (2006a: 159–160).

Chapter 7

Duties of a law-abiding citizen

The tension between legal authority and individual judgment is a theme that reoccurs throughout Arendt's report on the Eichmann trial. As discussed in Chapters 3 and 4, Eichmann was making decisions in the context of a military hierarchy and inside what Carl Schmitt (2006: 13–15) called, a 'state of exception'. That is, a state where ordinary laws and legal procedures were set aside and exceptional power was vested in the sovereign. 'This was the way things were' Arendt (2006a: 135) notes at the beginning of chapter 8 and the 'new law or the land' was grounded in the will of the Führer. In this context, Eichmann stressed to the court that he was a 'law-abiding citizen' who 'not only obeyed orders, he obeyed the law' (Arendt 2006a: 135).

It is easy for us to judge Eichmann for collapsing his self and capacity for individual judgment into the will of the sovereign. However, his example provides us with an opportunity to examine broader perspectives on the authority of law and the claim it makes to our obedience. In totalitarian regimes, the capacity for judgment is controlled through force and the threat of violence. Moreover, as the Eichmann case demonstrates, individuals living in Nazi Germany self-regulated their behaviour because of a desire for promotion, social ascendency and because they conflated morality with the will of the Führer. Self-regulation was assisted further when individuals adopted strong nationalist positions or assimilated myths about the historical destiny of the Aryan people and the thousand-year Reich.

While obviously distinct, one can note examples of self-regulation and conceptual confusion in open societies. Nationalism and national pride ('my country, right or wrong') are perhaps the most obvious examples. However, at a subtler level, one can also note a belief that if something is legal, it is also moral and vice versa. Lawyers are particularly susceptible to this conflation because of their training in reducing even the most complex social or political problem to its legal dimensions. Only rarely do law students have the opportunity to receive instruction on moral reasoning, as distinct from legal ethics (Kronman 2008: 8). Moreover, as critical theory continues to be jettisoned from law degrees in favour of instrumental training, many students graduate without basic tools for making independent moral judgments (Thornton 2012: 59–109). In this respect, law schools are contributing to the broader social phenomenon of 'thoughtlessness' which Arendt (1998: 5) described as the 'the heedless recklessness or hopeless confusion or complacent repetition of "truths"' rather than instructing people to think for themselves and encounter law with critical allegiance.

In this chapter I begin by presenting three different theoretical perspectives on the authority of law. While related, this discussion goes beyond conceptual claims about law and the Hart-Fuller debate described in Chapter 3. The perspectives analysed include philosophical anarchism, claims when an authority has an exclusive moral privilege to rule and inclusive legal positivism.[1] These theories are described to provide a context for Eichmann's views on legal authority and Arendt's subsequent engagement with Eichmann about the duties of citizens confronted with immoral law. To introduce this analysis, I recount a moment in the trial where Eichmann directly invokes Kant and suggests that, prior to the Final Solution, he had lived his life according to the dictates of practical reason. This was a scandalous moment for Arendt and caused her to directly engage Eichmann on the limits of unquestioned obedience to the law. In fact, I suggest that a great deal of Arendt's subsequent writing on judgment can be understood as an extended argument with Eichmann about a proper reading of Kant and as an attempt to deploy his work as a resource for individuals to think critically about authority. Finally, the chapter concludes by noting the virtues of civil disobedience as a means of renewing the State and establishing a democratic citizenship.

The authority of law

> It is not wisdom but Authority that makes a law (Hobbes 1997: 55).

To appreciate Arendt's analysis of Eichmann and the duties that attach to law-abiding citizens it is helpful to begin with a brief consideration of the dominant arguments legal theorists make when discussing the authority of law. To begin, it is important to underline that law *claims* immense power over citizens. The claim to this power is made without our explicit consent and regardless of whether the judgments of the State are morally or practically correct. 'In doing so', Scott Shapiro (2002: 383) notes, authorities 'appear to place themselves above the truth – their right does not seem to depend on their being right.'[2] Even if presented with unambiguous evidence of their error, legal authorities may deploy their monopoly on violence to demand that the law is carried out (Weber 1958: 83). Critics of natural law often point to this fact when responding to the suggestion that an immoral law is not a law. In what tangible sense is that claim true of authorities who still have the power to drag someone to prison or execute them?

In response to questions about law's purported authority over citizens, philosophical anarchists like Richard Wolff (1990: 5) claim that the phrase 'legitimate

1 For a broader discussion see Shapiro (2002: 382–439).

2 The anarchist writer William Godwin (1971: 122) made a similar point: 'There cannot be a more absurd proposition, than that which affirms the right of doing wrong.'

authority' is a contradiction. For Wolff, one's obligation to act morally should always take precedence over the law. According to Wolff (1990: 22), legal authorities should not be obeyed simply because they are authorities who have issued commands. Rather, authorities should attempt to convince citizens that their normative claim is worthy of obedience. From this perspective, an individual's decision to follow a particular law does not arise because of the command – but because I am a morally autonomous person with independent reasons for performing the act (Wolff 1990: 22).

Wolff (1990: 25) argues further that a morally autonomous person is someone who takes responsibility for his or her actions. They are also deeply thoughtful in that they have a duty to gather new information, analyse their motives and evaluate their options in light of this reflection.[3] Moral autonomy is a central aspect of one's humanity. William Godwin (1971: 122) agrees:

> [W]here I make the voluntary surrender of my understanding and commit my conscience to another man's keeping, the consequence is clear. I then become the most mischievous and pernicious of animals. I annihilate my individuality as a man, and dispose my force as an animal to him among my neighbours …

One obvious response to Wolff is that while there are real risks to blind obedience, the world is simply too complex for individuals to realise his standard of moral autonomy.[4] If autonomy is inconsistent with authority then it is difficult to see how autonomy can be realised (Shapiro 2002: 388). It is also interesting to note that Kant (whom I will be turning to in the next section) did not perceive a clash between moral autonomy and authority. He argued that those subject to some overweening authority should publicly ask questions. Indeed, he wrote that individuals do not contravene our 'civil obligations' by voicing 'thoughts on the impropriety of even injustice' of a command (1991: 56).

Robert Ladenson provides an alternative perspective on authority and focuses on circumstances when an authority has an exclusive moral privilege to rule.[5] Legitimate authorities are those with the (a) ability to force citizens to comply with their commands and (b) who have the moral authority to do so, i.e. elected under proper democratic process (Ladenson 1990: 38). From this perspective, laws are not seeking to build a consensus or appeal to individual moral judgment. Laws are threats, backed by force. Ladenson (1990: 38) justifies this appeal to force with reference to the work of Thomas Hobbes (1982), arguing that authority provides government institutions with the ability to solve social problems, i.e. law

3 For a critique of Wolff see Raz (1990: 3–6) and Shapiro (2002: 387–393).

4 Wolff (1990: 29) is keenly aware of this complexity: 'There are great, perhaps insurmountable, obstacles to the achievement of a complete and rational autonomy in the modern world.'

5 Here the term 'privilege' is interpreted in a way that is consistent with Hohfeld (1964).

and order. Only centralised power can ensure that important social institutions are maintained and that order persists (Ladenson 1990: 39).

This argument has curious implications when applied to the Nazi regime. For example, Ladenson argues that the Nazi party had a legitimate right to rule (at least between 1933 and 1944). Moreover, the fact that the Nazis dramatically abused their right to rule did not mean that right was voided in every instance. Ladenson (1990: 39) provides an example:

> One can, for example, believe that German citizens had a right to resist the Nazis and that German traffic police on the *Autobahn* had a right to detain speeding motorists which private citizens did not have. The latter right stemmed simply from the Nazi government's power and general acceptance, not from the moral worth of its ideological foundations.

In opposition to Ladenson, one might reasonably claim that the scale of violence initiated by the Nazi regime violated their legitimate right to rule in every instance. This argument might further be supported by the fact that the first concentration camp was opened in Dachau in 1933 and state sanctioned killings of Nazi opponents began that same year (Wachsmann 2015: 23–24). Moreover, while Ladenson's account solves some of the paradoxes of authority, he neglects one salient feature of law's preservation, namely that the reason that most citizens do not break the law is not because of fear of sanction (there is in fact, little evidence, that severe penalties deter crime)[6] but because the law is, for the most part, consistent with our own moral code (Hart 1997: 56–57; Raz 1990: 4). Even from the perspective of 'power politics' Ladenson ignores Weber's (1958: 57) argument that, even in the context of power politics, authorities must frame their actions in the context of a grand narrative or implement legitimating instruments such as law, if authority is to be maintained.

A final, and arguably more sophisticated, conception of authority is provided by Joseph Raz (1986). For Raz, an essential feature of law is that it *claims* to have legitimate authority and a moral right to direct or pre-empt the behaviour of citizens (Raz 1996: 212–213). However, while the law might claim authority, it does not necessarily possess it. In fact, Raz (1986: 56) argues that the law and political authorities are legitimate only to the extent to which they 'serve the governed' or help citizens 'act on reasons which bind them'. Governments legitimate their authority therefore, not by providing security or undertaking public works, but by producing and validating laws that conform to reason (Raz 1996: 214).

Two further points underpin Raz's service conception of legal authority. First, legal directives should be based on 'reasons which already independently apply to the subjects' and which are 'relevant to their action in the circumstances' (Raz 1986: 47). Thus, law should engage directly with the issue or problem which

6 See, for example, Radelet and Lacock (2009).

citizens face.[7] Second, Raz argues that it must be the case that a citizen 'is likely to better comply with reasons which apply to him ... if he accepts the directives of the alleged authority as authoritatively binding, and tries to follow them, than if he tries to follow the reasons which apply to him directly' (Raz 1996: 214). In other words, the legitimacy of authority is confirmed with reference to instrumental rationality – citizens are more likely to do what is right if they follow the law than if they were left to their own reasoning.

These are both stringent demands and it is unlikely that currently existing authorities would always meet Raz's standard for authority. However, Raz (1986: 73–75) does recognise the possibility of partial legitimacy – where a State is legitimate in some areas but not in others. Everything depends on context and whether or not society would function better with subjects who comply with the law rather than their own reason. In extreme cases, Raz (1979: 266–275) also recognises the morality of certain, limited forms of civil disobedience.

With this background in place, we are in a position to consider Eichmann's attitude toward the authority of Nazi law and Arendt's extended engagement with Eichmann about the responsibility of citizens. While differences exist, I suggest that Arendt's advocacy for the primacy of moral reasoning and civil disobedience shares similarities with the position articulated by the philosophical anarchist.

Eichmann contra Kant

> Man, insofar as he does anything at all, lays down the law; he is the legislator (Arendt 1989: 50).

Eichmann's own relationship to the law and authority are complex. In chapter 8 it is possible to read Eichmann's allegiance to law in purely instrumental terms. That is, as calculated and justified with regard to material gain for the Nazi war effort. Arendt's description of his work in Hungary and in particular his efforts to fleece Jewish prisoners of their money and goods support this reading (Arendt 2006a: 144). However, Arendt does not read Eichmann in this way. Instead, she portrays Eichmann as somebody who was motivated by the desire for professional ascendance and who had internalised many aspects of Nazi law. This latter point was strengthened with respect to Eichmann's allegiance to the Führer, cemented in part by the respect he felt Hitler's personal story of ascendance.[8] This was one of the reasons Eichmann continued to carry out deportations after Himmler had ordered him to stop the evacuations (Arendt 2006a: 147).

One of the most fascinating aspects of Eichmann's perspective on legal authority is that, at the start of the War, he described himself as someone who

7 In saying this, Raz (1986: 48) is also clear that a law or directive need not always be in their interests of citizens: 'A military commander, for example, should put the defence of his country above the interests of his soldiers. He may therefore order them to act against their own interests.'

8 See Arendt (2006a: 126 and 149).

had 'lived his whole life according to Kant's moral precepts and especially according to a Kantian definition of duty' (Arendt 2006a: 135). During his testimony, Eichmann also gave an 'approximately correct' definition of the categorical imperative: 'I meant by my remark about Kant that the principle of my will must always be such that it can be the principle of general laws' (Arendt 2006a: 136).[9] However, following this comment Eichmann acknowledged that once he was charged with carrying out the Final Solution, he ceased to live by Kantian principles. At this point, Eichmann seems to have adopted the degraded Kantianism promoted by Hans Frank, the Governor of Poland: 'Act in such a way that the Führer, if he knew your action, would approve it' (quoted in Arendt 2006a: 136). Picking up on this point, Fine (2001: 112) argues that 'Eichmann did not so much abandon the Kantian moral principle when he acted in line with the Leader principle, as adapt it to an absolute morality which declares that duty is duty, law is law, and Jews must perish – with no exceptions, not even for his own friends.'

It is not difficult to imagine Arendt's reaction to Eichmann's appropriation of Kant during his testimony to police and trial. Incensed, Arendt (2006a: 136) switched tone and offered the following rejoinder as though she were addressing Eichmann directly:

> Kant to be sure, had never intended to say anything of the sort; on the contrary, to him every man was a legislator the moment he started to act: by using his 'practical reason' man found the principles that could and should be the principles of law.

A year after the publication of *Eichmann in Jerusalem* Arendt (2013: 49) was still troubled by Eichmann's comments. During an interview with Joachim Fest, she commented:

> Quite an impertinent remark, of course, isn't it? On Herr Eichmann's part. After all, Kant's whole ethics amounts to the idea that every person, in every action, must reflect on whether the maxim of his action can become a general law. In other words … It really is the complete opposite, so to speak, of obedience! Each person is a lawgiver. In Kant, nobody has the right to obey.

Indeed, Kant argued that moral thinking and judgment was something anyone can participate in. It is implicit in common-sense deliberations concerning the moral worth of actions and the character they express. His book – *Grounding of the Metaphysic of Morals* – is simply an attempt to elucidate the underlying principles implicit in our common sense judgments of moral worth (1993: 16). Put another

9 Arendt (2006b: 216) provides a useful explanation of the categorical imperative: 'The principle of lawgiving, as laid down in the "categorical imperative" – "always act in such a manner that the principle of your action can become a general law" – is based upon the necessity for rational thought to agree with itself.'

way, Kant does not mean to teach us what is right and wrong (he would think that presumptuous) but to make us aware of the moral law as rooted in our free reason. A full awareness of this, he believes, arouses a strong desire to act for moral reasons. Moreover, because this desire belongs to us in our capacity as free, autonomous and reasonable persons, Kant argues that it has higher authority than the positive law of the state (Kant 1996: 133; Arendt 1989: 50).[10]

Arendt (1989) continued her analysis on practical reason and obedience to authority in the fall of 1970 during a during a series of lectures on Kant's political philosophy.[11] Indeed, we can understand a considerable portion of Arendt's later work as a continuation of her argument with Eichmann about his attempt to mobilise Kant as a resource for thoughtless obedience to a fascist system of government (Butler 2014: 156).

From Arendt's later writing it is possible to discern two models of judgment: the first is presented from the standpoint of the political actor – the person engaged in the public world. The second is more distant and emerges from the position of the spectator or observer (D'Entrèves 2002: 246). These models are somewhat at odds but are united by Arendt's consistent engagement with Kant's (1987: 160) aesthetics[12] and his theory of judgment. Arendt's appeal to Kant's aesthetic theory (rather than his moral philosophy) might, at first instance, seem like an odd choice.[13] However, Arendt (2006b: 216) claimed that the *Critique of Judgement* contained 'perhaps the greatest and most original aspect of Kant's political philosophy' and that his writings on aesthetic judgment[14] was a fruitful basis for the post-war reformulation of politics (Butler 2014: 156).

Judgment, according to Arendt, is a political act because it *requires* that we use our imaginations to see from another's perspective (Arendt 2013: 49). Kant (1987: 160) described this 'enlarged mentality' as the ability 'think in the place of everybody else'. While Kant theorised judgment with respect to taste, Arendt

10 Kant argues that citizens are obligated to obey the sovereign 'in whatever does not conflict with inner morality'.

11 Arendt's writing on judgment are scattered across a range of essays. See Arendt (1978b), (2005b), (2006b) and (2006c). Markell (2014: 65) argues further that Kant's third critique appears briefly in Arendt (1998).

12 Markell (2014: 62) convincingly illustrates that the Kantian presence in Arendt's thought predate her 1970 writings, extending as far back as the 1950s. This claim is contested by Wolin (2014): 'As most Arendt scholars are aware, Arendt only developed these Kantian precepts in earnest circa 1970, in the course of her Lectures on Kant's Political Philosophy and in the complementary essay "Thinking and Moral Considerations."'

13 According to Arendt (1989: 15), this thought is not contained in Kant's moral philosophy. She argues: 'For judgment of the particular – This is beautiful, This is ugly; This is right, This is wrong – has no place in Kant's moral philosophy. Judgment is not practical reason; practical reason "reasons" and tells me what to do and what not to do; it lays down the law and is identical with the will, and the will utters commands; it speaks in imperatives. Judgment, on the contrary, arises from "a merely contemplative pleasure or inactive delight".'

14 See Kant (1987: 41–43) and Bernstein (1992: 17–65).

thought that judgment was 'one of the most fundamental abilities of man [*sic*] as a political being' and that it enabled individuals to orient themselves to the public realm.[15] In fact, Arendt (2006b: 218) claimed:

> the Greeks called this ability [to judge] phronesis, or insight, and they considered it the principal virtue or excellence of the statesman in distinction from the wisdom of the philosopher. The difference between this judging insight and speculative thought lies in that the former has its roots in what we usually call common sense, which the latter constantly transcends. Common sense … discloses to us the nature of the world insofar as it is a common world; we owe to it the fact that our strictly private and 'subjective' five senses and their sensory data can adjust themselves to a non-subjective and 'objective' world which we have in common and share with others. Judging is one, if not the most, important activity in which this sharing-the-world-with-others comes to pass.

For Arendt, the validity of political judgments depended, not on their truth – truth is limited to the realm of cognition, logic, mathematics and the strict sciences.[16] Political judgment, by contrast, requires that a person purifies their thinking through public debate and engaging as many diverse opinions as possible. This cannot be done in isolation and requires active participation in the public realm so that an issue is 'flooded and made transparent by the full light of human comprehension' (Arendt 2006c: 242). Arendt (2006c: 241) argues further:

> The more people's standpoints I have present in my mind while I am pondering a given issue, and the better I can imagine how I would feel and think if I were in their place, the stronger will be my capacity for representative thinking and the more valid my final conclusions, my opinion.

Of course, one might find themselves in a situation where freedom of assembly and thought are prohibited – as it was in Nazi Germany. However, in this instance, Arendt (1989: 50) argues that person has an immediate obligation to challenge State authority: 'For Kant, the moment to rebel is the moment when freedom of opinion is abolished.' This was something that Eichmann was incapable of understanding (even as he claimed to be Kantian). He could not engage in

15 For academic debate on Arendt's employment of the Aristotelian notion of phronesis alongside Kant's idea of an 'enlarged mentality' see D'Entrèves (2002: 253). See also Bernstein (1986) and Benhabib (1992).

16 Arendt (2006c: 241): 'The trouble is that factual truth, like all other truth, peremptorily claims to be acknowledged and precludes debate, and debate constitutes the very essence of political life. The modes of thought and communication that deal with truth, if seen from the political perspective, are necessarily domineering; they don't take into account other people's opinions, and taking these into account is the hallmark of all strictly political thinking.'

practical reason or see the world from the perspective of his victims. His consignment of a portion of the world to the death camps was truly thoughtless. As Robin (2015) suggests, Eichmann's behaviour was consistent with 'someone who did not see a portion of the world because he could not see the world from their portion' (Robin 2015).

This, for Arendt (2006a: 279), was Eichmann's ultimate crime and the fact that legitimised his execution. Eichmann failed to think and distance himself from the requirements that Nazi law and policy had placed upon him. Moreover, once Eichmann became complicit in murder, he ceased any internal dialogue or deliberation about the morality of his actions (Arendt 2006a: 136). He let others decide for him and divorced himself entirely from practical reason and the dictates of morality. Judith Butler (2009) explains how a person's deeds might silence their capacity for moral thinking:

> [W]e can commit acts that make us want to cut ties with ourselves, to break up with ourselves, to disown and banish the self that committed such a deed. Indeed, we cease speaking to the self who committed such an act and we no longer recognise that self as having anything to do with us. This break-up of the self, banishes one part of the self to a location to which all lines of communication are stopped. Whatever we might mean by the remaining self, repudiates and disavows the other whose misdeeds were the cause of this rather stark divorce.

This banishment of the self and closure from moral thinking was obviously widespread throughout Germany. In fact, Arendt's (2006a: 150) final paragraph in chapter 8 is a powerful statement on how the dictates of practical reason were repressed in the murderous context of the Nazi regime:

> Many Germans and many Nazis, probably the overwhelming majority of them, must have been tempted not to murder, not to rob, not to let their neighbours go off to their doom … and not to become accomplices in all these crimes by benefiting from them. But God knows, they learned how to resist temptation.

For Arendt, no properly thinking person can have blind obedience. It is also clear that Arendt sees morality as primary to law or any claim to authority that the law might assume. While important differences exist, Arendt's position is closer to the philosophical anarchist than it is to Raz. Indeed, she would share with Wolff and Godwin the importance of individual judgment and affirm civil disobedience in the face of immoral law. However, unlike the anarchists, Arendt sees civil disobedience as a responsibility for all citizens and as a method of strengthening the State by correcting it in line with moral values. In fact, in the context of the United States, Arendt (1972: 101) recommended that protest groups be invited to 'influence and "assist" Congress by means of persuasion, qualified opinion and the numbers of their constituents'. This proposal, which effectively amounts to institutionalising civil disobedience, is unique in political theory.[17] However, it reflects Arendt's (2008: 467) firm conviction that citizenship required not patriotism but 'permanent opposition and criticism'.

For Arendt civil disobedience mediates the boundary between the need for change and the need for stability. The law both gains and retains its legitimacy through contestation and antagonism. The state gains its authority – not from our tacit consent (i.e. being born into a society) but only if we have the power to dissent. Dissent implies consent and it is for this reason that Jay Bernstein (2004: 116) claims: 'civil disobedience is the fulfilment of Arendt's political doctrine'. We have a responsibility to oppose immoral law and, under some conditions, to actively engage in civil disobedience. And by binding his loyalty to the will of Führer, Eichmann failed to grasp this elementary point.

17 For alternative proposals within the liberal tradition see Rawls (1999: 39); Habermas (1985: 106); and Lefkowitz (2007: 218–223).

Chapter 8

The deportation chapters

Chapters 9–12 mark an import shift in the narrative structure of Arendt's report of the Eichmann trial. Until now, Arendt has been concerned primarily with Eichmann's motivations for accepting his role in the Final Solution, the politics of the trial and questions of collaboration or resistance to authority. In chapter 9, Eichmann is introduced as the most important bureaucrat in the deportation process and as someone who has assimilated any moral or emotional problems he might have felt about the brutality of the Final Solution. Arendt (2006a: 153) captured the vacuous state of Eichmann's character in one of the most frequently quoted sentences in her book: '[W]hat for Eichmann was a job, with its daily routine, its ups and downs, was for the Jews quite literally the end of the world.'

Another important shift in this part of Arendt's report is that Eichmann gradually shifts to the background and Arendt turns her attention to the way material conditions – the law, social relations and governance – impacted the deportation process. These factors are often overshadowed by Arendt's description of Eichmann as a thoughtless bureaucrat and her brief comments on the banality of evil at the end of her report. In fact, some scholars have even interpreted Arendt as suggesting that thoughtlessness provides a sufficient explanation for the evil experienced during the Holocaust.[1] In contrast, I contend that this narrow reading of Arendt is unsustainable and contrary to the complex picture of the Holocaust Arendt presents, not only in her Eichmann report, but throughout her oeuvre.

While the 'end of the world' took many different forms, historians and political scientists have yet to produce an adequate explanation that accounts for the diverse way countries responded to the Final Solution. 'That we do not have an account of this gap' argues Jay Bernstein (2013) 'is a massive and dismal failure in human inquiry.' While not intending to fill this gap, this chapter develops Arendt's material analysis of the Holocaust by underlining the role played by the anti-Jewish legislation, the legal status of victims and the extent to which the Nazi government had infiltrated and controlled a territory. Implicit in this approach is the perspective that one cannot begin to understand territorial differences during the Holocaust by taking a determinist approach that favours a single explanation,

1 See for example Jay Bernstein's lecture 'Judgment in Extremis' (2013) and Lilla (2013).

i.e. evil as a banal phenomenon. Any serious analysis must shift away from totalities and engage across a range of distinctive moments. While not comprehensive, Arendt's chapters on the deportation of Jewish victims provides important clues from which we can begin this task.

Anti-Jewish legislation

> Legal stability and a totalitarian movement could not be reconciled (Arendt 2006a: 186).

In three short years, the Nazi regime had murdered 82 per cent of the Jewish population in Europe. The final total amounted to between five and six million people.[2] However, vast geographical differences existed in the extent to which exterminations were carried out. For example, 70–90 per cent of Jews in Poland, Latvia, the Netherlands and Hungary were killed. Corresponding figures for Romania, Norway, Belgium and Estonia are between 40 and 50 per cent. In Italy and France, approximately 20 per cent were killed while in Bulgaria and Denmark many Jews escaped or were protected by the local population.

New students of the Holocaust continue to be shocked by the extent of the slaughter. But for Nazi leadership, the surprising fact was that more Jews were not killed. Indeed, the Nazis believed that violent anti-Semitism could become a unifying theme across all of Europe. On this point, Arendt (2006a: 156) argues: 'The Nazis, always eager to generalise, thought they had demonstrated that Jews were "undesirables" everywhere and that every non-Jew was an actual or potential anti-Semite.' And yet 'to the never ending surprise' of Nazi officials even anti-Semites were inconsistent in carrying out orders and 'the German "radical" variety' of extermination was only appreciated in Eastern European countries whom the Nazis regarded as '"subhuman" barbarian hordes' (Arendt 2006a: 156, 154).

To begin to comprehend this situation, the role of law and anti-Jewish legislation needs to be put in its rightful place. With respect to deportations, the importance of law is mixed. Against the primacy of law, Arendt (2006a: 155) considers the first movement of Jews from Stettin, Baden and Saafpfalz in 1940. In total approximately 9,000 people were taken, including women, children and the elderly. An important fact about these first deportations is that they occurred without the elaborate legal preparations which proceeded later operations. Arendt (2006a: 155) notes:

> No laws had yet been passed depriving Jews of their nationality the moment they were deported from the Reich, and instead of the many forms Jews

2 Raul Hilberg (1985b) came up with a figure of 5.1 million. By contrast, Lucy Dawidowicz (1975: 402–404) used pre-war birth and death records to come up with a more precise figure of 5,933,900. One of the largest sources of uncertainty concerns the number of Jews murdered in the Soviet Union (Snyder 2012).

> eventually had to fill out in arrangement for the confiscation of their property, the Stettin Jews simply signed a general waiver, covering everything they owned.

This action was not designed to test the legality of their actions or the administrative dimension of the deportation. Rather, it was a display of power carried out to assess the 'general political conditions' (Arendt 2006a: 155). Could men, women, children and the elderly be forced to pack their bags, give up their worldly goods and walk in the middle of the night through the streets to board a train which was taking them into the unknown? Would their neighbours, friends and community countenance such a barbaric act? Would they revolt? And what about the foreign government who was expected to give access to a sudden influx of expelled people? Conforming to Nazi expectations, these tests were conducted successfully and as Arendt (2006a: 156) comments 'everything turned out satisfactorily'.

The success of subsequent deportations from the Reich was assisted by the gradual implementation of anti-Jewish legislation and the numerous exemption categories that protected prominent Jews.[3] However, as discussed in Chapter 6, anti-Jewish legislation also provided the Nazi state with a cloak of moral and legal legitimacy. For example, deportations could be justified, not just on racial grounds, but on the basis that those deported were legally stateless. Moreover, authorities could build a narrative that linked deportations to nationalism all through legal means.

Anti-Jewish legislation was implemented not only in areas under direct Nazi control but also amongst Axis allies. For example, Arendt (2006a: 191) argues that Romania implemented some of the harshest anti-Jewish legislation in Europe. In Romania, anti-Jewish legislation was aimed at the 'integral nationalism' of Romanian society. To achieve this it stripped Jews of citizenship which had been granted in 1923 and defined the nation as a 'cultural community based on the law of blood' (Wiesel Commission 2004: 182).[4] Exemption categories were extremely narrow and limited to war veterans and those Jews who had been Romanian citizens prior to 1918. In total, this amounted to approximately 1 per cent of the Jewish population (Arendt 2006a: 191). Moreover, unlike the Nuremberg Laws of 1940 a person with one Jewish parent who had converted to Christianity was still considered a Jew. Antonescu justified this on the following basis: 'mystery of baptism could not change the destiny of Jewish blood' (Wiesel Commission 2004: 183). Thus for the Romanian government, political racism was at the centre of anti-Jewish legislation. Jews were persecuted for who they were, not for any action (real or imagined).

3 For a comprehensive collection of anti-Jewish legislation enacted in Germany see Lemkin (2008).

4 The phrase 'law of blood' referred primarily to ethical, spiritual and cultural characteristics.

In contrast to Germany and Romania, other countries were able to implement legislation which, while unambiguously anti-Semitic, frustrated extermination efforts. Italy, for example, introduced legislation that deprived Jews of full citizenship rights, excluded them from large portions of the private sector and banished them from cultural institutions. While the legislation defined Jews in strict terms (Hilberg 1985b: 663), they also provided exemption categories that included war veterans, those with military decorations and members of the Italian Fascist party (Arendt 2006a: 178). This last exemption was particularly important because in 1938, approximately 6,900 Jews were members of the Fascist party and occupied positions of leadership (Cesarani 2016: 172; Hilberg 1985b: 664).

In her examination of Italy (which is generally positive) Arendt neglects to note that Mussolini personally insisted that Jews be expelled from the party and argued against calls from the Vatican to exempt Jews who had converted to Christianity (Cesarani 2016: 174).[5] Moreover, the legislation barred Jews from employment by the State, possession of farms and future membership in the party. 'Its victims must have felt the code severely' argues Raul Hilberg (1985b: 665) 'because in the past they had found in their country such complete acceptance.' Moreover, by 1940 Mussolini had reached the view that there was 'no room for the Jews in Europe, and eventually ... they would all have to go' (Cesarani 2016: 174).

A stronger example of law being used for protection can be noted in Bulgaria. Anti-Jewish legislation was introduced in December 1940[6] to exclude Jews from public service and professions.[7] The legislation also required Jews to live in certain areas, undertake segregated education and submit to crippling levels of taxation (Cesarani 2016: 573). Like other examples of anti-Jewish legislation, the term 'Jew' was defined in racial terms. However, after protests from politicians, intellectuals and the Orthodox Church, a broad exemption was created for baptised Jews regardless of when they converted (Cesarani 2016: 573). Arendt (2006a: 186) notes that this led to an 'epidemic of conversions' and 5,000 more Jews were granted 'special privileges'.

While Nazi officials found this legislation 'ridiculous' they could not offer the Bulgarian government sufficient incentive to deport the Jewish population (Arendt 2006a: 186). It was this fact, argues Hilberg (1985b: 744), that ultimately saved the majority of Bulgarian Jews: 'There was no need to preserve them and no reason to destroy them ... the Reich ... could not offer sufficient gain to the cautious Bulgarian rulers.' As the war progressed, the King of Bulgaria and other leading figures in the Church and government refused to assist the occupying forces (Todorov 2001: 8–14). However, rather than deporting the Jews, Bulgarian

5 Mussolini's hostility toward Jews was driven by the prominence of Italian Jews in anti-fascist organisations (Cesarani 2016: 172).

6 Note that Arendt (2006a: 186) claims that the legislation was introduced in January 1941.

7 See also Bar-Zohar (1998) and Todorov (2001).

officials put them to work in compulsory labour camps (Chary 1972: 35–84; Cesarani 2016: 573).

Legal status and national identity

Another key factor that determined the fate of Jewish people was their citizenship status and whether they were members of a national community.[8] Across Europe a similar theme played out where stateless Jews were rendered vulnerable to be murdered with impunity. Adopting the vernacular of Mark Curtis (2004: 2) – stateless Jews were 'Unpeople' and their lives were 'deemed worthless, expendable in the pursuit of power …'. Once Jews had been stripped of their legal status – as citizens and property holders – all they could do was appeal to the common humanity of their persecutors. This was insufficient in a context where Jewishness was a mark of inferiority. It was this fact that encouraged allied powers to develop post-war treaties aimed at limiting the freedom countries had to abandon their residents (Kadri 2015: 14).

A key example is France which demonstrated a callous indifference to what the Vichy government called 'those foreign Jews' (Arendt 2006a: 163). At first, stateless Jews were used as a bargaining chip or 'second line of defense' in negotiations with the Germans in order to protect French nationals (Hilberg 1985b: 609). Rather than admitting the relative power that Germany exerted over France, Pierre Laval, Premier under Philippe Pétain, presented the deportations as an opportunity: 'these foreign Jews had always been a problem in France and that the French Government was glad that a change in the German attitude towards them gave France an opportunity to get rid of them' (United States Department of State 1942: 464; Arendt 2006a: 163).

Here we see a coalescence of a legal and administrative structure that was prepared for deportation and a political objective that coincided with the demands being made on the French government. As a result, following Eichmann's two-day visit to Paris in 1942, 27,000 stateless Jews were deported to Auschwitz (Cesarani 2016: 548; Arendt 2006a: 164). Subsequently deportations were concentrated in refugee camps, the free zone and regional cities where stateless Jews were blamed for shortages and contributing to black market activity (Cesarani 2016: 551).

It was at this juncture that the German authorities made a critical mistake. Well short on their target for deportations, they commenced a frenzy of roundups which targeted Jews whose nationality had previously protected them. This included citizens from Romania, Belgium and Greece (Cesarani 2016: 554). It was only after these citizens were deported and German authorities sought to include French Jews in the next round of deportations that the French public found their voice. Citizenship made a person visible and the spectacle of 'women and children being herded through the streets and driven towards cattle trucks

8 Citizenship status remains a key protection from state violence. See Kadri (2015: 14).

heading towards an "unknown destination", provoked a wave of repulsion' (Cesarani 2016: 554). The most visible public outcry came from the Church. For example, on 23 August, Cardinal Saliège of Toulouse issued a powerfully worded letter which stated:

> In our own diocese, the most disturbing scenes have taken place in the camps of Noe and Recebedou. Jews are human beings. Foreigners are human beings. All is not permitted against them, against these men, against these women, against these fathers and these mothers of families. They belong to humankind; they are our brothers as are so many others. A Christian may not forget this (Cesarani 2016: 555).

Outside the Church, similar sentiments were expressed in the underground press and by civil society organisations. This pressure gave the Vichy politicians permission to reconsider their strategy of cooperation. As Arendt (2006a: 165) notes: 'the French now refused to take a step they had eagerly contemplated only a short time before, that is to revoke naturalisations' that had been granted to Jews in 1927 and 1933. Their caution was deepened by decisive turns in the war – in particular the Soviet counter-offensive at Stalingrad (Cesarani 2016: 556). As a result, French authorities ceased collaboration and created endless difficulties in deporting the 250,000 Jews who had remained in France.

Another key example of the importance of national identity is the Danish response to deportations. In fact, Arendt (2006a: 171) suggests that the story of Danish resistance should be 'required reading in political science for all students who wish to learn something about the enormous power potential inherent in non-violent action and in resistance to an opponent possessing vastly superior means of violence'. From the outset, it is important to note that Denmark had a relatively small Jewish population (around 8,000 people). Jews had lived there since the seventeenth century, were highly assimilated and gained full citizenship in the 1840s (Cesarani 2016: 687). The government also had very tight controls preventing Jewish refugees from entering and staying in Denmark.[9] Moreover, prior to occupation, the Danish government initiated a broad public education campaign to protect populations from the racist propaganda being perpetuated by the Nazi party. Bo Lidegaard (2014: 15) explains that from the mid-1930s:

> A broad national unity was meant to be forged around democracy and the national flag ... Gradually a strong sense developed of a national 'us', which included every citizen adhering to the principles of democracy and its

9 Only 5,000 refugees were allowed into Denmark between 1933 and 1939 and most were encouraged to leave quickly. Commenting on these numbers, Karl Steincke, the Minister of Justice, noted: 'One does not want to be humane, and one does not dare to be humane because of the consequences' (Cesarani 2016: 687).

> underlying humanitarian values, opposed to a 'them' of the political extremes not subscribing to those same ideas.

As Lidegaard notes, Danish nationalism was performed in civic terms. What mattered was a shared commitment to the state and dominant political ideology – not a common religion or ethnicity. One significant downside to this approach was that while the Danish government mobilised to protect its Jewish population, it did not protect or build a public defence for the communist community who were labelled un-Danish and deported for supporting Stalin and denouncing the Danish royal family (Lidegaard 2014: 15 and 21–22). Even those who held anti-Semitic attitudes understood politically loyal Jews to be part of the Danish community and regarded an attack on them as a transgression against the nation (Lidegaard 2014: 173).

As a result of these factors, there was no Jewish problem that needed to be addressed and no anti-Semitic movement with the power to push for radical measures (Lidegaard 2014: 11). Arendt (2006a: 171) provides an instructive example of the difficulties Nazi authorities faced extending the Final Solution to Denmark:

> When the Germans approached them rather cautiously about introducing the yellow badge, they were simply told that the King would be the first to wear it, and the Danish government officials were careful to point out that anti-Jewish measures of any sort would cause their own immediate resignation.

A popular myth even developed after this which had held that the King of Denmark had ridden through Copenhagen wearing a yellow star on his breast (Lidegaard 2014: xi). In fact, the king never did make such a grand public display of support and the Germans did not push the issue. Moreover, when in September 1943 the Germans sought to take control of deportations, members of the Danish government resigned from their post and refused to cooperate in any future government with the Germans. Politicians from rival parties also issued a joint statement after the first round-up of Jews was announced. Part of the statement read: 'The Danish Jews are an integral part of the people, and therefore all the people are deeply affected by the measures taken, which are seen as a violation of the Danish sense of justice' (Lidegaard 2014: 237).

Infiltration and control

While national identity was an important fact in saving many Danish Jews it is also important to note that German occupation in Denmark was significantly lighter than in other countries. The Nazis pursued a strategy of indirect rule because they viewed the Danes as fellow Aryans and a population which could benefit greatly in a unified Aryan Europe. As a result, the Danes were given unique privileges – they kept their king and most aspects of their governance structure throughout the war. Self-government provided the Danish leadership with the capacity to frustrate German goals and shut down operations in a way that was not possible for other occupied countries.

Another instructive example is the Netherlands whose 'Jews were destroyed with a thoroughness comparable to the relentless uprooting process in the Reich itself' (Hilberg 1985b: 570). With respect to Nazi control over governance, the Dutch royal family and government were evacuated to London at the start of the war (Cesarani 2016: 297; Warmbrunn 1963: 12). To fill this vacuum, Hitler effectively absorbed the Dutch into the Reich by appointing Arthur Seyss-Inquart to the position of civil administrator. Seyss-Inquart, who was a fanatical anti-Semite, built a new government and filled key positions with members from the German and Dutch Nazi parties (Cesarani 2016: 297; 314–315).[10] Moreover, at the start of 1941 the Dutch security police were placed under the control of SS-Gruppenführer Wilhelm Harster who answered directly to Himmler and Heydrich. As a consequence, 'there was no buffer between Berlin and the Nazi occupation bosses in The Hague and Amsterdam' (Cesarani 2016: 315).

Other extreme examples can be noted in fully annexed and partially incorporated territories like Poland which became the headquarters of the killing centres (Winstone 2014; Kochanski 2014). Nazi lawyers working in Berlin sought to describe these areas in a way that effectively treated them as part of the Reich, so German law applied, supposedly unconstrained by international law (Sands 2016: 214). In Poland, the Nazis had more time than in any other occupied country to implement anti-Semitic policies. While resistance did occur in these areas, the Nazi authorities had direct power to quash uprisings, replace noncompliant personnel and spread total terror (Gutman 1998). German soldiers committed war crimes in Poland from the beginning of their occupation. One soldier in the 41st infantry division noted: 'Polish civilians and soldiers are dragged out everywhere … When we finish our operation, the entire village is on fire' (Neitzel 2013: 85).

Hans Frank, Hitler's personal lawyer, took up the post of Governor General on 25 October 1939. Hitler's decree bypassed the usual structure for administering external territories and stated that Frank was to report directly to the Führer and ordered that the entire area 'be directed by the Governor General'. Under this decree, Frank set about transforming Poland into a nation of slaves (Jacobson 2012: 387; O'Connor 2014: 2). In fact, in an early interview Frank told a reporter that Poland was now a 'colony' and that the Polish people were the 'slaves of the Greater German World Empire' (quoted in Sands 2016: 214). In a further humiliation for the Poles, Frank established himself and his government at Wawel Castle in Kraków, the former home of Polish kings (Sands 2016: 214).

10 Arendt (2006a: 169) notes that the Dutch had a strong Nazi movement that 'could be trusted to carry out such police measures such as seizing Jews, ferreting out their hiding places and so on'. See also the Arrow Cross movement that was active in Hungary.

As Governor General, Frank acted like a sovereign. His Poland was not a constitutional state where people had rights and minority treaties were respected. Rather, Frank started issuing decrees which enabled him to put into effect ideas he first expressed in 1935 at the Berlin conference. In his General government, the 'community of the people' would be the only legal standard and all individuals would be subjected to the will of the Führer (Sands 2016: 216). The pride Frank felt about his ruthless regime is evident from the way he bragged to a foreign reporter in 1940: 'If I had to hang up a poster every time we shot seven Poles, we'd have to cut down all the Polish forests, and we still wouldn't be able to produce enough paper for all the posters I'd need' (O'Connor 2014: 2).

Those who survived the killing were subjected to crippling restrictions on movement, travel, assembly and speech. In May 1940 Himmler and Frank introduced programmes to make sure that 'the non-German peoples of the East may not receive any education beyond four-year elementary school' (Sontheimer 2011). Educational goals for the Poles were limited to the 'ability to do simple sums no higher than 500, write their name, and understand that it is their divine duty to obey Germans, be honest, diligent and well-behaved' (Sontheimer 2011). Following this, in October 1940 Hitler ordered 'all members of the Polish intelligentsia' to be killed (Sontheimer 2011). In support, Heydrich ordered lists of 'teachers, clergymen, noblemen, legionaries, returning officers' to be put together immediately and that whoever was left of the Polish elite and intelligentsia be placed in camps (Sontheimer 2011). While much more could be said, it is sufficient to note that occupied Poland became a site of total terror. Under these conditions, no amount of creative legislation, public education or resistance could match the level of infiltration and control the Nazi regime had in the territory.

While they move in and out of focus, the material factors discussed in this chapter are all circumstances that Arendt is attuned to and which she incorporates into her analysis of individuals like Eichmann. To understand Arendt, and the broader factors that contributed to the Holocaust, we must avoid looking for general explanations or fetishising debates about the extent to which Arendt moved away from a Kantian conception of radical evil. Rather, the challenge is to encounter specific instances and the myriad of material factors that explain how individual countries in Europe responded to the Final Solution as well as the pressures (legal, cultural and social) that made their desires easier or harder to realise. In chapters 9–12, the deportation chapters, Arendt offers the beginning of such an explanation.

Chapter 9

Did Eichmann receive a fair trial?

> [The] whole thing is so damned banal and indescribably low and repulsive (Arendt and Blucher 2000: 357).

In the early 1960s the future of the Israeli State was not guaranteed (Segev 2000: 328). Most Jews (including a significant number of survivors) had not come to live in Israel and political leaders had largely failed in their ambition to make the State the centre of Jewish cultural life (Segev 2000: 328; Grodzinsky 2004: vii). Hostilities with neighbours were also high and culminated in the disastrous war of 1967 which reshaped the entire region (Segev 2008). Despite these issues, by 1961 the State had worked consciously toward reinventing itself as a liberal democracy or 'nation among nations' (Zertal 2005: 94; Robinson 2013: 29–67). With respect to law, this reinvention was formally facilitated by the adoption of the Criminal Code Ordinance 1936 enjoining adherence to English law and precedent (Abrams 1972: 25). Moreover, in 1948 Israel adopted a Declaration of Independence, which promised: 'the State of Israel will be based on freedom, justice and peace and will grant complete equality to all its inhabitants without regard of religion, race or sex' (Rattner and Fishman 1997: 8).[1]

While far ranging, chapters 13 and 14 of *Eichmann in Jerusalem* contain key moments which test the extent to which Eichmann's trial confirmed with the government's stated goal – to provide a fair trial which conformed with the basic principles of justice expressed in a liberal criminal system. Despite points of similarity, this inquiry is distinct from arguments about whether proceedings in the District Court could properly be regarded as a 'show trial' (I rejected this argument in Chapter 1). Instead, in this chapter I am concerned only with matters inside the court room and the extent to which proceedings matched the express goals of the Israeli justice system.

To conduct this inquiry, I first describe the role of the criminal trial in a liberal democracy. Following this, I contend that there are three key credentials for a

1 Whether these principles were incorporated into the Israeli criminal justice system is debatable, particular in light of the treatment of Arab Israelis. See further Rattner and Fishman (1997: 8).

liberal trial: open justice, the existence of a jury system and mechanisms to enable the accused to participate in their defence. Reflecting on these credentials, I ultimately conclude that the Eichmann trial fell short of the standards of a liberal trial. The most significant shortcomings relate to participation. Specifically, I contend that Eichmann did not enjoy the presumption of innocence, that the historical dimensions of the trial forced Eichmann to respond to allegations outside of his conduct, that defence witnesses were deterred from travelling to Israel and that his lawyer was denied access to his client and not properly resourced. Taken together, these factors erode the prosecution's claim that Israel was the most appropriate venue to bring proceedings against the accused and lend support to claims that the trial was illegitimate.

The criminal trial

In a liberal criminal system, the separation of powers is reflected in the divide between the investigatory, prosecutorial and adjudicative functions. The criminal trial makes only a brief appearance at the end of this chain but it is significant because of its potential for controlling the coercive power of the executive to fine, detain or terminate of the life of a citizen (Lai 2010:2). Moreover, when a case reaches trial, 'what has hitherto been more or less shrouded in secrecy is thrust into the open, laid bare to the *public* gaze' (Lai 2010: 244–245). The public nature of a trial is vital and places a burden on the State to publicly produce evidence for their case and justify the assertion that a citizen is guilty and deserving of punishment. Arendt affirms this point. Echoing Lord Hewart CJ's famous dictum, she notes: 'Justice, in order to be done, "must be seen to be done," and for that justice demands a legal trial' (2006a: 277).

While the judiciary have described a criminal trial as a 'search for truth'[2] other commentators have focused more on the process through which the executive is called to account for exercising its powers (Lai 2010: 245). This shift from truth to process is underpinned by several important ideas. The first is the presumption of innocence and the doctrine that places on the prosecution the burden of proving guilt.[3] Second, most scholars have abandoned the idea that there is a 'right answer' to hard cases or truth waiting for a judge to discover (Dworkin 1986: 52; Fish 1990: 103–119; Sunstein 1996: 50). However, while we cannot expect a trial to render truth, we do have significant agency over the processes and procedures that undergird a criminal trial (Fuller 1969: 81). Thus, Lai (2010: 245) argues that a verdict's legitimacy depends on how the trial was conducted and the quality of the engagement between the accused and the State. If these aspects are open

2 *R v Nikolovski* [1996] 3 SCR 1197, 1206 (Cory J): 'The ultimate aim of any trial … must be to seek and to ascertain the truth.'

3 In *Woolmington v DPP* [1935] AC 462 the House of Lords famously described the presumption of innocence as the 'golden thread' that runs 'throughout the web of the … Criminal Law'.

and fair, we significantly increase the likelihood that the trial will conform with elementary principles of justice.

Credentials of a liberal trial

In the preceding section, I argued that the criminal trial represents a formal check on executive power. The court's role inside a liberal society reflects the government's commitment to the individual, freedom and limited government. To discharge this function, the court must satisfy certain credentials basic to constitutional liberalism (Allan 2001: 79). For the purpose of this chapter, I regard these credentials as the basic or minimum features of a liberal trial.

To begin, a liberal trial will respect the autonomy of the accused and enable them to participate in their own defence (Lai 2010: 251). Autonomy is realised through freedom of choice, i.e. can the accused plead guilty or not? Do they have the right to silence or the privilege against self-incrimination? Can the accused direct their lawyer in terms of trial strategy and the evidence to be presented? In a similar way, participation is linked to self-direction and the 'freedom which consists in being one's own master' (Berlin 1984: 23). At its most basic, participation requires that the accused is enabled to participate in their defence. For example, they should have the right to be heard, representation, legal professional privilege and the ability to challenge evidence produced against them.[4] According to Gérard Soulier (1995: 162), these ideas of participation are linked to equality:

> The judicial institution will pacify if everyone believes that they will freely be able to make their cause understood. We see here how the criminal trial and democracy are linked – there is a conflict which must be resolved through speech, based on a principle of equality.

Further to these explicit ideas, participation also contains implicit assumptions. For example, participation assumes that the verdict has not already been decided and that the accused has the ability to play a meaningful role in determining the outcome of the trial. Participation is a substantive (and not simply a formal) concept which reinforces the idea that citizens are not objects to be acted upon or compelled to 'play act' in a predetermined process. Participation should also relate directly to charges levelled against the accused and not to events or actions which the prosecution knows to be irrelevant. It is impossible to meaningfully respond to spurious accusations and the State has no legitimate authority to restrict the liberty of a citizen for that purpose.

A second credential of a liberal trial, common to many jurisdictions, is a right to be judged by a jury. A jury trial has been described as 'the crucible of democracy' (Burns 2004: 177). While that might be an overstatement and the

4 In some jurisdictions, the accused also has the right to confront witnesses. This is a constitutional right in the United States, see *Crawford v Washington* 541 US 36 (2004).

flaws of jury deliberation have long been understood (Miner 1946), a jury trial provides an accused the opportunity to be tried against the norms or standards of their community (Lai 2010: 252; Walker 1988: 366). Further, the jury system has also been regarded as an important safeguard of individual liberty: 'the jury furnishes a check against unbridled abuse by either the prosecution or the court' (Garcia 1992: 183).

The final credential with broad support is the principle of open or public justice (Jaconelli 2002: 4–5). The holding of proceedings in secret and without public oversight has 'long been regarded as an instrument of oppressive government' and a hallmark of totalitarian terror (Jaconelli 1997: 169). The importance of openness to a liberal trial can be understood when we recall that a trial 'is a process of public justification' (Lai 2010: 252). The executive must present their evidence and argument in a public forum where citizens have free access and journalists can report on proceedings. Reflecting the importance of public justice, some scholars have also argued that the grounds offered by the executive during a trial must aim at public acceptability to justify engaging the coercive powers of the State (Macedo 1991).

While other credentials might be suggested, we can see these factors as the minimum requirements for a criminal trial to be legitimate. When a criminal trial is evaluated as legitimate this means that the process was fair and worthy of our continued adherence. Lai (2010: 253) comments:

> … the legitimacy of a verdict, its claim to recognition, is seriously eroded when it is the result of a secret process; such a verdict calls for blind trust rather than reasoned acceptance. Also, the moral weight of a conviction depends partly but crucially on the quality of the interaction between state and citizen in the process by which the latter is found guilty. Where the accused is treated unfairly at the trial, the state's right to expect him or her, and the citizenry in general, to accept the resulting conviction is somehow undermined.

With this background in place we are in a position to evaluate the Eichmann trial against the basic credentials of a liberal trial. In conducting this evaluation, I am not superimposing abstract principles onto the Jerusalem court. Rather, while conscious of the precarious state of Israeli statehood, my interest is simply to compare aspects of the trial against the standards held out by the Israeli government. In other words, I seek to expand on Arendt and consider the extent to which events in the courtroom matched the rhetorical justifications provided.

Evaluating the trial

As we have noted, Arendt has a complicated relationship with the Eichmann trial. Notwithstanding her disdain for its show-like aspects, her overall impression of the court was positive. As discussed in Chapter 2, Arendt (2006a: 3–4) commented on the 'the scrupulous fairness of all technical arrangements for the trial' and openly expressed her admiration for the dignity and fair-mindedness of the judges, especially Moshe Landau. However, in chapters 13 and 14 of her report, Arendt elaborates on several points which complicate her initial positive assessment.

Starting with positive facts, it is undeniable that the Eichmann trial was open and subject to broad public scrutiny. The courtroom was accessible to all demographics and Jewish people were actively encouraged to attend and witness proceedings first hand. Moreover, large portions of the trial were broadcast on Kol Yisrael (Voice of Israel) radio station and subject to scrutiny from both the national and international press. Elaborate preparations, including hiding cameras in the walls of the courtroom, were also made to film and broadcast the trial to 56 countries for over four months.[5] While we might take such steps for granted today, the Eichmann trial was the world's first documentary series and provided people unprecedented access to the accused and the testimony of his victims. While the public nature of the trial furthered the political aims of the Israeli State, the authorisation to broadcast was also justified on the basis that the results would have significant public and historical importance and the pressing need to preserve the trial in its totality.

With respect to the next liberal credential, it is important to highlight that Israel does not have a jury system. Professional judges handle all aspects of the criminal justice process, including determinations of fact. The rationale for this is largely historical – when the court system was formed in 1949, the government thought that it would be impossible to constitute a jury who did not know each other or were sufficiently removed from the accused and counsel (Straschnov 1999: 528). Such familiarity would have made the creation of an unbiased jury impossible after statehood and provisions for a jury trial were explicitly excluded from consideration in the *Nazi and Nazi Collaborators Punishment Act* 1957. While it is unlikely that Eichmann (or other collaborators charged under the NNCL) would have opted for a jury trial, it is a curious feature of Israeli jurisprudence that the initial decision on jury trials has never been revisited.

The final credential of a liberal trial, and the one which occupies most of Arendt's attention, concerns participation. To begin, Arendt (2006a: 209–210) questions whether Eichmann enjoyed the presumption of innocence:

> In Israel, as in most other countries, a person appearing in court is deemed innocent until proved guilty. But in the case of Eichmann this was an obvious fiction. If he had not been found guilty before he appeared in Jerusalem, guilty beyond any reasonable doubt, the Israelis would never have dared, or wanted, to kidnap him … In contrast to normal arrests in ordinary criminal cases, where suspicion of guilt must be proved to be substantial and reasonable but not beyond reasonable doubt … Eichmann's illegal arrest could be

5 The Eichmann trial became the world's first documentary series. For a dramatisation see Williams (2015). See also Hartouni (2012).

> justified, and was justified in the eyes of the world, only by the fact that the outcome of the trial could be safely anticipated.

Arendt was not the only one making this point. Certainty over the court's verdict and death sentence dominated all major Israeli newspapers and Knesset member Moshe Sneh proclaimed:

> There is no room for legal considerations … there has to be a judicial procedure, and we will have it with all due order and process. But the verdict has already been determined (Segev 2000: 332).

What consequence does this have on the validity of the trial? At least two responses are possible. The first is that overwhelming evidence against an accused does not necessarily give rise to a miscarriage of justice. In fact, Lai (2010: 255) argues that it is important to conduct a criminal trial even when the guilt of the accused is not in doubt:

> That we insist in bringing notorious war criminals before a criminal trial, even though it is far simpler just to shoot them in the street, has less to do with doubts about the atrocities that they have perpetuated and more to do with abiding by certain values that define us as a society, the most basic of which must include respect for our common humanity and commitment to the rule of law. As Gaita puts it, 'no criminals are so foul that they may be denied justice.' Every accused person, however heinous the charges, deserves to be treated with dignity and remains worthy of reasoned engagement on the justice of his or her condemnation and punishment, this is, 'the most sublime aspect of our legal tradition'.[6]

But there is another aspect of this that Arendt does not consider in detail. It is possible to argue that Eichmann, regardless of what evidence was presented at the trial, was never going to leave Israel alive. Once the decision was taken to kidnap him from Argentina, Eichmann's life was forfeit. Arendt mentions this in a letter to Jaspers (1992: 430–431) just before she departed for Israel: 'Today an Israeli in the diplomatic corps, a decent, intelligent man, said in a discussion of the possibility that Eichmann might not be executed: That would cost significantly more lives; there won't be a village in Israel where heavy rioting won't break out immediately!' Once in Israel Arendt appears to put her trust in the ability of the judges to circumvent any political objective Ben-Gurion had for the trial. But perhaps this reasoning overplays the virtue of the judges, their capacity to be

6 See also Gaita (2002: 54): 'Justice was owed to the man in the glass booth, not just for the sake of the court, or for the sake of future legal or political goods, but because it was owed to him as a human being, even though there was no doubt about this identify and about his terrible guilt.'

impartial and their relative power vis-à-vis the State. Suffice to say, if a verdict of innocent was not just improbable but impossible, it is hard to say the criminal trial was legitimate.

Further to this point, Eichmann's participation was eroded by the historical dimensions of the trial and the consideration of evidence that went far beyond the charges brought against him (Arendt 2006a: 9 and 253). In chapter 13 of Arendt's report, the historical picture painted by the prosecution reached absurd proportions and the court was asked to consider evidence from the East where, as Arendt (2006a: 206) notes, the evidence was 'scanty'. Rather than limit proceedings, the poor quality of evidence gave the prosecution a 'welcome pretext for calling an endless procession of witnesses' including three sessions which were devoted to 'background witnesses' who had never seen the defendant (Arendt 2006a: 206). Perhaps the most extreme example was K-Zetnik who, after giving an explanation of his adopted name and a short statement on astrology, fainted once the prosecution and judges tried to steer him toward the case at hand (Arendt 2006a: 223–224).

Arendt is inconsistent in her assessment of what Yad Vashem called 'the right of the witnesses to be irrelevant' (Arendt 2006a: 225). For example, in reporting on the evidence of Zindel Grynszpan, Arendt (2006a: 227) noted that 'every once in a long while one was glad that Judge Landau had lost his battle' to keep proceedings relevant to the accused. After Grynszpan relayed his story of deportation and the horrors he endured at the hands of the SS, Arendt (2006a 229–230) was moved to write that '[e]veryone, everyone should have his day in court'.[7] A similar sentiment was expressed when Abba Kovner gave evidence on the resistance activities of Austrian conscript sergeant Anton Schmid (Arendt 2006a: 230–232). Schmid's story represented one of the rare glimmers of light that entered the Jerusalem courtroom. Arendt (2006a: 231) reports that in the two minutes it took to hear Schmid's story:

> a single thought stood out clearly, irrefutably, beyond question – how utterly different everything would be today in this courtroom, in Israel, in Germany, in all of Europe, and perhaps in all countries of the world, if only more such stories could have been told.

In these moments, we witness Arendt's principles about the legitimate functions of the court give way to her humanism or *humanitas*. More than truth, Arendt was interested in making space for those who appeared before her to disclose the world anew (Arendt 2006c: 229). Thus, if Arendt is inconsistent in her analysis of

7 See also Arendt's description of Grynszpan in a letter to Blucher (2000: 359): 'No gesticulating. Very impressive. I told myself – even if the only result was that a simple person, who would otherwise never have such an opportunity, is given the chance to say what happened, publicly, in ten sentences and without pathos, then this whole thing would have been worth it.'

the role of history in the trial, it is an inconsistency that she would have embraced in her commitment to plurality and the potential for other people disclosing reality as it appeared to them.

Another aspect of the trial that impacted Eichmann's participation was the numerous instances of hearsay evidence that were admitted by the court (Arendt 2006a: 220). Hearsay evidence refers to out of court statements which are provided in order to prove or disprove a particular fact asserted. In Australia and other liberal jurisdictions, hearsay evidence is generally inadmissible. There are good reasons for this, including the fact that out of court statements are not generally made under oath; there is usually an absence of testing by cross examination and there are dangers of inaccuracy or fabrication.

However, section 15(a) of the NNCL empowered the court to deviate from the rules of evidence if the judges were 'satisfied that this will promote the ascertainment of the truth and the just handling of the case'. While this deviation facilitated some erroneous investigations, such as circumstantial evidence that Eichmann took part in the murder of a Jewish boy caught taking fruit from a cherry tree (Arendt 2006a: 22; Rogat 2011: 7),[8] there was good reason for relaxing the rules of evidence in this particular instance. Specifically, many witnesses were no longer alive or able to come to the court to speak for themselves. Relaxed evidence rules enabled the journals and letters of deceased victims to be heard by the court. Moreover, evidence accepted under section 15(a) of the NNCL was usually independently corroborated and section 15(b) required the court to provide, on record, the reasons that prompted its admission of hearsay evidence.

Another fact which impacted Eichmann's participation in the trial was that many witnesses for the defence were deterred from travelling to Israel to give evidence. As Arendt (2006a: 220) notes, 'sixteen witnesses ... could not come to Jerusalem, because the Attorney General had announced that he "intended to put them on trial for crimes against the Jewish people"'. While it is unlikely that any of these witnesses would have come to Jerusalem in any case, it is worth underlining that the Attorney General could have granted immunity for the specific period required to give evidence before the court. By not taking this step, the government undermined its claim that an Israeli court was 'the most suitable for a trial against the implementers of the Final Solution' (Arendt 2006a: 221). In fact, Arendt states (2006a: 221) that 'it quickly turned out that Israel was the only country in the world where defence witnesses could not be heard' and where 'the accused and his lawyer could not obtain their own defence documents'. In response, several of the witnesses submitted written statements to the court (admissible under section 15a of the NNCL). But this is hardly a substitute for appearing before the court in person and being available to answer specific questions.

8 Eichmann was cleared of this charge for lack of evidence. However, this charge survives in the secondary literature and is even presented as fact in the popular movie *Eichmann* (2007).

The final issue with respect to participation concerns the quality of Eichmann's defence counsel. Servatius was the primary mechanism through which Eichmann 'spoke' in the court and he accepted responsibility for shaping Eichmann's defence and raising objections against the prosecution. The appointment of Servatius came after a long search inside Israel. Several applicants volunteered for the position, but the Ministry of Justice ultimately concluded that Israeli lawyers would be placing themselves in danger by acting for the defence (Lipstadt, 2011: 37) and that they lacked international credibility (Cesarani 2006: 246). The Israeli secret service (Mossad) vetted several other international applicants, including an American neo-Nazi (Hausner 1966: 301–302; Yablonka 2004: 124–126). While the secret service was undertaking their search, they were contacted by Servatius.

Servatius had served in the Germany military between 1935 and 1945 but had never joined the Nazi party. According to the Mossad report, Servatius had 'militaristic and right-wing inclinations, without it being possible to say that he has Nazi tendencies' (Ceserani 2006: 246). Post-war he established a mixed reputation for defending Nazi war criminals. Most notably, Servatius unsuccessfully defended Fritz Sauckel before the Nuremberg Tribunal in 1945–1946 and Karl Brandt during the 'doctors' trials' of 1946–1947. Reflecting on these experiences, Karl Jaspers noted that Servatius 'knows all the tricks in the book' and 'will not have a hard time of it legally' (Arendt and Jaspers 1992: 424).[9] Israel agreed and eventually offered to pay the legal costs of the defence. The total amount, approximately US$30,000, was also used to pay a legal assistant, Dieter Wechtenbruch, who Arendt described as 'charming' and 'very intelligent' (Arendt and Blucher 2000: 357, 360). However, Wechtenbruch was frequently in Europe interviewing witnesses and was unavailable to support Servatius for large portions of the trial (Arendt 2006a; 145).

The money paid to Servatius was 'ridiculously inadequate' even through Eichmann's family had agreed to pay him an additional US$15,000 (Arendt 2006a: 222; Arendt and Jaspers 1992: 286). Servatius ought to have had a clearer idea of the costs of running a long trial after his experience at Nuremberg (his decision to reside at the only luxury hotel in Jerusalem did help). However, rather than negotiating a higher fee, seeking more funding from Eichmann's family or using the international spotlight to put pressure on West Germany, Servatius sought to leverage his misfortune to his financial advantage. Arendt (2006a: 222) quotes Servatius as saying that for him the trial was a 'mere business manner' and that he sought to 'make money'. Arendt (2006a: 222) notes further that Servatius 'began complaining about being underpaid almost the first day of the trial, and soon thereafter he openly voiced the hope that he would be able to sell whatever "memoirs" Eichmann would write in prison "for future generations"'.

While financial or resource imbalance is not uncommon in criminal trials (the imbalance was greater at Nuremberg), one might reasonably question Servatius's

9 Arendt describes Servatius as 'oily, greasy, clever, concise and to the point – he knows what he wants' (Arendt and Jaspers 1992: 285).

motives for offering himself as defence council. Was he seeking to uphold the rights of the accused or line his own pockets? While those goals are not necessarily incompatible, Servatius's comments before the trial indicate that he sought to personally benefit from his client's situation. Plainly, the value of Eichmann's memoirs would rise if he were executed. Further to this point, Yablonka (2004: 129) argues that not only did Israel underpay Servatius[10] but also interfered with his access to Eichmann and monitored all of their interactions (Cesarani 2006: 247). According to a top secret police report:

> Servatius complained bitterly that he wasn't allowed to meet with Eichmann 'not, as it were, eye to eye, but ear to ear.' Servatius explained that he could not oppose having a glass partition between [himself and Eichmann] ... and he was even prepared to believe us that no listening device was being used, if we so declare ... In this regard, [Servatius] mentioned the presence of a Mossad agent during his last visit [to Eichmann], who listened with great attention (Yablonka 2004: 129).

As a result of these factors, by January 1961, Servatius had not been able to properly prepare the defence strategy. By contrast, the prosecution team had been working for over seven months. 'This' notes Yablonka (2004: 129) 'was a manifest disproportion.' Moreover, while Servatius and Wechtenbruch were briefed on local jurisprudence (Cesarani 2006: 247) they were not properly acquainted with the specifics of Israeli criminal law and trial procedure. This was evident during the trial where Servatius was criticised for being 'clumsy and unimaginative'. In particular, he was unprepared during cross-examination and often unfamiliar with how to handle evidence from interrogatories. Throughout the trial, Servatius conducted almost no cross-examination and lacked a detailed knowledge of the evidence against his client. At times Servatius's incompetence in court led to direct confrontations with Eichmann. Lipstadt (2011: 116) recounts one example:

> Servatius often stumbled, mixed up documents, and could not locate the proper reference. On occasion, Eichmann corrected him or passed him a document from his booth so he could make a particular point. When this happened, one observer noted, 'Eichmann's voice sharpened: the cold snarl, the bark that many of the witnesses remembered was there, one tone beneath what we heard.'

Scenes like this occurred more frequently as the trial progressed and reached its climax.[11] Given the manifest shortcomings of the trial, this was not surprising.

10 Yablonka (2004: 128) notes that the Israeli government agreed to pay Servatius $20,000 but that his expenses totalled $27,000.

11 See for example Jewish Telegraphic Agency (1961).

However, can we conclude that the State of Israel failed to meet the standards of a liberal trial? I would argue in the affirmative and point specifically to the many ways Eichmann's participation was limited or supressed. More than 50 years later, it is baffling that Israel did not more fully resource Servatius or remove basic impediments to Eichmann's defence strategy. Such measures would have legitimated the trial in the eyes of the international community and furthered whatever historical and political goals lay behind Eichmann's kidnapping.

In response, some commentators have followed Justice Jackson in his justification of the Nuremberg trial: 'They have been given the kind of a Trial which they, in the days of their pomp and power, never gave to any man [sic]' (McKeown 2014: 119). While one can understand the impulse behind this sentiment, it is ultimately self-defeating and a poor standard upon which to measure our own behaviour. Judged against Israeli's own stated goals, the trial fell short and that is one reasons it was so controversial and is still debated today.

Chapter 10

Judgment

> Great deeds are not done by strength or speed or physique; they are the production of thought and character and judgment (Cicero 2016: 39).

The relationship between thoughtfulness and judgment is a persistent theme throughout Arendt's political writing (Bernstein 2000: 277–292). This concern motivates her early engagement with authoritarian ideology (Arendt 1973a) and the problem of understanding phenomena without precedent (Arendt 2005d). Following the Eichmann trial, Arendt's interest in judgment was further developed in a series of essays that considered the links between opinion, facts and deliberation (2006b and 2006c) and in her posthumously published lecture series on Kant's political philosophy (Arendt 1989). However, while Arendt was clearly concerned with judgment throughout her career, it was during the Eichmann trial that her writing is most closely linked to what Jerome Kohn (2000: 113) called 'the priority of the political'.[1]

In this chapter I describe and contrast two kinds of judgment. To begin I look at the judgments handed down by the Israeli District and Supreme Courts. These judgments, which are bounded by the law and enforced through the State's assumed monopoly on violence, are both formal and narrow in scope. The judgments permit only some kinds of questions and while they appear objective, they also play a political role in providing a legitimating narrative for events. I consider this with respect to the way the District Court sought to distance its judgment from the spectacle of survivor testimony it permitted in evidence and the way the Supreme Court adopted the prosecution's description of Eichmann as a central figure in the Holocaust who sought to surpass his superiors.

Following this discussion, I unpack Arendt's performative judgment of Eichmann which she delivers at the end of her report. This judgment, which is articulated through the invocation of a plural 'we', embodies something of the theatrical elements of justice discussed in Chapter 2. While legal judgment is narrow and formal, Arendt models a version of philosophical judgment whose fidelity is to

1 Villa (2000: 16) argues that Arendt's writing on judgment shifts during the late sixties and early seventies to focus on the detached spectator. See also Beiner (1989).

practical reason. Arendt asks big questions and seeks to understand the stakes of decisions where one party has the power to determine with whom they wish to share the earth. Arendt also considers judgment from the perspective of individual plurality and what it means to keep company with oneself. The notion of conscience is central in Arendt's thinking about how evil can be avoided and she develops this idea in relationship to the practice of thinking and moral judgment.

The District Court and the Supreme Court

It was mid-December 1961 before the District Court reconvened for the judges to issue their decision. The courtroom at Beit Ha'am was packed with survivors and international press waiting behind the auditorium to broadcast the news to the world. The judgment of the District Court began with comments that were consistent with Arendt's perspective on legal justice. While some parties had sought to use the trial as a 'forum for the clarification of questions of great import' the court's responsibility, they insisted, was to focus on the defendant's actions and to 'entirely eliminate' anything foreign to this process. The court noted:

> It cannot allow itself to be enticed into provinces which are outside its sphere. The judicial process has ways of its own, laid down by law, and which do not change, whatever the subject of the trial may be. Otherwise, the processes of law and of court procedure are bound to be impaired, whereas they must be adhered to punctiliously, since they are in themselves of considerable social and educational significance, and the trial would otherwise resemble a rudderless ship tossed about by the waves (Nizkor 1991).

While consistent with our analysis of the liberal trial, this statement abstracts from the experience of those involved in the Eichmann trial and the numerous instances where the court considered evidence or allowed questions far outside the scope of its legitimate sphere. For example, while the court permitted witnesses to 'pour their heart out … in the witness box' they reduced the testimony to a 'by-product of the trial' and ancillary to the court's decision. Such is the distance between rhetoric and reality that one is tempted to suggest that the judges are acting in bad faith and using their judgment to establish a legitimating narrative before the international community.

Having begun with a rebuke of the prosecution, the judges returned to the objections raised by Servatius at the beginning of the trial (discussed in Chapter 3). As noted, the court rejected each of Servatius's claims and restated the basis for their standing to sit in judgment of the accused. The court held:

> Our jurisdiction to try this case is based on the Nazis and Nazi Collaborators (Punishment) Law, a statutory law the provisions of which are unequivocal. The Court has to give effect to the law of the Knesset, and we cannot entertain the

> contention that this law conflicts with the principles of international law (Nizkor 1991).

Despite this response, the court spent several sessions reviewing, in exhaustive detail, a litany of cases that supported their authority to judge Eichmann and the consistency of the *Nazis and Nazi Collaborators (Punishment) Law* 1950 (NNCL) with international law.

Having established its legitimacy and the foundations for their judgment, the court considered Eichmann's contention that there existed 'mitigating circumstances' which should be taken into account in sentencing. As noted in Chapter 2, the NNCL is characterised by strict liability and in most instances, it is sufficient for the prosecution to prove that the act itself was committed (Segev 2000: 335). Section 11 of the NNCL limits mitigating factors to circumstances where the accused did their best to 'reduce the gravity of the consequences of the offence' and when the offence was committed to avert 'consequences more serious than those which resulted from the offence'.

Such provisions were clearly written with Jewish collaborators in mind and it is difficult to imagine that the legislature ever envisioned that Nazis would seek refuge in section 11. Nonetheless, the court considered several of Servatius's arguments, including that Eichmann's work in Vienna had been for the 'mutual benefit' of Jews and Nazis and that had the Madagascar plan 'materialized, everything would have been in perfect order to the satisfaction of the Germans and the Jews'. Neither argument was accepted and the court put together an accurate description of Eichmann's job, including his role in organising timetables, ordering deportations and filling trains with Jewish bodies. As Lipstadt (2011: 143) contends, it was Eichmann who 'commanded those who rounded up Jews, packed them onto the freight cars, without subsistence for the trip, and ensured that they arrived at the killing places in sufficient numbers so that the extermination equipment would operate at maximum capacity'. For the court, the distinction Eichmann sought to draw between his activities and those who physically murdered inmates was immaterial:

> … the legal and moral responsibility of a person who delivers the victim to his death is, in our opinion, no less, and maybe even greater, than the liability of the one who does the victim to death (Nizkor 1991).

And yet, the court did not convict Eichmann for every incident alleged. For example, they did not believe that the prosecution had proved that Eichmann had personally murdered a child in Budapest. The prosecution also did not prove that Eichmann was connected to the Kristallnacht, had helped establish the Reinhardt camps, participated in the sterilisation programme or arranged the death marches. Moreover, while Eichmann's deportation activities at the start of the war were brutal (such as the Nisko plan discussed in Chapter 4), the judges concluded that they did not constitute crimes against the Jewish people.

Revealing a significant degree of separation from the State, the court 'found [Eichmann] guilty of what the evidence could prove and rarely ventured beyond that' (Lipstadt 2011: 144).

At the end of their judgment, the District Court ventured to offer some thoughts on Eichmann's character. As Arendt (2006a: 26) noted early in her report, these were shallow reflections that failed to adequately grasp how totalitarian law and its components of ideology and terror impacted individual subjectivity and people's ability to render judgments that were critical of the Nazi regime.[2] An example of the District Court's failure can be noted in their attempt to examine the oral evidence presented by Eichmann. Rather than grappling with the context in which Eichmann was operating, the court focuses on Eichmann's character and concludes that he was lying:

> The Accused's evidence in this case was not truthful evidence, in spite of his repeated declarations that he was reconciled to his fate, knowing the gravity of the activities to which he had confessed of his own will, and now his only desire was to reveal the truth, to correct the wrong impression which had been created in the course of time in regard to his activities in the eyes of his people and of the whole world. In various sections of this Judgment, we have pointed out where the Accused was found to be lying in his evidence. We now add that his entire testimony was nothing but one consistent attempt to deny the truth and to conceal his real share of responsibility, or at least to reduce it to a minimum (Nizkor 1991: 243).

Following this portion of the trial, the court provided Eichmann with an opportunity to make a long statement. Unsurprisingly, Eichmann maintained his argument that he had simply followed orders and that he was only guilty of 'having been obedient, having subordinated myself to my official duties and the obligations of war service and my oath of allegiance and my oath of office, and in addition, once the war started, there was also martial law'. Eichmann also expressed his misfortune in having 'become entangled in these atrocities' (Nizkor 1991). It was as though the Nazi party and his role in the Holocaust was something that happened to Eichmann, as opposed to something that he chose or took conscious steps toward. In short, Eichmann framed himself (and other subordinates) as one of the 'victims':

> It is said that I could and should have refused to be obedient. That is a consideration with hindsight. Under the circumstances then prevailing such an attitude was not possible. Nor did anyone behave in this fashion. From my experience I know that the possibility, which was alleged only after the

2 Arendt (2006a: 26): 'They preferred to conclude from occasional lies that he was a liar – and missed the greatest moral and even legal challenge of the whole case.'

> War, of opposing orders is a self-protective fairy tale. An individual could secretly slip away. But I was not one of those who thought that permissible.

Curiously, Eichmann also thought it relevant that nobody came to him and reproached him for his conduct. This is striking and reveals a deeper contradiction. While Eichmann sought to 'strive and achieve ethical values' it is also clear that he required direction and guidance from moral authorities. Put another way, Eichmann required explicit remonstration from his superiors and could not tell from the faces of those he deported or visited in camps that his actions were wrong. The court was not sympathetic with this position and need to understand it to pass judgment.

In the end, Eichmann was found guilty of all fifteen counts. With respect to sentencing, the court was not obliged to impose the death penalty and had not done so for other persons charged under the NNCL. However, the court concluded 'with a deep feeling of the burden of responsibility' that 'in order to punish the Accused and deter others, the maximum penalty laid down in the law must be imposed.' Far from simply following commands, the court found that Eichmann had 'acted out of an inner identification with the orders' and with a 'fierce will to achieve the criminal objective'. Importantly, the court also noted that the same sentence would have been passed even if they had accepted Eichmann's claims to blind obedience.

Eichmann instructed Servatius to appeal the decision and three months later proceedings began in the Israeli Supreme Court. During the appeal, Servatius ran exactly the same objections and was unable to produce any new evidence (Arendt 2006a: 248). These proceedings lasted only one week before the Court adjourned for two months for deliberation. The appeal judgment was brief and confirmed the decision of the District Court. However, in a striking revision, the appeal judgment stated:

> As a matter of fact, the Appellant did not receive any orders 'from above' at all; it was he who was supreme, he who was the commander in all that pertains to Jewish Affairs. He ordered and commanded, not only without orders from his superiors in the hierarchy of the service, but also, at times, in absolute conflict with such orders (Nizkor 1991: 17).

While the District Court described Eichmann as an important bureaucrat, the Supreme Court positioned him as a central figure that sought to 'outdo and surpass even his "illustrious masters"'. The court concluded:

> It is clear that the idea of the Final Solution was not his own, but the Fuehrer's. Yet that idea might not have assumed so satanic and infernal an expression – in the bodies of millions of tortured and martyred Jews – but for the thorough planning, the zeal, the fanatical enthusiasm, and the insatiable bloodthirstiness of the Appellant and those who did his bidding ... The

> Appellant was no nondescript entity amongst the activators, but was among the leaders and played a central and decisive part among them all (Nizkor 1991: 17).

In reaching this conclusion Arendt (2006a: 249) notes that the court of appeal 'not only accepted the arguments of the prosecution, it had adopted its very language'. In the days between this final judgment and Eichmann's execution, several requests for clemency were heard. In 2016 Eichmann's personal request was released. The letter, dated 29 May 1962, read:

> There is a need to draw a line between the leaders responsible and the people like me forced to serve as mere instruments in the hands of the leaders. I was not a responsible leader, and as such do not feel myself guilty. I am not able to recognise the court's ruling as just, and I ask, Your Honour Mr President, to exercise your right to grant pardons, and order that the death penalty not be carried out (ABC 2016).

Eichmann was hanged just two hours after his final appeal had been denied. Outside of his family in Argentina and those like Martin Buber who opposed the death penalty,[3] there was little sympathy for Eichmann. His body was cremated and his ashes scattered in the Mediterranean outside Israeli waters.

Arendt's judgment of Eichmann

In the final pages of her report Arendt offers her own performative judgment of Eichmann. Her judgment is both theatrical (in the sense articulated in Chapter 1) and a direct challenge to the narrowness of legal reasoning offered by the court.[4] In writing her judgment, Arendt is unbounded by the law and the rules of precedent. She enjoys this liberty as a philosopher who can engage directly with the new kind of subject she contends was produced under totalitarianism – a framework that sought to eradicate all notions of subjectivity and thus legal responsibility. For this reason, Arendt positions Eichmann as a new kind of criminal and argues that the mechanisms and terms of justice need to be rethought to address the new reality

3 Some of Israel's leading scholars, including Martin Buber, Yesayahu Leibowitz and Gershom Scholem, petitioned Israeli president Ben-Zvi to commute the death sentence. They were joined by the poet Leah Goldberg, and the artist Yehuda Bacon. Professor of Philosophy Shmuel Hugo Bergmann found the protest deeply moving and commented: 'This was, in my eyes, proof that the Judaism of love and compassion still lived and breathed even after the Holocaust' (Lipstadt 2011: 145).

4 Writing with respect to the courts in Jerusalem, Arendt (2006a: 374) noted that 'the justice' of their actions 'would have emerged to be seen by all if the judges had dared to address their defendant in something like the following terms'. The direct address that follows is obviously intended to be courageous, compensating for the judgments that have been handed down.

(Arendt 2006a: 26; Arendt 2013: 43; Seymour 2010: 213–214 and Butler 2014: 288). Her report on the trial does not attempt to sketch out alternatives to the criminal trial but her judgment does perform an alternative response to the court.

Arendt's judgment is proceeded by a dramatic shift in tone as she abandons the first person narrative and speaks through the plural 'we'. Arendt (2006a: 279) writes:

> You also said that your role in the Final Solution was an accident and that almost anybody could have taken your place, so that potentially almost all Germans are equally guilty. What you meant to say was that where all, or most all, are guilty, nobody is. This is an indeed quite common conclusion, but one we are not willing to grant you … guilt and innocence before the law are of an objective nature, and even if eighty million Germans had done as you did, this would not have been an excuse for you.

Whose is the plural voice that emerges here? Is Arendt making a performative judgment on behalf of all humanity? Is it the voice of civil society? Is it what the judges should have said as officers of the State of Israel? It is not clear but her use of the term 'we' suggests a relationship between human plurality and the act of judgment (Butler 2014: 160–162).

Continuing in this fashion, Arendt rejects Eichmann's assertion that he found himself in his role by accident. Arendt might have engaged with this argument further and considered its consistency with her contention that totalitarianism erased individual subjectivity and responsibility. Instead, Arendt focused on Eichmann's concrete actions and returned to her strict perspective that law is not concerned with the inner life or motives of the accused. The crucial point for Arendt is that while we will never know the life Eichmann would have led had he not sought out a career within the Nazi regime, the fact remains that he did commit actions for which he must be held personally responsible. As Arendt (2006a: 279) states: 'Let us assume for the sake of argument, that it was nothing more than misfortune that made you the willing instrument in the organisation of mass murder; there still remains the fact that you have carried out, and, therefore, actively supported, a policy of mass murder.'

This argument has obvious appeal to lawyers because it enables a kind of justice to be enacted against Eichmann. However, as Seymour (2010: 214) contends, Arendt's appeal to objectivity does not resolve the tension she has set up between totalitarianism and judging the unprecedented: 'Paradoxically, [Arendt's] dependence on the absence of subjectivity … as a means of allocating personal responsibility articulates precisely the equivocations inherent in the attempt to judge the unprecedentedness of totalitarianism by reference to the precedent of prior liberal law and liberal legality; of grounding legal responsibility in those situations in which any distinction between subjectivity and the environment appears to have vanished.' This is a clear shortcoming in Arendt's attempt to perform a radically different kind of judgment that responds to the unprecedented context which Eichmann and others existed and acted within. However, it also suggests that Arendt would uphold or retain some elements of liberal law in judging the unprecedented (Seymour 2010: 214).

Following this discussion, Arendt (2006a: 279) brings her report to a close with the following pronouncement:

> [J]ust as you supported and carried out a policy of not wanting to share the earth with the Jewish people and the people of a number of other nations – as though you and your superiors had any right to determine who should and who should not inhabit the world – we find that no one, that is, no member of the human race, can be expected to want to share the earth with you. This is the reason, and the only reason, you must hang.

There is a lot to unpack here but we can see already Arendt's judgment of Eichmann contains two themes. First, Arendt faults Eichmann for his failure to be critical of positive law and distance himself from the demands which Nazi law and policy placed upon him. Put another way, she criticises Eichmann for his obedience to the law and his failure to think for himself. Second, Eichmann's ultimate crime is that he took as a right the ability to determine with whom he wanted to share the earth.[5] As Butler (2014: 288) suggests, there is a principle at work here which states that 'those who seek to eradicate the plurality of human life lose the right to life and that the death penalty is justified only in cases where genocide has been established'.[6]

As I discuss in Chapter 12, Arendt's instantiation of the 'death penalty' here can be reconciled with reference to her earlier writing on punishment and forgiveness. Here Arendt argues that you can only punish what you can forgive because forgiving represents a beginning again. If an event is unforgivable then you cannot punish it and thus the death sentence comes into play. In my view, this reasoning is austere but ultimately unacceptable. The death penalty is clearly one method for deciding with whom to cohabit the earth. However, its appeal to legitimacy and the attempt it makes to distinguish itself from other kinds of violence drops away somewhat when we realise that they all represent attempts to choose with whom we wish to share the earth (Butler 2011: 292). This is an obvious point and one of which Arendt was surely cognisant. However, despite engaging with colleagues on this issue, Arendt did not critically examine her support for the death penalty or connect Eichmann's death with her critique of the political aims of the trial.

Eichmann's crime against cohabitation is obviously different from Arendt's prior judgment on his thoughtlessness. Indeed, the two can only be reconciled if

5 Benhabib (2013: 194) reads this as Arendt accepting the role of international law and human rights.

6 Young-Bruehl (2004: 59) defines the crime against plurality as 'denying [others] the right to have rights'.

there is some intimate relationship between thinking and cohabitation (Butler 2014: 172). Does thinking commit us to the preservation of plurality such that if we seek to destroy plurality we cease to be thinking beings (Butler 2014: 153)? Such a direct link is difficult to trace. Arendt theorises two types of plurality – the plurality of the self and the plurality of the social. This distinction is not absolute and indeed, both are important for responsibility and the exercise of a plural self (Arendt 2005b: 106). We are, according to Arendt, internally divided and must remain in this state if we are to engage fully in the practice of thinking (Arendt 1978b: 185; Butler 2009). She writes for example, 'even in the singularity or duality of thinking processes, plurality is somehow germinally present insofar as I can think only by splitting up into two although I am one' (Arendt 2005b: 106).[7] Arendt's self is simultaneously redoubled and didactic. This redoubling occurs in relation to other people and without this relationship our ability to think cannot develop or mature (Butler 2009) 'This two in one' Arendt (2005b: 106) writes, 'looked upon from the standpoint of human plurality, *is like* the last trace of company even when being one by oneself I am or can become two, which becomes so very important only because we discover plurality where we would least expect it.'

Arendt's notion of the plural self is a condition of conscience and of responsibility. She writes: 'Conflicts of conscience are actually nothing but deliberations between me and myself. They are not resolved through feeling but through thinking. Conscience means no more than this being at peace with myself which is the *sine qua non* of thinking' (Arendt 2005b: 108). In making this pronouncement, Arendt follows Kant's (2008) first critique and his assertion that the 'I' has the capacity to assert its equivalence and so is the precondition of thought.[8] Arendt (2005b: 184) writes: 'The curious thing that I am, needs no plurality in order to establish difference, it carries the difference within itself when it says "I am I", so long as I am conscience, that is conscience of myself, I am inevitably two in one.' For Arendt this split is the foundation for conscience and responsibility. But, figures like Eichmann can also split off or detach from their inner plurality and this is the end of conscience. If the dialogic relation to the self is broken, that constitutes the failure of responsibility (Butler 2009).

Before concluding this section, it is important to note that Arendt believed that the activity of thinking could condition human beings against evil doing. In Arendt's (1978b: 5) final and unfinished book, *The Life of the Mind* she argued:

> Might the problem of good and evil, our faculty for telling right from wrong, be connected with our faculty of thought? … Could the activity of thinking

7 Butler (2014: 173): '[W]ithout the animating trace of social company, there can be no self-reference, which means that sociality precedes and enables what is called thinking. One becomes capable of having a dialogue with oneself only on the condition that one has already been engaged in dialogue by others.' See also Brunner (2000: 445–448).

8 Hegel (1997) develops this further, asserting that identity cannot be asserted without redoubling the identity at issue.

> as such, the habit of examining whatever happens to come to pass or attract attention, regardless of results and specific contents, could this activity be among the conditions that make men abstain from evil-doing or even actually 'condition' them against it?

Thinking interrupts our everyday and sometimes automatic judgments and initiates an internal dialogue (Arendt 2005b: 181). It was this internal dialogue (grounded in the duality of consciousness) that Socrates tried to awaken in his discussant (Arendt 2005b: 187–188; Canovan 1994: 269). Only through cultivating our inner duality can individuals awaken the voice of conscience and fully realise themselves as political beings. Judith Butler (2009) summarises Arendt's position as follows:

> If to think is to be in dialogue with oneself and so to maintain one's own proper duality, in composing genocidal policy one fails to think because, thinking it would appear, is not just a dialogue with one's self but is also related to the plurality of the human – that differentiated many that belong to the realm of sociality. So to maintain a dialogue with oneself must imply maintaining a relationship to that plurality. Thinking must require both and implicate us in both.

Seen in this light, it might be possible to interpret Arendt's final judgment of Eichmann (and perhaps judgment in general) not simply as an individual act but an implicit recognition of human plurality (Young-Bruehl 2009: 26–27; Jackson 1987: 97; Butler 2009). By adopting the plural 'we' Arendt presents herself as a subject that is connected to a broader sociality. She judges Eichmann for seeking to deny the right of European Jewry to coexist in a plurality of subjects. Eichmann's crime was against plurality and it is in the name of this plurality that Arendt judges Eichmann and sentences him to death (Butler 2009).

Arendt's final judgment is performative and reflects deep dissatisfaction with the judgment of the District Court. She does not accept the court's obligation to bind their analysis to the norms of criminal procedure and she refuses to invoke any concept of natural or vernacular law in handing down her sentence (Weston and Bollier 2014: 104). Rather she relies on a pre-legal understanding of responsibility or practical reason to ground her judgment. Her shift from 'I' to 'we' seeks to expand her authority and provide a legitimate foundation for her alternative judgment. Arendt exercises practical judgment not as a way of subordinating an individual to an existing rule, but as a creative act which is still captured within the accepted norms of public critique (Butler 2009). Arendt asks us to consider human judgment not as bound by existing law or norms but as something which produces its own virtue through the act itself. However, whether her invocation of 'we' does the work of instantiating a post-national framework for conceiving of plurality that can also serve as the basis for legal decision-making is highly doubtful (Butler 2014: 169).

In summary, Arendt follows no law when she judges Eichmann and condemns him to death. Just as she faults him for following existing law, rather than questioning its legitimacy, she bases her judgment against him on an independent perspective of what she thinks law should be. She is an autonomous judge who positions practical reason as the source of law (Butler 2014: 169). This perspective is part of a long tradition in legal and political philosophy and represents a rational response to the existence of immoral law. Those who uphold this view are sometimes accused of being unpatriotic, but as Arendt explained in a letter to Gershom Scholem: 'there can be no patriotism without permanent opposition and criticism' (Arendt quoted in Smith 2009: 105). From this perspective, disobedience in the face of immoral law mediates the boundary between the need for change and the need for stability. The law both gains and retains its legitimacy through contestation and antagonism. That was precisely what Eichmann failed to understand (Arendt 2006a: 133). If we ask according to what norms or what criteria we decide whether or not a specific law should be followed, the answer according to Arendt has to do with whether or not we can continue to live with ourselves, to keep company with ourselves after having committed such an act.[9] This point is powerfully articulated in Arendt's (2005a: 44) essay 'Personal Responsibility Under Dictatorship'. She writes:

> The nonparticipants, called irresponsible by the majority, were the only ones who dared *judge by themselves*, and they were capable of doing so not because they disposed of a better system of values or because the old standards of right and wrong were still firmly planted in their mind and conscience but … because their conscience did not function in this, as it were, automatic way … they asked themselves to what extent they would still be able to live in peace with themselves after having committed certain deeds; and they decided that it would be better to do nothing, not because the world would then be charged for the better, but because only on this condition could they go on living with themselves.[10]

9 In making this argument Arendt understates the dark side of human potentiality. See further Burdon (2015).

10 See further de Wall (2012).

Chapter 11

Reading Eichmann today

In the 40 years since her death, Hannah Arendt remains a major figure in Western political thought. For many scholars she is the analyst of totalitarian regimes, revolutionary types, forms of violence and war. She is a touchstone for those interrogating issues that concern citizenship, the nation state and international relations. Her vision of the possibilities for freedom and political life have inspired writing on mass surveillance and the weakening of democratic institutions. And her report on the Eichmann trial and reflections on thoughtless evil remain the subject of intense debate and have inspired scholarship in areas such as climate change, refugee policy and the status of whistleblowers (Burdon *et al.* 2014).

Arendt, to borrow a phrase from Ezra Pound (1960: 29) is 'news that stays news'. The reason for this is not because Arendt was always correct or that history bore out all of her insights. Rather, it is because of Arendt's ability to square traditional concepts with new realities and the model she presented as an intellectual who sought to engage with her own time. Arendt wanted thoughts and deeds that responded to present circumstances and challenged her peers to abandon passively received ideas and see past bureaucratic doubletalk. Crucial to this task was Arendt's ability to hold a place in her mind for the unprecedented and her refusal to collapse new events into traditional concepts or recognisable tendencies. For example, in the preface to the first edition of *The Origins of Totalitarianism* Arendt (1973a: viii) castigated political scientists for 'denying the outrages, deducing the unprecedented from precedents … explaining phenomena by such analogies and generalities that the impact of reality and the shock of experience are no longer felt'.[1] Later, as Arendt was making revisions to that same work, she argued that many social scientists did not appreciate the careful distinctions she made about aspects of totalitarianism: 'There exists … a silent agreement in most discussions amongst political scientists that we can ignore distinctions and proceed on the assumption that everything can eventually be called anything else, and that distinctions are meaningful only to the extent that each of us has the right "to define

1 For a sociological investigation into the meaning of unprecedented see Baehr (2002: 820–826).

his terms'" (Arendt 1956: 413).[2] For Arendt, it was theoretically misguided and morally obtuse to extrapolate totalitarianism to previous experiences or historical institutions.[3]

In the decades since Arendt's death, her emphasis on fostering a habit of thinking and identifying what is unprecedented (as opposed to looking for historical analogies) remains a fundamental challenge (Baehr 2002). Recently, this failure to confront the unprecedented and draw distinctions was most powerfully expressed in the reflexive way Donald Trump has been labelled a fascist (Kinsley 2016; Watson 2016)[4] or the way intellectuals have sought to understand Trump through Max Weber's description of charismatic leadership (Lane 2016).[5] This tendency to substitute and shuffle ideas or assimilate conventional categories, destroys the boundaries between discrete objects and is something which the historically minded should resist.

With this in mind, and conscious of the opposite danger that exaggerating the novelty of events can be distorting, I turn now to consider two current political problems. First, I return to Arendt's analysis of thoughtlessness and a warning she issued toward the end of her report on the Eichmann trial about the re-emergence of totalitarianism in the future. Drawing on Arendt's warning, I draw on Sheldon Wolin and Wendy Brown to argue that corporate dominance in western democracies has given rise to an inverted totalitarianism where human subjects are constituted as *homo oeconomicus* and are unfree in novel ways. Following this, I consider Arendt's early essays on the establishment of the State of Israel and her advocacy for a binational solution or federated structure which draw attention to the rights of the stateless Palestinian population. While Arendt's analysis might be faulted for its naivety, it prefigures her later writing on spaces of freedom based on 'the direct participation of every citizen in the public affairs of the country' (2006d: 264). I argue further that Arendt's writing on Binationalism was prescient in understanding how the condition of statelessness would lead to continued territorial violence in Palestine and Israel. Moreover, her attempt to go beyond nationalism and identitarian politics offers a way forward which draws from the shared history of dispossession and violence common to Israeli Jews and Palestinians.

Inverted totalitarianism

One of the most pertinent thoughts Arendt raises in her report on the Eichmann trial relates to the 'general atrophy in our powers of judgment' (Villa 1997: 184).

2 See for example Adler who sought to use the sociology of slavery to understand the Nazi camps (Baehr 2002: 809). Against this interpretation Arendt (1973a: 444) persuasively claimed that the camps were unprecedented and served a fundamentally different purpose than slavery.

3 For a critique of Arendt's portrait of totalitarianism see Brinton (1966) and Aron (1993).

4 For a thoughtful response to this claim see Paxton (2016).

5 Arendt (1973a: 361–362) thought it was a 'serious error' to employ Weber to comprehend totalitarian rule. See also Young-Bruehl (2004: 43).

As the distance between our participation in decision-making widens in mass technological society, our capacity to think and express judgment on moral and political matters has diminished (Villa 1997: 184). With this distance comes an increased reliance on popular ideas or 'banisters' to help us navigate the complexities of everyday life without needing to pause and reflect (Arendt 1979: 314). Common banisters today might be located inside the dominant ideology of a society or pertain more directly to a person's political identity, i.e. whether they are left or right. The trouble, Arendt claimed, was that these banisters make it difficult for individuals to identify and reflect upon significant changes in the public sphere. Moreover, they 'lull us into a kind of automatic judgment' in which the singularity of an individual event loses its import (Villa 1997: 184).

What Arendt feared most was not the possibility that each of us would realise our potential for evil.[6] Rather, she was concerned about the increasingly automatic and unreflective quality of our judgments and she described thoughtlessness as the 'outstanding characteristic of our time' (Arendt 1998: 5). Arendt (1979: 314) articulated this worry in a letter to her colleague and friend, Hans Jonas:

> If you go through such a situation [totalitarianism] the first thing you know is the following: you never know how somebody will act. You have the surprise of your life! This goes through all layers of society and it goes throughout various distinctions between men. And if you want to make a generalisation then you could say that those who were still very firmly convinced of the so-called old values were the first to be ready to change their old values for a new set of values, provided they were given one. And I am afraid of this, because I think that the moment you give anybody a new set of values – of this famous 'banister' you can immediately exchange it. And the only thing that the guy gets used to is having a 'banister' and a set of values, no matter.

In relying on these banisters ordinary people can unreflectively turn to fascism. It is important that we take heed of Arendt's concern because, as she warns in her report on Eichmann, 'once a specific crime has appeared for the first time, its reappearance is more likely than its initial emergence could ever have been' (Arendt 2006a: 273). In what must be the most chilling passage in her report, Arendt (2006a: 273) writes:

> The particular reasons that speak for the possibility of a repetition of the crimes committed by the Nazis are even more plausible. The frightening coincidence of the modern population explosion with the discovery of technical devices that, through automation, will make large sections of the population

6 In 1972 Arendt spoke at a conference at the University of Toronto dedicated to her work. Speaking at the close of the conference, Arendt forcibly repudiated the idea that her report on the Eichmann trial suggested that we could all behave like the accused (Villa 1997: 184).

> 'superfluous' even in terms of labor, and that, through nuclear energy, make it possible to deal with this twofold threat by the use of instruments beside which Hitler's gassing installations look like an evil child's fumbling toys, should be enough to make us tremble.

That murder has not been made fully bureaucratic on the scale witnessed during the Second World War is not grounds for optimism.[7] As Max Weber (1978: 24–25) recognised, modern life continues to be subject to the protocols of bureaucratic instrumental rationality. Alongside this are the disciplining effects of contemporary surveillance and the imperatives of technological progress. Reflecting on contemporary politics, Sheldon Wolin (2011: xvii) has characterised contemporary politics as 'inverted totalitarianism' – a political hybrid, where economic and state powers are conjoined and virtually unbridled. Wolin (2011: 47) writes:

> The Nazi and Fascist regimes were powered by revolutionary movements whose aim was not only to capture, reconstitute and monopolize state power but also gain control over the economy … In contrast, inverted totalitarianism is only in part a state-centred phenomenon. Primarily it represents the political coming of age of corporate power and the political demobilization of the citizenry.

At best, Wolin argues, Western democracies are 'managed' and the public is no longer sovereign. At worst, democracies have become so hollowed out that corporate powers are no longer bound by the State. The result is not a 'system of codetermination by equal partners' but rather a situation where the demos is dominated by private interests and notions of the common good are reduced to individual desires (Wolin 2011: xxi). This is exacerbated where the corporate entity has greater resources than the country they are negotiating with, i.e. the relationship between Exxon Mobil and the Republic of Chad in northern Central Africa (Coll 2013: 154–176). While Wolin makes it clear that 'inverted totalitarianism' is not morally or politically comparable to Nazi Germany, he warns that neoliberal capitalism seeks total power and gives rise to its own unique pathologies.

The corporate interests driving inverted totalitarianism speak in the language of freedom and represent themselves in a manner which suggests a deep respect for democratic institutions and the rule of law. However, these same forces corrupt and manipulate democracies as to make representative governance impossible (Chomsky 2005: 24). Thus Wendy Brown (2015: 9) argues that western

7 In connection to this point Pinker (2012) argues that the current era is less violent, less cruel and more peaceful than any previous period of human existence. The decline in violence holds for violence in the family, in neighbourhoods, between tribes and between states.

democracies have grown 'gaunt, ghostly' and that their future is 'increasingly hedged and improbable'. In agreement, the editorial team at *The Economist* (2014) have published essays claiming that: 'Democracy has always had its critics, but now old doubts are being treated with renewed respect as the weaknesses of democracy in its Western strongholds, and the fragility of its influence elsewhere, have become increasingly apparent.' While the specifics vary according to location, Peter Mair (2013) provided an important survey of the hollowing out of the political system in Europe, measured with respect to sharp drops in party membership, a decline in electoral voting, the collapse of social organisations such as trade unions and increased hostility to major political parties.[8]

While Wolin stresses that his notion of inverted totalitarianism is a 'tentative' or 'hypothetical' construction, he also argues that certain tendencies in our society indicate a shift away from democratic principles such as representation and toward a 'managed democracy' (Wolin 2011: xxiv and 136–158). This is a situation where governance is directed by private interests and democratic values are saturated with market values. Rather than sharing power, Brown (2015: 10) argues that citizens are being shaped into *homo oeconomicus:* 'an intensely constructed and governed bit of human capital tasked with improving and leveraging its competitive positioning and with enhancing its (monetary and nonmonetary) portfolio across all of its endeavours and venues'. Inverted totalitarianism challenges the conviction that democracy should aspire to the shared rule of the people. It is a politics, but as Wolin (2011: 63) contends, it is largely untempered by traditional political concerns: 'What is absent is the political, the commitment to finding where the common good lies amidst the welter of well-financed, highly organized, single-minded interests rabidly seeking governmental favours and overwhelming the practices of representative government and public administration by a sea of cash.'

Like traditional examples of totalitarianism, inverted totalitarianism is perpetuated by individuals who may not fully comprehend the deeper meaning or consequences of their actions (Wolin 2011: xvii). Market values replace individual judgment and convictions like growth or privatisation are held up as immutable laws around which everything else must fit. Thoughtlessness spreads and few seem interested in taking seriously the extent to which a pattern of consequences is emerging without having been preconceived. This pattern 'disseminates the model of the market to all domains and activities … and configures human beings exhaustively as market actors' (Brown 2015: 31). The subject formed in this environment has significantly reduced experiences of self-governance and reduced capacities for democratic life. Their orientation is also increasingly directed at

8 Humphreys and Tietze (2013). Antonio Gramsci (1971: 2010) presciently described this process in his prison writings: 'At a certain point in their historical lives, social classes become detached from their traditional parties. In other words, the traditional parties in that particular organisational form, with the particular men who constitute, represent, and lead them, are no longer recognised by their class (or fraction of a class) as its expression.'

instrumental goals which are concentrated on individuality and macro-economic goals. In short, the subject formed under inverted totalitarianism may be limited in novel ways and have reduced capacities not only to exercise moral judgment but also in their capacity to think about what an authentic egalitarian politics might look like.

Returning to Arendt, inverted totalitarianism risks destroying social relations that are important to maintaining the public sphere and the conditions under which the plural self has developed. As described in Chapter 9, the plural self represents a split of the individual. This internal exchange between 'me and myself' is required for a person to exercise judgment (Arendt 2005b: 108). However, judgment is not a splitting off from the self – this distinction is crucial. For Arendt plural or dialogic self is the condition from which conscience and responsibility emerge. But the splitting off is the end of conscience. Should this new emerging form of totalitarianism succeed in conditioning us as *homo oeconomicus* then, following Arendt's warning, we all have cause to tremble. This offers at least some indication for Arendt's urgent philosophical claim (not in *Eichmann* but in everything else she wrote), that the most powerful way to combat evil is not through morals but by defending the public sphere as a site for political expression.

Israel–Palestine

The second contemporary political problem that requires attention concerns the political situation in Israel and Palestine. This topic was of great concern to Arendt in a series of essays she wrote during the 1940s (2008: 342–416). Moreover, as mentioned in the introduction, it is a topic that motivates much of the current criticism of Arendt's report.[9] In her introduction to the 2006 edition of *Eichmann in Jerusalem*, Amos Elon (2006: viii) comments on the book's reception in Israel:

> A new Hebrew translation was recently published to considerable acclaim. In the past, the difficulty of many Israelis to accept Arendt's book ran parallel to another difficulty – foreseen by Arendt early on – the difficulty of confronting, morally and politically, the plight of the dispossessed Palestinians. The Palestinians bore no responsibility for the collapse of civilization in Europe but ended up being punished for it.[10]

The origin of the Israeli-Palestinian conflict is usually dated from the end of the nineteenth century when political Zionists sought to resolve what we have been calling 'the Jewish question'. In 1917 Zionist leaders won the support of a great power for its project – in this case Great Britain through the issuance of what was

9 See Ezrahi (2004).
10 See Arendt (2006a: x)

called the Balfour Declaration. The Balfour Declaration was a letter from Arthur James Balfour, the United Kingdom's Foreign Secretary to Baron Rothschild, the leader of the British Jewish community (Segev 1998: 27). The declaration stated: 'His Majesty's government view with favour the establishment in Palestine of a national home for the Jewish people, and will use their best endeavours to facilitate the achievement of this object' (Schneer 2012: 334).

Following the declaration, the main challenge was the indigenous population because Palestine at the end of the nineteenth century was overwhelmingly Muslim (Pappe 2007: 29–30). The Zionist movement (in particular the World Zionist Organization and the Jewish Agency) understood from the very beginning that there was no way that the Indigenous population would acquiesce to the creation of a Jewish state over land that they both occupied and had connection with. Given this state of affairs there were two main options that were considered by the Zionist movement. Benny Morris (2001: 39–40) summarises the options as follows:

> The Zionist movement can choose between one of two options. The first is the way of South Africa – the establishment of an apartheid state with a settler minority lording it over a large exploited native majority. The second is the way of transfer – to expel the indigenous population and in that way to solve the dilemma.

While other proposals were debated, these were the two dominant options considered during the first phase of the occupation between 1917 and 1948. As has been well documented, the Zionist movement opted for the second option – the way of transfer (Morris 2001: 40). On 14 May 1948, David Ben-Gurion proclaimed Israeli independence. He also used the aftermath of the Second World War as an opportunity to expel the Palestinian population. This was one of the factors that contributed to the first Arab–Israeli War which ended in 1948 with the expulsion of approximately 80 per cent of Arabs from the Israeli boarders (Allan 2013: 5). Those expelled were juridical made foreigners and became what is called the 'The Palestinian refugee question' (Said 2001). Many went to live in refugee camps in what came to be called the West Bank and Gaza while others went to live in neighbouring countries such as Lebanon, Jordan, Syria and Egypt.

During the 1940s Arendt wrote several editorials, essays and unfinished pieces concerning the creation of the State of Israel and the fate of the Palestinian population. Her commentary on these events changes over time but reflects the perspective of a refugee who took seriously the history of displacement and exile and sought to secure rights for the stateless. In saying this, it is also important to note that Arendt's early writing reflects a Eurocentrism common to the period and a typology that marginalising the Sephardim and Mizrachim Jews whom she described as the 'oriental mob' (Arendt 2006a: 435; Butler 2014: 139–140).

In 1940 Arendt (2008: 130) developed a critique of nationalism grounded in secular or religious values. A just society is flexible and will expand equality to all people that reside in its zone of influence. Arendt also worried about the emergence of Judaism as a major political identity.[11] 'Those Jews', Arendt (2008: 162) wrote 'who no longer believe in their God in a traditional way but continue to consider themselves "chosen" in some fashion or other can mean by it nothing other than that by nature they are better or wiser or more rebellious or salt of the earth. And that would be, twist and turn it as you like, nothing other than a version of racist superstition.' Although Arendt understood the importance of establishing a safe area for victims of the Holocaust, she also found it unacceptable that survival trumped egalitarian values such as freedom and equality. For this reason, Arendt (2008: 130) argued that the Jewish people might form a nation (without territory) and become part of a federated Europe:

> The notion that nations are constituted by settlement within borders and are protected by their territory is undergoing a crucial correction. Spaces that can truly be maintained economically and politically are constantly expanding. There may soon come a time when the idea of belonging to a territory is replaced by the idea of belonging to a commonwealth of nations whose politics are determined solely by the commonwealth as a whole.

For Arendt, an arrangement like this would give Jews a voice inside a European parliament and an army which could join the resistance against fascism (2008: 136–139; Jacobson 2013: 362–365). When Arendt recognised that her vision of a federated plurality within Europe was unlikely and she later morphed aspects of her proposal in favour of a federated Jewish-Arab state which would guarantee equal political rights for the two peoples (2008: 193; Young-Bruehl 2004: 183; Butler 2014: 137). Drawing on the history of Jewish oppression, Arendt argued that a state founded on Jewish sovereignty would inevitably produce massive injustice for whatever minority groups lived inside its boarders. In a sweeping statement, Arendt (2008: 194) argued: 'Palestine can be saved as the national homeland of Jews only if (like other small countries and nationalities) it is integrated into a federation.'[12]

In 1943 Arendt (2008: xxv and 193) became engaged in debates (alongside figures such as Martin Buber and Judah Magnes) about the formation of a binational

11 From this analysis it is clear how Arendt would analyse and critique recent attempts to define Israel as a Jewish state. The proposed basic law would have defined Jewishness as the default nature of the state in any instance, legal or legislative, in which the state's Jewishness and its democratic aspirations clash (Ravid *et al.* 2014). See also attempts to increase the role of Jewish law in the Israeli legal system (Lis 2016).

12 Arendt (2008: 141–142) cites a Jewish religious leader Hillel to support this position: 'As Jews we want to fight for the freedom of the Jewish people, because "If I am not for me who is for me?" As Europeans we want to fight for the freedom of Europe, because "If I am only for me who am I?" (Hillel) [first century A.D. Jewish sage].'

state.[13] The radical democratic elements of this debate would reoccur later in *On Revolution* as Arendt recalled the lost treasure of citizens' councils where individuals 'protect the island of freedom they have come to inhabit against the surrounding sea of necessity' (2006d: 267). With respect to Binationalism, Arendt's engagement can be traced through the Ihud (unity) movement which unilaterally opposed the formation of a single Jewish commonwealth. Binationalism for Ihud meant a single Jewish-Arab political confederation where Jewish emigration, at first instance, would be matched to equal the Palestinian population (Jacobson 2013: 366).[14] The eventual aim would be to secure Jewish minority rights inside of a greater Arab commonwealth. Arendt agreed with aspects of Ihud's platform but argued against a discourse of majority/minority rights which she felt was destined to become reduced to a call for 'population transfers' which would 'never work without fascist organizations' (2008: 195).

'The only realistic position' Arendt (2008: 206) wrote in May 1944, 'would be a policy of alliances with other Mediterranean peoples, which would strengthen the Jewish status in Palestine and secure the sympathies of our neighbours.' Also in 1944, Arendt (2008: 343) returned to her argument that founding the Israeli State on the basis of exclusive Jewish sovereignty would aggravate the problem of statelessness and lead to a 'tragic conflict' which could only be solved through the displacement of the Palestinian population ('cutting the Gordian knot'). She also described as 'absurd' the idea of establishing a Jewish state in a 'sphere of interest' of external superpowers (2008: 345 and 371). Such a state would live in the 'delusion of nationhood' and she argued that it is 'folly' to 'dictate a policy which trusts a distant imperial power for protection, while alienating the goodwill of neighbours' (2008: 371 and 372; Butler 2007).[15]

Here we see Arendt seeking to think through two political tensions. On the one hand, she is obviously concerned to find a solution which does not result in the displacement of the Palestinians and their subjugation as stateless refugees. Moreover, she is troubled by the thought that a state founded on the basis of

13 Arendt was strongly condemned by the mainstream Zionist establishment for this argument: 'Any program which denies these fundamental principles such as advanced by the Ihud or any other group, is unacceptable to the Zionist Organization of America and Hadassah, the Women's Zionist Organization of America' (quoted in Kohn 2008: lxxiv). For Arendt's response see (2008: 414).

14 The Ihud declaration sought a government based on 'equal political rights for the two peoples' and which would 'guarantee the national rights of all peoples within it' (Jacobson 2013, 368–369).

15 On this point, Arendt (2008: 344) argued further: 'Nationalism is bad enough when it trusts in nothing but the rude force of the nation. A nationalism that … depends on the force of a foreign nation is certainly worse. This is the threatened fate of the Jewish nationalism and of the proposed Jewish state, surrounded inevitably by Arab states and Arab peoples. Even a Jewish majority in Palestine – nay, even a transfer of all Palestine Arabs, which is openly demanded by the Revisionists – would not substantially change a situation in which Jews must either ask protection from an outside power against their neighbors or come to a working agreement with their neighbors.'

Jewish sovereignty will escalate tension and render the prospects for peaceful coexistence more distant:

> … if the Jewish commonwealth is proclaimed against the will of the Arabs and without the support of the Mediterranean peoples, not only financial help but political support will be necessary for a long time to come. And that may turn out to be very troublesome indeed for Jews in this country, who after all have no power to direct the political destinies of the Near East (Arendt 2008: 373).[16]

The Arab–Israeli War confirmed many of Arendt's fears. Writing in 1948 she noted that 'even if the Jews were to win the war, its end would find the … achievements of Zionism in Palestine destroyed … The "victorious" Jews would live surrounded by an entirely hostile Arab population, secluded inside ever threatened borders, absorbed with physical self-defence to a degree that would submerge all other interests and activities' (2008: 396). In an attempt to undercut nationalism and the problem of statelessness, Arendt once again argued in favour of a federated state under the temporary trusteeship of the United States. In her view, such an arrangement:

> would have the advantage of preventing the establishment of sovereignty whose only sovereign right would be to commit suicide. It would provide a cooling off period. It could initiate the Jordan Valley Authority project as a government enterprise and it could establish for its realization local Arab-Jewish committees under the supervision and the auspices of an international authority. It could appoint members of the Jewish and the Arab intelligentsia to posts in local and municipal offices. Last but not least, trusteeship over the whole of Palestine would postpone and possibly prevent partition of the country (2008: 399–400).

This did not eventuate and by the 1950s Arendt was describing Israel as a colonial occupation founded on the basis of anti-democratic citizenship requirements. Judith Butler (2014: 142–143) summarises the development in Arendt's thinking: 'If, in the 1930's, she worried about the Jews becoming increasingly stateless, in the late 1940's and early 50's she was attuned to the displacement of Palestinians and developed a more comprehensive account of statelessness.' This account was most forcefully articulated in Arendt's 1951 book *The Origins of Totalitarianism.* Here Arendt argued that, for structural reasons, a nation-state founded on hegemonic nationalism must produce large numbers of refugees. With regard to the establishment of Israel, Arendt (1973a, 290) wrote:

16 Arendt (2008: 345) noted: 'Jews who know their own history should be aware that such a state of affairs will inevitably lead to a new wave of Jew-hatred.'

> After the war it turned out that the Jewish question, which was considered the only insoluble one, was indeed solved – namely by means of a colonized and then conquered territory – but this solved neither the problems of the minorities nor the stateless. On the contrary, like virtually all other events of our century, the solution for the Jewish question merely produced a new category of refugees, the Arabs, thereby increasing the number of stateless and rightless by another 700,000 to 800,000 people.

While the actual number of displaced Palestinians was higher, Arendt's underlying point about the risks minority groups face when living within states (or occupied territories) founded on a narrow understanding of national belonging, remains persuasive. In adopting this perspective, we must also be careful not to equate Zionism with Nazism. This was not Arendt's position and it ignores the obvious fact that debates surrounding Binationalism emerged from within Zionist politics. However, as Butler (2014: 121) notes, there are 'principles of social justice that can be derived from the Nazi genocide that can and must inform our contemporary struggles, even though the contexts are different and the forms subjugating power are clearly distinct.'

Moreover, Arendt's focus on statelessness, regardless of cultural or national identify, offers a useful lens through which one might engage with debates about Binationalism today. These debates seek to imagine a Binationalism infused with substantive principles of equality. This Binationalism is thus premised on the end to settler colonialism and demands more than the 'wretched Binationalism' or unequal cohabitation that occurs today (Butler 2014: 18). While this discussion is dramatically at odds with the current direction of Israeli politics I contend it is still worth discussing. As Butler (2014, 30) notes: 'It may be that Binationalism is an impossibility, but that mere fact does not suffice as a reason to be against it.' Beyond impossibility, we should also remain open to the unexpected and political developments which are outside the limits of our imagination.

Chapter 12

The last Nazi trials and forgiveness

'There are no tidy endings following mass atrocity' (Minow 1999: 102).

On a cold morning in February 2016, Reinhold Hanning, a former SS guard at the Auschwitz concentration camp, was wheeled into a courtroom in Detmold, Germany. Hanning, who is 94 years old, looks frail and keeps his eyes downcast as he listens with strained attention to the judge and sips from a plastic cup of water. Hanning is a shadow of the 18-year-old youth who volunteered in 1942 to work as a guard at Auschwitz. While none of the witnesses remember Hanning personally, he is charged with being an accessory to the murder of 170,000 people who were killed at the death camps while he worked there between January 1943 and June 1944. At Auschwitz Hanning was assigned to register work details, but he later accepted a post in the guard tower. According to the indictment, Hanning played a role in selecting who would be chosen to work or sent to the gas chambers. In a statement read by Hanning's lawyer to the court, the accused denied personal involvement but admitted knowing of the killing process:

> Nobody talked to us about it in the first days there, but if someone, like me, was there for a long time, then one learned what was going on ... People were shot, gassed and burned. I could see how corpses were taken back and forth or moved out. I could smell the burning bodies (Gray 2016).

Hanning, who was sentenced to five years in prison, is one of dozens of Nazis who have stood trial in recent years.[1] In 2016 ten Nazi trials were held across Europe and the Simon Wiesenthal Center (2015) maintains a list of the most wanted Nazi war criminals. Recent trials in Germany have gained momentum after the trial of John Demjanjuk (91) who was sentenced to five years in prison in 2011 for

1 Other high profile cases include Oskar Groening (94) who was sentenced to four years in prison in 2015 for his role in the murder of 300,000 Jews. Groening did not kill anyone directly but sorted the bank notes from trainloads of arriving Jews (ABC 2015). Also important is Hubert Zafke (95) who was charged with 3,681 counts of accessory to murder at Auschwitz but the court determined that he was medically unfit to stand trial (Rising 2016).

assisting in the murder of 28,060 Jews while acting as a guard at the Sobibór extermination camp, Poland (Douglas 2016; Solomon 2016). Demjanjuk died after his lawyers appealed his conviction and under German law, no conviction stands until all appeal rights have been exhausted (Douglas 2016: 3). Despite this, the Demjanjuk case set an important precedent as the first case where a Nazi guard was convicted solely on the basis of having served as a camp guard, without specific evidence of violence against an identified victim.

The resurgence of Nazi war trials provides an opportunity for reflecting on the merits of criminal process in the aftermath of large-scale violence. To do this, I first consider how Arendt, in light of her judgment of Adolf Eichmann, might think about current criminal cases against camp guards. I argue that these cases also involve crimes against cohabitation and seek to fragment the plurality of humankind. To exercise judgment concerning with whom one will cohabit the earth is to undertake an unforgivable action. In these circumstances the death penalty is apparently justified. However, with respect to current cases, I argue that Arendt would strongly oppose attempts to convict defendants without evidence of specific criminal acts. Rather than allow former guards to evade responsibility for their actions, I next consider Arendt's writing on forgiveness as a mechanism for reversing past harm. While Arendt does see forgiveness as a mechanism for mutual release, I argue that she gives it a narrow application which would not extend to willed evil or mass crimes committed with thoughtless or banal intentions. For those complicit in genocide, Arendt appears to recommend the death penalty, not as a punishment, but because those individuals have placed themselves beyond the reach of forgiveness. While Arendt theorised forgiveness as a limited and conditional faculty, I contrast her writing with alternative perspectives offered during the South African Truth and Reconciliation Commission and writers such as Desmond Tutu and Martha Nussbaum. Drawing on these perspectives I argue that legal and political institutions need to be cultivated so that they are forward looking and leave open the opportunity for reconciliation and mutual release.

Current Nazi trials

The dominant debate concerning the continued prosecution of Nazi war criminals tends to break down along the following lines. Those against prosecution point to the age and fragility of the accused; the time that has elapsed since the alleged actions were committed; concerns about the quality of evidence (in particular, the veracity of witness testimony); the good behaviour of the accused since the alleged actions; the criminal context in which the actions were committed;[2] the expense of bringing the accused to trial and the desire to put history to rest.[3]

2 Arendt (2006a: 26) levelled this objection against proceedings against Eichmann.

3 Rieff (2016: 79) argues that in some circumstances, it might be more moral to forget mass violence: ' … sooner or later the brute reality of the passage of time all but guarantees that the mantra to remember a given event … does not fully respond'.

Those against proceedings also see the criminal trial as an important limit on executive power and, contrary to the Demjanjuk case, prefer to see camp guards prosecuted with reference to specific acts.

The opposing view is most forcefully articulated by Kurt Schrimm, the prosecutor leading the renewed effort to bring the Nazi criminals to justice: '[I]n view of the monstrosity of these crimes, one owes it to the survivors and the victims not to simply say "a certain time has passed, it should be swept under the carpet"' (*Der Spiegel* 2013).[4] In response to the tactical shift to broaden the definition of a crime, proponents of continued prosecution point to flaws in domestic law and the historical failure to convict SS members who worked at death camps. Andreas Eichmüller (*Der Spiegel* 2013), for example, has calculated that of the 6,500 members of the SS who served in Auschwitz and survived the war, only 49 have been convicted. The failure of the German judiciary was described by Ralph Giordano (1987: 14) as a 'second guilt' which demands continued rapprochement.[5]

Where does Arendt fit into this picture? As noted in Chapter 10, Arendt's judgment of Eichmann grapples directly with the limits of judging totalitarian systems and subjects whose capacity for subjectivity and responsibility have been acutely reduced. While Arendt ultimately employs liberal notions of responsibility in judging Eichmann, she did not think that legal processes were sufficient or equipped to answer greater moral, historical and political challenges.[6] This was particularly true when the law was put in the service of history or explicit political objectives. Moreover, it is clear that Arendt would have rejected the practice in German courts to prosecute camp guards for the crime of murder or manslaughter. Against this approach Arendt (2006a: 272) argued that the most important political aspect of the Eichmann trial was the challenge it posed to the 'emergence of an international penal code' that could come to terms with the new criminality that totalitarian regimes had unleashed into the world. For Arendt, such a code would provide a proportional response and bring into focus what she believed were unprecedented crimes.

Further insight can be gained by returning to Arendt's judgment of Eichmann (discussed in Chapter 10). In sentencing Eichmann, Arendt's underlying principle (*ratio decidendi*) is that individuals have no right to choose with whom to cohabit the earth. Cohabitation is a necessary characteristic of the human condition.

4 See also Zuroff (2012): 'Had these criminals been prosecuted decades ago, when they were far younger, the importance of the effort to bring them to justice would not have been questioned. They are just as guilty today as the day they committed their crime – and they do not deserve a prize for eluding justice for so long.' For a response to this perspective and a reflection on the relationship between anger and payback see Nussbaum (2016a).

5 See also (Beste *et al.* 2012).

6 As Arendt wrote to Karl Jaspers before the trial began: 'We have no tools to hand except legal ones with which we have to judge and pass sentence on something that cannot even be adequately represented either in legal terms or in political terms' (Arendt and Jaspers 1992: 417). See also Luban (2011: 623–626).

Those who violate this characteristic engage in genocidal acts and might be sentenced to death. Arendt's application of this principle to Eichmann is also suggestive and indicates that she would support the death penalty in a wide range of circumstances and not just for the Nazi leadership. Just how far her reasoning would extend is not clear. In thinking about its application to defendants like Reinhold Hanning the appropriate question would be something like: *did the defendant engage directly in acts against cohabitation or make decisions in furtherance of a genocidal policy?*

While it is fraught to imagine how a particular thinker might judge current events it is arguable that Arendt would have supported the death penalty in circumstances where the factual matrix was broader than those she encountered in Jerusalem. If she sentenced Eichmann to death, why not someone like Hanning or other guards who voluntarily chose to work in death camps? Are these not both examples where an individual deliberately ruptured the plurality of humankind?

However, while Arendt might have supported a broader application of the death penalty, she would also be extremely critical of attempts to convict defendants on the basis of their association to the Nazi party or whether they worked in a particular location. Arendt is unequivocal on this point and her judgment of Eichmann indicates that she would prefer an approach which required prosecutors to present evidence related to specific deeds. This will no doubt be interpreted as conservative or an overly legalistic position but it is consistent with Arendt's perspective on the legitimate function of a court as a check on state power (2005a: 21–22). If this reasoning were applied then most of the current Nazi trials would not take place. There is simply not enough quality evidence for prosecutors to bring specific charges in most instances.

Where does this leave us? If Arendt would not support the prosecution of camp guards like Hanning, is there another way they might be held to account and the victims provided a forum to be heard? What other possibilities exist for victims to be released from their traumatic relationship with perpetrators? With these questions in mind I turn to consider Arendt's writing on forgiveness and the potential it provides for mutual release.

Arendt on forgiveness

Arendt most fully explored the notion of forgiveness in her 1951 book *The Human Condition.* Starting with definitions, Arendt (1998: 215) described forgiveness as the human faculty for undoing or reversing harmful actions. In her own words, forgiveness is 'the necessary corrective for the inevitable damages resulting from action' and it arises out of action to address 'the predicament of irreversibility'.[7]

7 In similar terms Nussbaum (2016a: 63) defines forgiveness as 'a change of heart on the part of the victim, who gives up anger and resentment in response to the offender's confession and contrition'.

The predicament of irreversibility refers simply to our inability to turn back time and 'undo what one has done' (1998: 215). Forgiveness addresses itself to past actions and provides some degree of security that we might restore relations in the future.

Because of Arendt's narrow typology of what phenomena count as 'action'[8] she draws an important distinction between 'action' and 'behaviour'. Action, which Arendt (1998: 9) positions as the *differentia specifica* of human beings, refers to the public initiation of new beginnings (natality) and the condition of plurality. Behaviour, by contrast, refers to daily repetitive activities and is judged with reference to norms and moral standards. Forgiveness does not apply to ordinary behaviour and does not belong in the ordinary moral domain in which most philosophical discussions of forgiveness are grounded. More importantly, Arendt's concept of forgiveness does not apply with respect to radical evil or the 'the extremities of crimes and willed evil' (1998: 239).[9] While the focus here is on intention, Arendt's judgment of Eichmann suggests that forgiveness is not available to those who thoughtlessly commit evil or commit evil with banal intentions.

Arendt's treatment of radical evil and thoughtlessness in her Eichmann report reflects a significant shift in her thinking on forgiveness. In *The Human Condition* Arendt used the verb 'trespass' to describe actions that could be forgiven.[10] Trespass, which is derived from the Greek word *hamartane*, means 'to miss the mark' or 'go astray' rather than a deliberate intention to do evil (Arendt 1998: 215, 362 n. 80). Here it is intention, rather than just the enormity of the crime that provides the basis for forgiveness. However, following the Eichmann trial, the reverse was true. It was the unsettling image of Eichmann – in all of his ordinariness – that became the proper image of evil for the twenty-first century.[11] Reading Arendt generously, it is likely that she intended her comments on the unforgivability of thoughtless evil to apply only with respect to mass crimes like genocide or crimes against humanity. At no time does she seek to displace the role of intention for lesser crimes such as murder or manslaughter.

Thus, for Arendt, when people knowingly or thoughtlessly engage in genocidal acts, they take leave from human plurality and put themselves outside the bounds of forgiveness. Drawing on the New Testament, Arendt (1998: 241) argues that

8 For Arendt (1998: 7), action is one of the fundamental categories of the human condition and constitutes the highest realization of the *vita activa*.

9 For a discussion on Arendt's view on radical evil see Bernstein (2002).

10 Arendt's touchstone for reflecting on forgiveness was the New Testament Gospels and in particular the teachings that are attributed to Jesus of Nazareth as a historical figure. See Arendt (1998: 238–241). Other scholars would argue that, contra Arendt, Jesus was every bit as much political as religious (Yoder 1994). Arguably Jesus's most powerful affirmation of forgiveness was because 'they know not what they do' (Luke 23:34); the very thoughtlessness Arendt accuses Eichmann of performing.

11 On this point Jay Bernstein (2013) argues: 'What modernity has made emphatic is that the stakes of evil with respect to the victim can be put in place without thought and temptation … those stakes can be realised with the same gestures that make railroads dependable and factories models of efficiency.' See also Neiman (2001: 89).

such people will be taken care of by God at the Last Judgment.[12] This is not an affirmation of Christian doctrine but a statement that such people are beyond human redemption. To make this point Arendt (1998: 241) draws on Luke 17:2 where Jesus says to his disciples that for one who offends unforgivably: 'it would be better for him to be thrown into the sea with a millstone tied around his neck'. Arendt endorses this position by affirming the death penalty for Eichmann. It is also consistent with her early writing on the unforgivability of totalitarian systems of oppression:

> [I]n their effort to prove that everything is possible, totalitarian regimes have discovered without knowing it that there are crimes which men can neither punish nor forgive. When the impossible was made possible it became the unpunishable, unforgivable absolute evil which could no longer be understood and explained by the evil motives of self-interest, greed, covetousness, resentment, lust for power, and cowardice; and which therefore anger could not revenge, love could not endure, friendship could not forgive. Just as the victims in the death factories or the holes of oblivion are no longer 'human' in the eyes of their executioners, so this newest species of criminals is beyond the pale even of solidarity in human sinfulness (1973a: 459).

For Arendt, the alternative to forgiveness and punishment was death. The death sentence for Arendt is not a punishment; it is what you do when the terms of having a future life with someone are unavailable. It might also be the appropriate response when encountering a human subject whose capacity for subjectivity and personal responsibility have been dramatically reduced. Seen in this light, the death sentence is different to vengeance which Arendt described as re-enacting the original offence and perpetuating a cycle of damage (1998: 240–241; 2006a: 254, 277). A similar sentiment was expressed by Niklas Frank, son of Hans Frank, the governor general of Poland during the Nazi period. Niklas, who carries a photograph of his recently hanged father in his pocket noted: 'I am opposed to the death penalty, except for my father' (quoted in Sands 2016: 360).

Arendt's articulation of the unforgivable nature of evil leaves unexplored many important issues. For example, while noting the unique horrors inflicted by totalitarian regimes, on what basis does Arendt claim that persons are beyond punishment or rehabilitation? What conditions does a person (a trespasser), to whom punishment is available, need to meet to merit forgiveness? Here Arendt (1998: 241) mentions repentance, but it is difficult to see how changing one's mind merits forgiveness?[13] Further, why does repentance make a difference for a trespasser but not someone who commits a deliberate crime? What is it about

12 This is also the starting point for Martha Nussbaum's genealogy of forgiveness (2016a: 57–88).

13 Note that the verb translated 'repent' in this passage is *metanoein*, which literally means 'to change one's mind' (Young-Bruehl 2009: 102).

repentance that qualifies an actor for forgiveness? Does repentance require a positive act such as a promise to change one's behaviour in the future (Young-Bruehl 2009: 102)? Or is Martha Nussbaum (2016a: 96) correct in her argument that we should abandon the idea of conditional forgiveness, conditioned as it is on receiving remorse and contrition in exchange.

While there can never be a strict code of guidelines governing forgiveness (the authenticity of forgiveness stems from the fact that it is unbounded and freely given) a person who does seek to forgive another might expect that person to show some repentance and have a sense of what that repentance might involve.[14] This is important also for legal and political systems that seek to incorporate forgiveness mechanisms into their structure (either formally or informally). While there was no such system in place when *The Human Condition* appeared in print, her writing helped initiate a discussion about forgiveness in the post-totalitarian world she was describing. Most important, 15 years after Arendt's death, her ideas about forgiveness influenced the South African Truth and Reconciliation Commission (TRC), which, for the first time, made forgiveness a guiding principle for a state (Young-Bruehl 2009: 111).[15]

Truth, reconciliation and the transition

> Forgiveness does not mean ignoring what has been done or putting a false label on an evil act. It means, rather, that the evil act no longer remains as a barrier to the relationship (King 1957).

The TRC brought forgiveness into the public realm in a way that went beyond Arendt's conceptualisation. Members of the commission understood clearly that the post-war trials were not adequate to the task of judging mass violence or balancing the 'requirements of justice, accountability, stability, peace and reconciliation' (Tutu 2000: 23). Neither the Nuremberg trials nor the Eichmann trial had such ambition or provided a context where the accused was tried by fellow nationals who were required to live together afterwards in the same society.

Another important distinction was that the TRC was not a court and had greater flexibility in terms of evidence and procedure. Moreover, the TRC had the authority to issue amnesty to individuals (not groups) and thus a significant portion of events was removed from the retributivist framework of the criminal trial. To be considered for amnesty, individuals were required to make a public statement which provided a full account of their actions (Hayner 2010: 29–31 and 99–102). Through this method, the TRC brought to light more information than an adversarial criminal trial where the accused has an incentive to keep quiet (Tutu 2000: 23). After the amnesty applications had been assembled, the

14 Arendt (1998: 218) ruled out the religious idea of unconditional forgiveness.

15 Note also the Truth and Reconciliation Commission of Canada. See Sinclair *et al.* (2015).

TRC could also arrange meetings between perpetrators and their victims. These meetings had a set structure. First the offenders spoke and then the victims could, if they chose, tell their own story and ask questions. After this, the victim could decide whether or not they wished to forgive the offender. Forgiveness could not be requested or coerced. It had to be freely offered by the person who had been wronged (Young-Bruehl 2009: 115).

Pumla Gobodo-Madikizela (2004) provides several moving examples of this process in her memoir *A Human Being Died That Night.* In one instance, the widows of two black policemen agreed to meet with Eugene de Kock (Prime Evil), the former South African police colonel who was responsible for the deaths. In response to de Kock's apology, Gobodo-Madikizela (2004: 14; Young-Bruehl 2009: 115–116) narrates:

> Both women felt that de Kock had communicated to them something he felt deeply and had acknowledged their pain [Mrs Feral Faku said]: 'I couldn't control my tears. I could hear him but I was overwhelmed by emotion and I was just nodding as a way of saying yes, I forgive you. I hope that when he sees our tears he knows that they are not only tears for our husbands, but tears for him as well … I would like to hold him by the hand and show him there is a future, and that he can still change.'[16]

Central to Mrs Faku's act of forgiveness is a release from the past and an invitation to a new beginning. Like Eichmann, de Kock made decisions about who he wished to share the earth with. However, rather than casting him outside the reach of forgiveness, Mrs Faku and the Commission accepted his repentance as the first step for his eventual re entry back into society (Young-Bruehl 2009: 116).

With examples like this in mind, Desmond Tutu considered the relationship between repentance and forgiveness. His answer, which draws primarily on a problematic Pauline interpretation of Christian forgiveness,[17] is that repentance is the most beneficial process for forgiveness (Tutu 2000: 270). However, Tutu also notes that unconditional forgiveness is possible on the following grounds: if the offender has died and cannot repent; if the person doing the forgiving determines that the offender should be restored to the community; or if the person doing the forgiving understands that forgiveness offers a release to the forgiver and a way to transcend their role as victim (Young-Bruehl 2009: 117). With respect to this last point, Tutu (2000: 272) contends:

16 De Kock was granted amnesty for all his crimes except for two for which he received a double life sentence. He was released from prison in 2015, see Smith (2015). See also Young-Bruehl (2009: 115–116).

17 I am indebted to Ron Engel for this point. Arguably the influence of Paul on Tutu is implicit in the TRC's work. See also Lull and Cobb (2005) who interpret Romans as concerned with community salvation rather than focused on individual salvation.

> If the victim could forgive only when the culprit confessed, then the victim would be locked into the culprit's whim, locked into victimhood, whatever her own attitude or intention. That would be palpably unjust.

Tutu expands on the idea of unconditional forgiveness in a more recent book, co-authored with his daughter, Mpho Tutu (2015). Here the authors present a critical view of the conditional model of forgiveness, likening it to a gift 'with strings attached' which may breed 'mutual resentment' (2015: 21 and 20). They note further that conditional forgiveness binds the victim to the wrongdoer.[18] The method Tutu now prefers is totally unconditional and centres around four steps: Admitting the wrong and acknowledging the harm; Telling one's story and witnessing the anguish; Asking for forgiveness and granting forgiveness; and Renewing or releasing the relationship. While aspects of this method are directed at intimate personal relations, the authors clearly have their sights on politics and the aftermath of political violence. Outside of the TRC, Tutu and Tutu (2015: 216) argue that the Gacaca traditional community courts established after the Rwandan genocide was an 'extraordinary example of the ability of a nation that once was convulsed in genocidal violence to heal itself through reconciliation and forgiveness'.

Perhaps the most explicit argument against conditional forgiveness is presented by Nussbaum (2016a: 96) who describes forgiveness based on repentance as a kind of covert retaliation.[19] Nussbaum (2016a: 238) argues further that the 'apparatus of abasement, confession, contribution and eventual forgiveness' often gets in the way of reconciliation by producing strong feelings of humiliation and resentment. In response, Nussbaum highlights the power and moral value of freeing oneself from the self-harm caused by corrosive anger. She argues:

> If one is focused on well-being and the future, then forgiveness of the classic transactional sort will not be useful, and may be quite harmful, leading parties to focus excessively on relative status and causing harms to dignity and self-respect that mar the future. What is useful is some type of generous and constructive future-directed response. Another sort of forgiveness – namely, a struggle within the self to release oneself from anger – may prove quite valuable as a way of approaching the Transition and a productive future (2016b).

18 Gobodo-Madikizela (2004: 117) makes a similar point when reflecting on interviews she conducted with de Kock: '[T]he victim becomes the gatekeeper to what the outcast desires – readmission into the human community … forgiveness is a kind of revenge … I felt a sense of power over him as a person who needed my understanding.'

19 This is particularly true in intimate relationships. See Nussbaum (2016b): '[T]he whole ritual of apology and forgiveness is a bit grim and laboured in a relationship where love and generosity could and should dominate.' This perspective marks a significant evolution in Nussbaum's thought. See Nussbaum (2004 and 2012).

Of course, some people who attended the TRC chose not to forgive the perpetrator. Similar experiences were collated by the Nazi hunter Simon Wiesenthal (1998) in his biographical book *The Sunflower*. In this text, Wiesenthal recounted a moment when a dying Nazi solider requested forgiveness for participating in a massacre of Jewish victims who were trapped inside a church. After hearing the soldier's confession, Wiesenthal turned and left the room without saying a word. Reflecting on the event, Wiesenthal concluded that he had no right to offer forgiveness on behalf of the victims. Those invited to reflect on this scene and Wiesenthal's decision have offered different perspectives and most comment on the difficulty of speaking on behalf of another (Wiesenthal 1998: 191–196).

By contrast, Tutu (2000: 272) offers a contribution which is particularly relevant to current Nazi trials. While understanding of Wiesenthal's dilemma, Tutu argued that if we took his actions to their logical conclusion, it would mean that there was nothing that former Nazi soldiers could do today to help the process of reconciliation – including offering reparations which some survivors have accepted (Young-Bruehl 2009: 118). Speaking about the situation in South Africa, Tutu (2000: 279) noted:

> If the present generation could not legitimately speak on behalf of those who are no more, then we could not offer forgiveness for the sins of South Africa's racist past, which predates the advent of apartheid in 1948 … True forgiveness deals with the past, all the past, to make the future possible … We have to accept that what we do we do for generations past, present and yet to come. That is what makes a community a community or a people a people – for better or worse.

From Tutu's perspective, just as victims have the right to bring a perpetrator before a court of law they also have the opportunity to offer moral forgiveness for the disabling memory of past deeds of radical evil. The dead cannot fulfil either function and so require the living to act on their behalf in order for the community to persist and make new commitments for the future. While Arendt would not support such a psychologising of politics, she does describe forgiveness as a type of action that provides the basis for mutual release (1998: 240). However, while Arendt places a firm limit on forgiveness, Tutu and Nussbaum argue that the health of a political community depends on the possibility that every human subject might become worthy of forgiveness. This appeal to worthiness simply opens the door to the possibility of forgiveness. It does not seek to displace political processes or make demands of the victim. Thus, a politics grounded in forgiveness must be differentiated from theological claims that have described the Jews as stubborn in their refusal to accept the teachings of Christ.[20] This would be the

20 Desmond Tutu was accused of transgressing this line when he offered a prayer at Yad Vashem for those responsible for the Nazi Genocide. Tutu (Cowell 1989) said: 'Our Lord would say that in the end the positive thing that can come is the spirit of

antithesis to Arendt's overtly political thinking and a barrier to substantive reconciliation.

Clearly there is a significant difference between a forgiveness process and a criminal trial. However, in the context of crimes which are over half a century old and where the evidence against them is too weak to seek prosecution for specific acts, an *option* for forgiveness could offer the opportunity for mutual release without sweeping the past under the rug. Nussbaum (2016a: 6, 31) calls this a Transition – a movement from anger, with all its defects, into forward-looking and constructive project. A Transition, which would provide a framework for the victim to be heard and acknowledged, ought to be the goal of law and represents a proper self-caring response to a breach of trust (Nussbaum 2016a: 125, 135, 238). It also returns the conflict back into the realm of politics and recognises that great trauma is only soluble by political means.

This takes us back to Arendt's urgent philosophical claim that the only way to combat evil is through the practice of politics. Psychologising political problems is a misguided response and does nothing to confront the power dynamics that are shaping and forming the public realm. Allen Frances, chairman of the task force that wrote the *Diagnostic and Statistical Manual of Mental Disorders* IV, recognised this point in response to suggestions that Donald Trump is incapable, on psychiatric grounds, of serving as president.[21] Confronting the limits of his profession, Frances noted:

> Psychiatric name-calling is a misguided way of countering Mr. Trump's attack on democracy … His psychological motivations are too obvious to be interesting, and analyzing them will not halt his headlong power grab. The antidote to a dystopic Trumpean dark age is political, not psychological.

Arendt would surely agree and her advocacy for a political response is captured most fully in her appeal to 'promise making' as a method for restoring plurality and providing respite from unpredictability. Promise making is the foundation for the covenantal tradition. It seeks to rescue action from unpredictability and 'the impossibility of foretelling the consequences of an act within a community of

forgiving, not forgetting, but the spirit of saying: God, this happened to us … pray for those who made it happen, help us to forgive them and help us so that we in our turn will not make others suffer …' In response, Rabbi Marvin Hier of the Simon Wiesenthal Center described Tutu's prayer as a 'a gratuitous insult to Jews and victims of Nazism everywhere' (Shaw 2013). I am indebted to David Seymour for this point.

21 See for example Dodes and Schachter (2017): 'Mr. Trump's speech and actions demonstrate an inability to tolerate views different from his own, leading to rage reactions. His words and behavior suggest a profound inability to empathize. Individuals with these traits distort reality to suit their psychological state, attacking facts and those who convey them (journalists, scientists). In a powerful leader, these attacks are likely to increase, as his personal myth of greatness appears to be confirmed. We believe that the grave emotional instability indicated by Mr. Trump's speech and actions makes him incapable of serving safely as president.'

equals where everybody has the same capacity to act' (Arendt 1998: 244). Connected to this, Arendt describes 'the force of mutual promises or contract' which has the power to join together those who engage in the public realm within a particular political community (1998: 244). Promise making provides certainty not by planning for the future but by establishing 'islands of predictability' and building 'guide-posts of reliability' in what would otherwise be an 'ocean of uncertainty' (1998: 244). Reconciliation, in this sense, requires us to overcome alienation and restore just relationships through a pledge to a new beginning. This is not a quid pro quo whereby repentance grants forgiveness. Rather, Arendt proposed a new covenant as the political means for securing the future.[22]

For a Transition or new covenant to be established, forgiveness needs to be cultivated at the political level. Anger and notions of payback need to be understood as destructive so that we can turn ourselves to the future and ask, *what next?* What can we do to make things better in the future (Nussbaum 2016a: 31–33)? What is critical is a commitment to a final conciliation and an understanding that my happiness is intimately linked to the happiness and well-being of my enemy. Our political and legal structures should never rule out the possibility of forgiveness no matter the person or the assault unleashed against humanity. In agreement Elizabeth Young-Bruehl (2009: 119) writes:

> No one is born evil or, having become a doer of evil deeds is necessarily fundamentally corrupted and incapable of change, restoration. No one is born banal and thoughtless, or is incapable of being restored to thoughtful-ness. No one who becomes dehumanized is incapable of re-humanization or re-entry into the human community.[23]

This thought takes us beyond Arendt and the limits she sets for the scope of for-giveness. However, perhaps when Arendt (1998: 241) suggested that we 'neither punish nor forgive' radically evil deeds she underestimated the human potential to forgive. This potential cannot be destroyed as long as we cultivate forgiveness in our community and are committed to a politics where the worth of each is made essential.

22 For a deeper investigation into covenant see Engel (2004 and 2008).
23 See further Baron-Cohen (2012).

Appendix

Nazis and Nazi Collaborators (Punishment) Law (1950)

Crimes against the Jewish people, crimes against humanity and war crimes.

1. (a) A person who has committed one of the following offences –

(1) done, during the period of the Nazi regime, in an enemy country, an act constituting a crime against the Jewish people;
(2) done, during the period of the Nazi regime, in an enemy country, an act constituting a crime against humanity;
(3) done, during the period of the Second World War, in an enemy country, an act constituting a war crime, is liable to the death penalty.

(b) In this section –

"crime against the Jewish people" means any of the following acts, committed with intent to destroy the Jewish people in whole or in part:

(1) killing Jews;
(2) causing serious bodily or mental harm to Jews;
(3) placing Jews in living conditions calculated to bring about their physical destruction;
(4) imposing measures intended to prevent births among Jews;
(5) forcibly transferring Jewish children to another national or religious group;
(6) destroying or desecrating Jewish religious or cultural assets or values;
(7) inciting to hatred of Jews;

"crime against humanity" means any of the following acts:

murder, extermination, enslavement, starvation or deportation and other inhumane acts committed against any civilian population, and persecution on national, racial, religious or political grounds;

"war crime" means any of the following acts:

murder, ill-treatment or deportation to forced labour or for any other purpose, of civilian population of or in occupied territory; murder or ill-treatment of prisoners of war or persons on the seas; killing of hostages; plunder of public or private property; wanton destruction of cities, towns or villages; and devastation not justified by military necessity.

Crimes against persecuted persons.

2. If a person, during the period of the Nazi regime, committed in an enemy country an act by which, had he committed it in Israel territory, he would have become guilty of an offence under one of the following sections of the Criminal Code, and he committed the act against a persecuted person as a persecuted person he shall be guilty of an offence under this Law and be liable to the same punishment to which he would have been liable had he committed the act in Israel territory:

(a) section 152 (rape, sexual and unnatural offences);
(b) section 153 (rape by deception);
(c) section 157 (indecent act with force, etc.);
(d) section 188 (child stealing);
(e) section 212 (manslaughter);
(f) section 214 (murder);
(g) section 222 (attempt to murder);
(h) section 235 (acts intended to cause grievous harm or prevent arrests)
(i) section 236 (preventing escape from wreck);
(j) section 238 (grievous harm);
(k) section 240 (maliciously administering poison with intent to harm);
(l) section 256 (abducting in order to murder);
(m) section 258 (abducting in order to subject person to grievous hurt);
(n) section 288 (robbery and attempted robbery);
(o) section 293 (demanding property with menaces with intent to steal).

Membership in enemy organisation.

3. (a) A person who, during the period of the Nazi regime, in an enemy country, was a member of, or held any post or exercised any function in, an enemy organisation is liable to imprisonment for a term not exceeding seven years.

(b) In this section, "enemy organisation" means –

(1) a body of persons which, under article 9 of the Charter of the International Military Tribunal, annexed to the Four-Power Agreement of the 8th August, 1945, on the trial of the major war criminals, has been declared, by a judgment of that Tribunal, to be a criminal organisation;
(2) any other body of persons which existed in an enemy country and the object or one of the objects of which was to carry out or assist in carrying out actions of an enemy administration directed against persecuted persons.

Offences in places of confinement.

4. (a) A person who, during the period of the Nazi regime, in an enemy country and while exercising some function in a place of confinement on behalf of an enemy administration or of the person in charge of that place of confinement, committed in that place of confinement an act against a persecuted person by which, had he committed it in Israel territory, he would have become guilty of an offence under one of the following sections of the Criminal Code, shall be guilty of an offence under this Law and be liable to the same punishment to which he would have been liable had he committed the act in Israel territory:

(1) section 100 (c) (threatening violence);
(2) section 162 (procuring defilement of females by threats, fraud or administering drugs);
(3) section 241 (wounding and similar acts);
(4) section 242 (failure to supply necessaries);
(5) section 249 (common assault);
(6) section 250 (assault causing actual bodily harm);
(7) section 261 (unlawful compulsory labour);
(8) section 270 (theft).

(b) "Place of confinement", in this section, means any place in an enemy country which, by order of an enemy administration, was assigned to persecuted persons, and includes any part of such a place.

Delivering up persecuted person to enemy administration.

5. A person who, during the period of the Nazi regime, in an enemy country, was instrumental in delivering up a persecuted person to an enemy administration, is liable to imprisonment for a term not exceeding ten years.

Black-mailing persecuted persons.

6. A person who, during the period of the Nazi regime, in an enemy country, received or demanded a benefit –

(a) from a persecuted person under threat of delivering up him or another persecuted person to an enemy administration; or
(b) from a person who had given shelter to a persecuted person, under threat of delivering up him or the persecuted person sheltered by him to an enemy administration, is liable to imprisonment for a period not exceeding seven years.

Application of General Criminal Code.

7. The provisions of the First Part of the Criminal Code shall, save as this Law otherwise provides, apply to offences under this Law.

Certain sections not to apply.

8. Sections 16, 17, 18 and 19 of the Criminal Code shall not apply to offences under this Law.

Res judicata.

9. (a) A person who has committed an offence under this Law may be tried in Israel even if he has already been tried abroad, whether before an international tribunal or a tribunal of a foreign state, for the same offence.

(b) If a person is convicted in Israel of an offence under this Law after being convicted of the same act abroad, the Israel court shall, in determining the punishment, take into consideration the sentence which he has served abroad.

Release from criminal responsibility.

10. If a persecuted person has done or omitted to do any act, such act or omission constituting an offence under this Law, the Court shall release him from criminal responsibility –

(a) if he did or omitted to do the act in order

to save himself from the danger of immediate death threatening him and the court is satisfied that he did his best to avert the consequences of the act or omission; or

(b) if he did or omitted to do the act with intent to avert consequences more serious than those which resulted from the act or omission, and actually averted them; however, these provisions shall not apply to an act or omission constituting an offence under section 1 or 2(f).

Extenuating circumstances.

11. In determining the punishment of a person circumstances. convicted of an offence under this Law, the court may take into account, as grounds for mitigating the punishment, the following circumstances:

(a) that the person committed the offence under conditions which, but for section 8, would have exempted him from criminal responsibility or constituted a reason for pardoning the offence, and that he did his best to reduce the gravity of the consequences of the offence;

(b) that the offence was committed with intent to avert, and was indeed calculated to avert, consequences more serious than those which resulted from the offence; however, in the case of an offence under section 1, the court shall not impose on the offender a lighter punishment than imprisonment for a term of ten years.

Prescription.

12. (a) The rules of prescription laid down in the Fifth Chapter of the Ottoman Code of Criminal Procedure shall not apply to offences under this Law.

(b) No person shall be prosecuted for an offence under this Law, except offence under section 1 or 2(f), if twenty years have passed since the time of the offence.

General amnesty not to apply.

13. The provisions of the General Amnesty Ordinance, 5709–1949, shall not apply to offences under this Law.

Institution of prosecution.

14. A prosecution for an offence under this Law may only be instituted by the Attorney General or his representative.

Evidence.

15. (a) In an action for an offence under this Law, the court may deviate from the rules of evidence if it is satisfied that this will promote the ascertainment of the truth and the just handling of the case.
(b) Whenever the court decides to deviate, under subsection (a), from the rules of evidence, it shall place on record the reasons which prompted its decision.

Interpretation.

15. In this Law –

"the period of the Nazi regime" means the period which began on the 3rd Shevat, 5693 (30th January, 1933) and ended on the 25th Iyar, 5705 (8th May, 1945);

"the period of the Second World War" means the period which began on the 17th Elul, 5699 (1st September, 1939) and ended on the 5th Elul, 5705 (14th August, 1945);

"the Allied Powers" means the states which signed the Declaration of the United Nations of the 1st January, 1942, or acceded to it during the period of the Second World War;

"Axis state" means a state which during the whole or part of the period of the Second World War was at war with the Allied Powers; the period which began on the day of the beginning of the state of war between a particular Axis state and the first, in time, of the Allied Powers and ended on the day of the cessation of hostilities between that state and the last, in time, of the Allied Powers, shall be considered as the period of the war between that state and the Allied Powers;

"enemy country" means

(a) Germany during the period of the Nazi regime;
(b) any other Axis state during the period of the war between it and the Allied Powers;
(c) any territory which, during the whole or part of the period of the Nazi regime, was de facto under German rule, for the time during which it was de facto under German rule as aforesaid;
(d) any territory which was de facto under the rule of any other Axis state during the whole or part of the period of the war between it and the Allied Powers, for the time during which that territory was de facto under the rule of that Axis state as aforesaid;

"enemy administration" means the administration which existed in an enemy country;

"persecuted person" means a person belonging to a national, racial, religious or political group which was persecuted by an enemy administration;

"the Criminal Code" means the Criminal Code Ordinance, 1936.

Implementation.

17. The Minister of Justice is charged with the implementation of this Law.

DAVID BEN-GURION

Prime Minister

PINCHAS ROSEN
Minister of Justice

YOSEF SPRINZAK
Chairman of the Knesset
Acting President of the State

*Passed by the Knesset on the 18th Av, 5710 (1st August, 1950) and Published in Sefer Ha-Chukkim No. 57 of the 26th Av, 5711 (9th August, 1950). p. 281; the Bill and an Explanatory Note were published in Hatza'ot Chok No. 36 of the 11th Adar, 5710 (28th February, 1950), p. 119.

I.R. No. 50 of the 12th Shevat, 5709 (11th February, 1949), Suppl. I, p. 173.

P.G. No. 652 of the 14th December, 1936, Suppl. I, p. 285 (English Edition). LSI vol. II, p. 115.

Nazis and Nazi Collaborators (Punishment) Law (Amendment) 5723–1963*

Amendment of section 12.	1. Section 12(b) of the Nazis and Nazi Collaborators (Punishment) Law, 5710–1950) is hereby repealed retroactively as from the day of its enactment.

LEVI ESHKOL

Prime Minister

DOV JOSEPH
Minister of Justice

SHNEUR ZALMAN SHAZAR
President of the State

*Passed by the Knesset on the 16th Av, 5723 (6th August, 1963) and published in Sefer Ha-Chukkim No. 404 of the 26th Av, 5723 (16th August, 1963), p. 140; the Bill and an Explanatory Note were published in Hatza'ot Chok No. 576 of 5723, p. 350.

Sefer Ha-Chukkim No. 57 of 5710, p. 281; LSI vol. IV, p. 154.

Bibliography

Books

Agamben, Giorgio, *Homo Sacer: Sovereign Power and Bare Life* (Stanford University Press, 1998)

Agamben, Giorgio, *Means Without End: Notes on Politics* (University of Minnesota Press, 2000)

Agamben, Giorgio, *Remnants of Auschwitz: The Witness and the Archive* (Zone Books, 2002)

Agamben, Giorgio, *State of Exception* (Stanford University Press, 2005)

Allan, Diana, *Refugees of the Revolution: Experiences of Palestinian Exile* (Stanford University Press, 2013)

Allan, TRS, *Constitutional Justice – A Liberal Theory of the Rule of Law* (Oxford University Press, 1st edn, 2001)

Aly, Götz, *Why the Germans? Why the Jews?: Envy, Race Hatred, and the Prehistory of the Holocaust* (Picador, 2015)

Arendt, Hannah, *Men in Dark Times* (Mariner Books, 1970)

Arendt, Hannah, *Crises of the Republic* (Harcourt Brace Jovanovich, 1972)

Arendt, Hannah, *The Origins of Totalitarianism* (Harcourt, Brace, 1973a)

Arendt, Hannah, *The Jew as Pariah: Jewish Identity and Politics in the Modern Age* (Grove Press, 1978a)

Arendt, Hannah, *The Life of the Mind* (Harcourt, 1978b)

Arendt, Hannah, 'Hannah Arendt on Hannah Arendt' in MA Hill (ed), *Hannah Arendt: The Recovery of the Public World* (St Martin's Press, 1979)

Arendt, Hannah, *Lectures on Kant's Political Philosophy* (University of Chicago Press, 1989)

Arendt, Hannah, *The Human Condition* (University of Chicago Press, 1998)

Arendt, Hannah, 'Personal Responsibility Under Dictatorship' in *Responsibility and Judgment* (Schocken, 2005a)

Arendt, Hannah, 'Thinking and Moral Considerations' in *Responsibility and Judgment* (Schocken, 2005b)

Arendt, Hannah, 'Some Questions of Moral Philosophy' in *Responsibility and Judgment* (Schocken, 2005c)

Arendt, Hannah, 'Understanding and Politics' in *Essays in Understanding, 1930–1954: Formation, Exile, and Totalitarianism* (Schocken, 2005d)

Arendt, Hannah, 'On the Nature of Totalitarianism' in *Essays in Understanding, 1930–1954: Formation, Exile, and Totalitarianism* (Schocken, 2005e)

Arendt, Hannah, *Eichmann in Jerusalem: A Report on the Banality of Evil* (Penguin, 2006a)

Arendt, Hannah, 'The Crisis of Culture: Its Social and Its Political Significance' in *Between Past and Future* (Penguin Classics, 2006b)

Arendt, Hannah, 'Truth in Politics' in *Between Past and Future* (Penguin Classics, 2006c)

Arendt, Hannah, *On Revolution* (Penguin, 2006d)

Arendt, Hannah, *The Jewish Writings* (Schocken, 2008)

Arendt, Hannah, *The Last Interview: And Other Conversations* (Melville House, 2013)

Arendt, Hannah, and Karl Jaspers, *Correspondence 1926–1969* (Houghton Mifflin Harcourt, 1992)

Arendt, Hannah, and Mary McCarthy, *Between Friends: The Correspondence of Hannah Arendt and Mary McCarthy 1949–1975* (Harcourt, 1995)

Arendt, Hannah, and Heinrich Blucher, *Within Four Walls: The Correspondence Between Hannah Arendt and Heinrich Blucher, 1936–1968* (Harcourt, 2000)

Arenson, Kenneth, Mirko Bagaric and Peter Gillies, *Australian Criminal Law in the Common Law Jurisdictions: Cases and Materials* (Oxford University Press, 2015)

Arnold, Matthew, *Culture and Anarchy* (Cambridge University Press, 1932)

Ashworth, Andrew, 'Testing Fidelity to Legal Values: Official Involvement and Criminal Justice' in Stephen Shute and Andrew Perry Simester (eds), *Criminal Law Theory: Doctrines of the General Part* (Oxford University Press, 2002) 299

Austin, John, *The Providence of Jurisprudence Determined* (Library of Ideas, 1954)

Bar, Bat-Ami, 'Women in Dark Times: Rachel Varnhagen, Rosa Luxemburg, Hannah Arendt, and Me' in Larry May and Jerome Kohn (eds), *Hannah Arendt: Twenty Years Later* (The MIT Press, 1997)

Bar-Zohar, Michael, *Beyond Hitler's Grasp: The Heroic Rescue of Bulgaria's Jews* (Adams Media Corporation, 1998)

Baron-Cohen, Simon, *The Science of Evil: On Empathy and the Origins of Cruelty* (Basic Books, 2012)

Bascomb, Neal, *Hunting Eichmann: How a Band of Survivors and a Young Spy Agency Chased Down the World's Most Notorious Nazi* (Mariner Books, 2010)

Bauer, Yehuda, *Rethinking the Holocaust* (Yale University Press, 2002)

Bazyler, Michael and Frank Tuerkheimer, *Forgotten Trials of the Holocaust* (NYU Press, 2015)

Beiner, Ronald, 'Interpretative Essay' in Hannah Arendt, *Lectures on Kant's Political Philosophy* (University of Chicago Press, 1989)

Bendersky, Joseph, *Carl Schmitt: Theorist for the Reich* (Princeton University Press, 1983)

Benhabib, Seyla, 'Judgment and the Moral Foundations of Politics in Hannah Arendt's Thought' in *Situating the Self* (Polity Press, 1992)

Benhabib, Seyla, *The Reluctant Modernism of Hannah Arendt* (Rowman & Littlefield Publishers, 2003)

Benhabib, Seyla, 'International Law and Human Plurality in the Shadow of Totalitarianism: Hannah Arendt and Raphael Lemkin' in Marco Goldoni and Christopher McCorkindale (eds) *Hannah Arendt and the Law* (Hart Publishing, 2013)

Bentham, Jeremy, *Rights, Representation, and Reform: Nonsense upon Stilts and Other Writings on the French Revolution* (Oxford University Press, 2002)

Berk, Stephen, *Year of Crisis, Year of Hope: Russian Jewry and the Pogroms of 1881–1882* (Greenwood, 1985)

Berlin, Isaiah, 'Two Concepts of Liberty' in Michael J Sandel (ed), *Liberalism and Its Critics* (Blackwell, 1984)

Bernstein, Jay, *The Fate of Art: Aesthetic Alienation from Kant to Derrida and Adorno* (Pennsylvania State University Press, 1992)

Bernstein, Jay, 'Promising and Civil Disobedience: Arendt's Political Modernism' in Roger Berkowitz and Thomas Keenan (eds), *Thinking in Dark Times: Hannah Arendt on Ethics and Politics* (Fordham University Press, 2004)

Bernstein, Richard J, 'Judging – the Actor and the Spectator' in *Philosophical Profiles* (Polity Press, 1986)
Bernstein, Richard J, *Hannah Arendt and The Jewish Question* (The MIT Press, 1996)
Bernstein, Richard J, 'Arendt on Thinking' in Dana Villa (ed), *The Cambridge Companion to Hannah Arendt* (Cambridge University Press, 2000)
Bernstein, Richard J, *Radical Evil: A Philosophical Interrogation* (Polity, 2002)
Bernstein, Richard J, 'Foreword' in Marco Goldoni and Christopher McCorkindale (eds), *Hannah Arendt and the Law* (Hart Publishing, 2013)
Botstein, Leon, 'Liberating the Pariah: Politics, the Jews, and Hannah Arendt' in Jeffrey Katz, Thomas Keenan and Roger Berkowitz (eds), *Thinking in Dark Times: Hannah Arendt on Ethics and Politics* (Fordham University Press, 2009)
Bracher, Karl, *The German Dictatorship: The Origins, Structure and Effects of National Socialism* (Holt Rinehart & Winston, 1970)
Bradley, Craig M, *Criminal Procedure: A Worldwide Study* (Carolina Academic Press, 2nd edn, 2007)
Breen, Keith, 'Law Beyond Command? An Evaluation of Arendt's Understanding of Law' in Marco Goldoni and Christopher McCorkindale (eds), *Hannah Arendt and the Law* (Hart Publishing, 2013)
Brinton, Crane, *The Anatomy of Revolution* (Random House, 1966)
Browder, George, *Hitler's Enforcers: The Gestapo and the SS Security Service in the Nazi Revolution* (Oxford University Press, 1996)
Brown, Wendy, *Undoing the Demos: Neoliberalism's Stealth Revolution* (Zone Books, 2015)
Browning, Christopher, *Ordinary Men: Reserve Police Battalion 101 and the Final Solution in Poland* (Harper Perennial, 1994)
Browning, Christopher, 'Introduction' in Leonard Newman and Ralph Erber (eds), *Understanding Genocide: The Social Psychology of the Holocaust* (Oxford University Press, 2002)
Burns, Elizabeth, *Theatricality: A Study of Convention in Theatre and Social Life* (Harper and Row, 1972)
Burns, Robert P, 'The Distinctiveness of Trial Narrative' in Antony Duff *et al.* (eds), *The Trial on Trial (Volume 1) – Truth and Due Process* (Hart, 2004)
Buruma, Ian, *The Wages of Guilt: Memories of War in Germany and Japan* (New York Review Books, 2015)
Butler, Judith, *Parting Ways: Jewishness and the Critique of Zionism* (Columbia, 2014)
Butler, Judith, *Notes Toward a Performative Theory of Assembly* (Harvard University Press, 2015)
Canovan, Margaret, *Hannah Arendt: A Reinterpretation of Her Political Thought* (Cambridge University Press, 1994)
Canovan, Margaret, 'Arendt's Theory of Totalitarianism: A Reassessment' in Dana Villa (ed), *The Cambridge Companion to Hannah Arendt* (Cambridge University Press, 2000)
Césaire, Aimé, *Discourse on Colonialism* (Monthly Review Press, 2000)
Cesarani, David, *Becoming Eichmann: Rethinking the Life, Crimes, and Trial of a "Desk Murderer"* (Da Capo Press, 2006)
Cesarani, David, *Final Solution: The Fate of the Jews 1933–49* (Macmillan, 2016)
Chary, Frederick, *The Bulgarian Jews and the Final Solution, 1940–1944* (University of Pittsburgh Press, 1972)
Chomsky, Noam, *Government in the Future* (Seven Stories Press, 2005)
Cicero, Marcus Tullius, *How to Grow Old: Ancient Wisdom for the Second Half of Life* (Princeton University Press, 2016)
Coll, Steve, *Private Empire: ExxonMobil and American Power* (Penguin Books, 2013)

Culbert, Jennifer, 'Judging the Events of Our Time' in Jeffrey Katz, Thomas Keenan and Roger Berkowitz (eds), *Thinking in Dark Times: Hannah Arendt on Ethics and Politics* (Fordham University Press, 2009)

Curtis, Mark, *Unpeople: Victims of British Policy* (Vintage Books, 2004)

d'Entrèves, Maurizio Passerin, 'Arendt's Theory of Judgment' in Dana Villa (ed), *The Cambridge Companion to Hannah Arendt* (Cambridge University Press, 2002)

Dawidowicz, Lucy, *The War Against the Jews* (Weidenfeld & Nicolson, 1975)

Doris, John, *Lack of Character: Personality and Moral Behaviour* (Cambridge University Press, 2005)

Douglas, Lawrence, *The Memory of Judgment: Making Law and History in the Trials of the Holocaust* (Yale University Press, 2005)

Douglas, Lawrence, *The Right Wrong Man: John Demjanjuk and the Last Great Nazi War Crimes Trial* (Princeton University Press, 2016)

Durkheim, Emile, *The Division of Labor in Society* (Free Press, 1997)

Dworkin, Ronald, *Laws Empire* (Belknap Press, 1986)

Elon, Amos, 'Introduction' *Hannah Arendt, Eichmann in Jerusalem* (Penguin, 2006a)

Engel, J Ron, 'What Covenant Sustains Us?' in Laura Westra, Klaus Bosselmann and Richard Westra (eds), *Reconciling Human Existence with Ecological Integrity: Science, Ethics, Economics and Law* (Routledge, 2008)

Ezrahi, Yaron, 'Arendt's Banality of Evil Thesis and the Arab-Israeli Conflict' in Roger Berkowitz and Thomas Keenan (eds), *Thinking in Dark Times: Hannah Arendt on Ethics and Politics* (Fordham University Press, 2004)

Felman, Shoshana, *The Juridical Unconscious: Trials and Traumas in the Twentieth Century* (Harvard University Press, 2002)

Fine, Robert, *Political Investigations: Hegel, Marx, Arendt* (Routledge, 2001)

Finkelstein, Norman, *The Holocaust Industry* (Verso, 2015)

Fischer-Lichte, Erika, *The Transformative Power of Performance: A New Aesthetics* (Routledge, 2008)

Fish, Stanley, *Is There a Text in This Class? The Authority of Interpretive Communities* (Harvard University Press, 1982)

Fish, Stanley, *Doing What Comes Naturally: Change, Rhetoric and the Practice of Theory in Literary and Legal Studies* (Duke University Press Books, 1990)

Frank, Hans, *Nationalsozialistisches Handbuch für Recht und Gesetzgebung* [National Socialist Handbook on Law and Legislating] (Zentralverlag der NSDAP, 1935)

Frankl, Viktor, *Man's Search for Meaning* (Beacon Press, 2006)

Friedländer, Saul, *Nazi Germany and the Jews: Volume 1: The Years of Persecution 1933–1939* (Harper Perennial, 1997)

Fuller, Lon L, *The Morality of Law* (Yale University Press, 1969)

Gaita, Raimond, *A Common Humanity: Thinking about Love and Truth and Justice* (Routledge, 2002)

Garcia, Alfredo, *The Sixth Amendment in Modern American Jurisprudence – A Critical Perspective* (Greenwood Press, 1st edn, 1992)

Garner, Helen, *This House of Grief* (Allen & Unwin, 2015)

Gerwarth, Robert, *Hitler's Hangman: The Life of Heydrich* (Yale University Press, 2012)

Giordano, Ralph, *Die Zweite Schuld oder von der Last Deutscher zu Sein* (Kiepenheuer & Witsch, 1987)

Gobodo-Madikizela, Pumla, *A Human Being Died That Night: A South African Woman Confronts the Legacy of Apartheid* (Mariner Books, 2004)

Godwin, William, *Enquiring Concerning Political Justice* (Clarendon Press, 1971)
Goldoni, Marco and Christopher McCorkindale (eds), *Hannah Arendt and the Law* (Hart, 2013a)
Goldoni, Marco and Christopher McCorkindale, 'Introduction' in Marco Goldoni and Christopher McCorkindale (eds), *Hannah Arendt and the Law* (Hart Publishing, 2013b)
Gramsci, Antonio, *Selections from the Prison Notebooks of Antonio Gramsci* (Lawrence & Wishart, 1971)
Gray, J Glenn, *The Warriors: Reflections on Men in Battle* (Bison Books, 1998)
Grodzinsky, Yosef, *In the Shadow of the Holocaust: The Struggle Between Jews and Zionists in the Aftermath of World War II* (Common Courage, 2004)
Gross, Jan, *Neighbors: The Destruction of the Jewish Community in Jedwabne, Poland* (Penguin Books, 2002)
Gross, Michael, *The War against Catholicism: Liberalism and the Anti-Catholic Imagination in Nineteenth-Century Germany* (University of Michigan Press, 2005)
Gutman, Israel, *Resistance: The Warsaw Ghetto Uprising* (Mariner Books, 1998)
Hall, Kermit and Peter Karsten, *The Magic Mirror: Law in American History* (Oxford University Press, 2008)
Hart, HLA, *The Concept of Law* (Oxford University Press, 1997)
Hartouni, Valerie, *Visualizing Atrocity: Arendt, Evil, and the Optics of Thoughtlessness* (New York University Press, 2012)
Harvey, David, *A Companion to Marx's Capital* (Verso, 2011)
Hatzfeld, Jean, *Machete Season: The Killers in Rwanda Speak* (Picador, 2006)
Hausner, Gideon, *Justice in Jerusalem* (Harper & Row, 1966)
Hayner, Priscilla, *Unspeakable Truths: Transitional Justice and the Challenge of Truth Commissions* (Routledge, 2010)
Hedges, Chris, *Death of the Liberal Class* (Nation Books, 2010)
Hegel, GWF, *Phenomenology of Spirit* (Oxford University Press, 1997)
Herman, Edward, *Beyond Hypocrisy: Decoding the News in an Age of Propaganda* (South End Press, 1992)
Hett, Benjamin, *Crossing Hitler: The Man Who Put the Nazis on the Witness Stand* (Oxford University Press, 2008)
Hilberg, Raul, *The Destruction of the European Jews: Student Edition* (Holmes & Meier, 1985a)
Hilberg, Raul, *The Destruction of the European Jews: Volume 1* (Holmes & Meier, 1985b)
Hilberg, Raul, *The Politics of Memory: The Journey of a Holocaust Historian* (Ivan R Dee, 2002)
Hobbes, Thomas, *Leviathan* (Penguin Classics, 1982)
Hobbes, Thomas, *A Dialogue between a Philosopher and a Student of the Common Laws of England* (University of Chicago Press, 1997)
Hodos, George, *Show Trials: Stalinist Purges in Eastern Europe, 1948–1954* (Praeger, 1987)
Hohfeld, Wesley Newcomb, *Fundamental Legal Conceptions* (Yale University Press, 1964)
Hohfeld, Wesley Newcomb, *The Speeches of Oliver Wendell Holmes* (Cornell University Library, 2009)
Horsman, Yasco, *Theatres of Justice: Judging, Staging, and Working Through in Arendt, Brecht, and Delbo* (Stanford University Press, 2010)
Hyde, Charles, *International Law: Volume 1* (Little, Brown and Company, 1947)
Jacobson, Arthur and Bernhard Schlink, *Weimar: A Jurisprudence of Crisis* (University of California Press, 2002)
Jacobson, Douglas, *The Katyn Order* (McBooks Press, 2012)

Jaconelli, Joseph, *Open Justice: A Critique of the Public Trial* (Oxford University Press, 1st edn, 2002)

Jarrow, Gail, *Robert H. Jackson: New Deal Lawyer, Supreme Court Justice, Nuremberg Prosecutor* (Calkins Creek, 2008)

Jockusch, Laura and Gabriel N Finder, *Jewish Honor Courts: Revenge, Retribution, and Reconciliation in Europe and Israel after the Holocaust* (Wayne State University Press, 2015)

Joseph, Sarah and Melissa Castan, *The International Covenant on Civil and Political Rights: Cases, Materials, and Commentary* (Oxford University Press, 2014)

Kant, Immanuel, *Critique of Judgement* (Hackett Publishing, 1987)

Kant, Immanuel, *Political Writings* (Cambridge University Press, 1991)

Kant, Immanuel, *Grounding for the Metaphysics of Morals: With On a Supposed Right to Lie because of Philanthropic Concerns* (Hackett Publishing Company, 1993)

Kant, Immanuel, *The Metaphysics of Morals* (Cambridge University Press, 1996)

Kant, Immanuel, *Critique of Pure Reason* (Penguin Classics, 2008)

Kasztner, Rezsö, *The Kasztner Report. The Report of the Budapest Jewish Rescue Committee 1942–1945* (Yad Vashem, 2014)

Kelsen, Hans, *Pure Theory of Law* (The Lawbook Exchange, 2009)

Kershaw, Ian, *Hitler: 1889–1936 Hubris* (WW Norton & Company, 2000)

Kochanski, Halik, *The Eagle Unbowed: Poland and the Poles in the Second World War* (Harvard University Press, 2014)

Kohn, Jerome, 'Freedom: The Priority of the Political' in Dana Villa (ed), *The Cambridge Companion to Hannah Arendt* (Cambridge University Press, 2000)

Kohn, Jerome, 'Preface: A Jewish Life: 1906–1975' in Hannah Arendt, *The Jewish Writings* (Schocken, 2008)

Kronman, Anthony T, *Education's End: Why Our Colleges and Universities Have Given Up on the Meaning of Life* (Yale University Press, 2008)

Lacey, Nicola, 'The Resurgence of Character: Responsibility in the Context of Criminalization' in RA Duff and Stuwart Green (eds), *Philosophical Foundations of Criminal Law* (Oxford University Press, 2013)

Ladenson, Robert, 'In Defense of a Hobbesian Conception of Law' in Joseph Raz (ed), *Authority* (NYU Press, 1990)

Lang, Jochen von, *Eichmann Interrogated: Transcripts from the Archives of the Israeli Police* (Vintage, 2009)

Lemkin, Raphael, *Axis Rule in Occupied Europe: Laws of Occupation, Analysis of Government, Proposals for Redress* (The Lawbook Exchange, 2008)

Levi, Primo, *Survival in Auschwitz* (Touchstone, 1996)

Lidegaard, Bo, *Countrymen: How Denmark's Jews Escaped the Nazis* (Atlantic Books, 2014)

Lidtke, Vernon L, *The Outlawed Party: Social Democracy in Germany, 1878–1890* (Princeton University Press, 1966)

Lipstadt, Deborah, *The Eichmann Trial* (Schocken, 2011)

Llewellyn, Karl, *The Bramble Bush* (Oxford University Press, 2008)

Lull, David, and John Cobb, *Romans* (Chalice Press, 2005)

Macedo, Stephen, *Liberal Virtues – Citizenship, Virtue, and Community in Liberal Constitutionalism* (Clarendon Press, 1st edn, 1991)

Mair, Peter, *Ruling the Void: The Hollowing of Western Democracy* (Verso, 2013)

Malkin, Peter and Harry Stein, *Eichmann in My Hands: A Compelling First-Person Account by the Israeli Agent Who Captured Hitler's Chief Executioner* (Warner Books, 1990)

Marcus, Jacob, *The Rise and Destiny of the Germany Jew* (Union of American Hebrew Congregations, 1934)

Markell, Patchen, 'Arendt, Aesthetics' in Nikolas Kompridis (ed), *The Aesthetic Turn in Political Thought* (Bloomsbury, 2014)

Mayer, Arno J, *Why Did the Heavens Not Darken?: The Final Solution in History* (Verso, 2012)

Milgram, Stanley, *Obedience to Authority: An Experimental View* (Harper Perennial Modern Classics, 2009)

Milgram, Stanley, *The Individual in a Social World: Essays and Experiments* (Pinter & Martin Ltd, 2010)

Miller, Richard, *Nazi Justiz: Law of the Holocaust* (Praeger, 1995)

Minow, Martha, *Between Vengeance and Forgiveness: Facing History after Genocide and Mass Violence* (Beacon Press, 1999)

Morris, Benny, 'Revisiting the Palestinian Exodus of 1948' in Eugene L Rogan and Avi Shlaim (eds), *The War for Palestine: Rewriting the History of 1948* (Cambridge University Press, 2001)

Mosse, George, *Nazi Culture: Intellectual, Cultural, and Social Life in the Third Reich* (Grosset & Dunlap, 1966)

Müller, Ingo, *Hitler's Justice: The Courts of the Third Reich* (Harvard University Press, 1992)

Murphy, Mark, *Natural Law in Jurisprudence and Politics* (Cambridge University Press, 2006)

Neiman, Susan, 'Theodicy in Jerusalem' in Steven E Aschheim (ed), *Hannah Arendt in Jerusalem* (University of California Press, 2001)

Neiman, Susan, *Evil in Modern Thought* (Princeton University Press, 2015)

Neitzel, Sönke, *Tapping Hitler's Generals: Transcripts of Secret Conversations 1942–45* (Frontline Books, 2013)

Nelson, Deborah, 'Suffering and Thinking' in Lauren Berlant (ed), *Compassion: The Culture and Politics of an Emotion* (Routledge, 2004)

Noakes, Jeremy, and Geoffrey Pridham (eds), *Nazism, a History of Documents and Eyewitness Accounts, 1919–1945* (Schocken, 1984)

Novick, Peter, *The Holocaust in American Life* (Mariner Books, 1999)

Nussbaum, Martha C, *Hiding from Humanity: Disgust, Shame, and the Law* (Princeton University Press, 2004)

Nussbaum, Martha C, *Anger and Forgiveness: Resentment, Generosity, Justice* (Oxford University Press, 2016a)

O'Connor, Garry, *The Butcher of Poland: Hitler's Lawyer Hans Frank* (Spellmount, 2014)

Orwell, George, *1984* (Harcourt, 2009)

Osiel, Mark, *Mass Atrocity, Collective Memory, and the Law* (Transaction Publishers, 1999)

Pappe, Ilan, *The Ethnic Cleansing of Palestine* (Oneworld Publications, 2007)

Pinker, Stephen, *The Better Angels of Our Nature: Why Violence Has Declined* (Penguin Books, 2012)

Plato, *Five Dialogues: Euthyphro, Apology, Crito, Meno, Phaedo* (Hackett Publishing Company, 2002)

Plato, *The Republic* (Penguin Classics, 2003)

Pound, Ezra, *ABC of Reading* (New Directions, 1960)

Rabinovici, Doron, *Eichmann's Jews: The Jewish Administration of Holocaust Vienna, 1938–1945* (Polity, 2011)

Radbruch, Gustav, 'Five Minutes of Legal Philosophy' in J Feinberg and H Gross (eds), *Philosophy of Law* (Wadsworth Publishing Company, 3rd edn, 1986)

Rawls, John, *A Theory of Justice* (Oxford University Press, 1999)

Raz, Joseph, *The Authority of Law: Essays on Law and Morality* (Oxford University Press, 1979)

Raz, Joseph, *The Morality of Freedom* (Oxford University Press, 1986)

Raz, Joseph, *Authority* (NYU Press, 1990)

Raz, Joseph, *Ethics in the Public Domain: Essays in the Morality of Law and Politics* (Clarendon Press, 1996)

Rieff, David, *In Praise of Forgetting: Historical Memory and Its Ironies* (Yale University Press, 2016)

Robin, Corey, *Fear: The History of a Political Idea* (Oxford University Press, 2004)

Robinson, Shira, *Citizen Strangers: Palestinians and the Birth of Israel's Liberal Settler State* (Stanford University Press, 2013)

Rogat, Yosal, *The Eichmann Trial and the Rule of Law* (Literary Licensing, 2011 [originally published in 1961])

Roseman, Mark, *The Villa, The Lake, The Meeting: Wannsee and the Final Solution* (Penguin, 2002)

Rosen, Lawrence, *Law as Culture: An Invitation* (Princeton University Press, 2008)

Ryback, Timothy, *Hitler's First Victims: The Quest for Justice* (Knopf, 2014)

Safrian, Hans, *Eichmann's Men* (Cambridge University Press, 2009)

Said, Edward W, *Representations of the Intellectual: The 1993 Reith Lectures* (Vintage, 1996)

Said, Edward W, 'Introduction: The Right of Return at Last' in Naseer Aruri (ed), *Palestinian Refugees: The Right of Return* (Pluto Press, 2001)

Salter, Michael, *Nazi War Crimes: US Intelligence and Selective Prosecution at Nuremberg* (Routledge, 2007)

Sands, Philippe, *East West Street: On the Origins of "Genocide" and "Crimes Against Humanity"* (Knopf, 2016)

Schlink, Bernhard, *Guilt About the Past* (House of Anansi Press, 2009)

Schmitt, Carl, *Staat, Großraum, Nomos. Arbeiten aus den Jahren 1916 bis 1969* (Duncker & Humblot, 1995)

Schmitt, Carl, *Political Theology: Four Chapters on the Concept of Sovereignty* (University of Chicago Press, 2006)

Schneer, Jonathan, *The Balfour Declaration: The Origins of the Arab-Israeli Conflict* (Random House, 2012)

Schoenbaum, David, *Hitler's Social Revolution: Class and Status in Nazi Germany, 1933–1939* (WW Norton & Company, 1997)

Schwab, George, *The Challenge of the Exception: An Introduction to the Political Ideas of Carl Schmitt Between 1921 and 1936* (Praeger, 1989)

Segev, Tom, *1949: The First Israelis* (Owl Books, 1998)

Segev, Tom, *The Seventh Million: The Israelis and the Holocaust* (Picador, 2000)

Segev, Tom, *1967: Israel, the War, and the Year that Transformed the Middle East* (Picador, 2008)

Sereny, Gitta, *Cries Unheard: Why Children Kill: The Story of Mary Bell* (Metropolitan Books, 1999)

Seymour, David M, *Law, Antisemitism and the Holocaust* (Routledge-Cavendish, 2007)

Shapiro, Scott, 'Authority' in Jules Coleman and Scott Shapiro (eds), *The Oxford Handbook of Jurisprudence and Philosophy of Law* (Oxford University Press, 2002)

Shklar, Judith, *Legalism: An Essay on Law, Morals, and Politics* (Harvard University Press, 1964)

Sinclair, Murray, Chief Wilton Littlechild, and Marie Wilson, *What We Have Learned: Principles of Truth and Reconciliation* (CreateSpace, 2015)

Smith, JC and David Weisstub, *The Western Idea of Law* (Butterworths, 1983)

Smith, Verity, 'Dissent in Dark Times: Hannah Arendt on Civil Disobedience and Constitutional Patriotism' in Roger Berkowitz and Thomas Keenan (eds), *Thinking in Dark Times: Hannah Arendt on Ethics and Politics* (Fordham University Press, 2004)

Snyder, Timothy, *Bloodlands: Europe Between Hitler and Stalin* (Basic Books, 2012)

Sofsky, Wolfgang, *The Order of Terror: The Concentration Camp* (Princeton University Press, 1993)

Sontag, Susan, 'Reflection on the Deputy' in Eric Bentley (ed), *The Storm over the Deputy* (Grove Press, 1964)

Sontag, Susan, *On Photography* (Picador, 2001)

Sophocles, *Antigone* (Prestwick House, 2005)

Soulier, Gérard, 'Equality of Speech, A Principle of a Democracy and of a Criminal Trial' in Mireille Delmas-Marty (ed), *The Criminal Process and Human Rights – Toward a European Consciousness* (Martinus Nijhoff, 1995)

Stangneth, Bettina, *Eichmann Before Jerusalem: The Unexamined Life of a Mass Murderer* (Knopf, 2015)

Steinweis, Alan, and Robert D Rachlin, *The Law in Nazi Germany: Ideology, Opportunism, and the Perversion of Justice* (Berghahn Books, 2015)

Stolleis, Michael, *The Law under the Swastika: Studies on Legal History in Nazi Germany* (University of Chicago Press, 1998)

Sunstein, Cass, *Legal Reasoning and Political Conflict* (Oxford University Press, 1996)

Thornton, Margaret, *Privatising the Public University: The Case of Law* (Routledge, 2012)

Todorov, Tzvetan, *The Fragility of Goodness: Why Bulgaria's Jews Survived the Holocaust* (Princeton University Press, 2001)

Trunk, Isaiah, *Judenrat: The Jewish Councils in Eastern Europe under Nazi Occupation* (University of Nebraska Press, 1996)

Tusa, Ann and John Tusa, *The Nuremberg Trial* (Skyhorse Publishing, 2010)

Tutu, Desmond, *No Future Without Forgiveness* (Image, 2000)

Tutu, Desmond and Mpho Tutu, *The Book of Forgiving: The Fourfold Path for Healing Ourselves and Our World* (HarperOne, 2015)

Villa, Dana, *Arendt and Heidegger* (Princeton University Press, 1995)

Villa, Dana, 'The Banality of Philosophy: Arendt on Heidegger and Eichmann' in Larry May and Jerome Kohn (eds), *Hannah Arendt: Twenty Years Later* (Cambridge University Press, 1997)

Villa, Dana, 'The Development of Arendt's Political Thought' in Dana Villa (ed), *The Cambridge Companion to Hannah Arendt* (Cambridge University Press, 2000)

Wachsmann, Nikolaus, *KL: A History of the Nazi Concentration Camps* (Farrar, 2015)

Waldron, Jeremy, 'Arendt's Constitutional Politics' in Dana Villa (ed), *The Cambridge Companion to Hannah Arendt* (Cambridge University Press, 2000)

Walker, Geoffrey, *The Rule of Law – Foundations of Constitutional Democracy* (Melbourne University Press, 1st edn, 1988)

Warmbrunn, Werner, *The Dutch Under German Occupation, 1940–1945* (Stanford University Press, 1963)

Watson, Don, *Enemy Within: American Politics in the Time of Trump* (Quarterly Essay, 2016)

Weber, Max, *From Max Weber: Essays in Sociology* (Oxford University Press, 1958)

Weber, Max, *Economy and Society: An Outline of Interpretive Sociology, Volume 1* (University of California Press, 1978)

Weston, Burns H, and David Bollier, *Green Governance: Ecological Survival, Human Rights, and the Law of the Commons* (Cambridge University Press, 2014)

Whitman, James, *Hitler's American Model: The United States and the Making of Nazi Race Law* (Princeton University Press, 2017)

Wiesenthal, Simon, *The Sunflower: On the Possibilities and Limits of Forgiveness* (Schocken, 1998)

Wieviorka, Annette, *The Era of the Witness* (Cornell University Press, 2006)
Williams, AT, *A Passing Fury: Searching for Justice at the End of World War II* (Jonathan Cape, 2016)
Winstone, Martin, *The Dark Heart of Hitler's Europe: Nazi Rule in Poland under the General Government* (IB Tauris, 2014)
Wolff, Robert, 'The Conflict between Authority and Autonomy' in Joseph Raz (ed) *Authority* (NYU Press, 1990)
Wolin, Richard, *Heidegger's Children: Hannah Arendt, Karl Löwith, Hans Jonas, and Herbert Marcuse* (Princeton University Press, 2001)
Wolin, Sheldom, *Democracy Incorporated: Managed Democracy and the Specter of Inverted Totalitarianism* (Princeton University Press, 2011)
Wuthnow, Robert, *Meaning and Moral Order* (University of California Press, 1987)
Yablonka, Hanna, *The State of Israel vs. Adolf Eichmann* (Schocken, 2004)
Yavnai, Lisa, 'U.S. War Crimes Trials in Germany, 1945–1947' in Patricia Heberer and Jurgen Matthaus (eds), *Atrocities on Trial: Historical Perspectives on the Politics of Prosecuting War Crimes* (University of Nebraska Press, 2008)
Yoder, John, *The Politics of Jesus* (Eerdmans, 1994)
Young-Bruehl, Elisabeth, *Freedom and Karl Jasper's Philosophy* (Yale University Press, 1981)
Young-Bruehl, Elisabeth, *Hannah Arendt: For Love of the World* (Yale University Press, 2004)
Young-Bruehl, Elisabeth, *Why Arendt Matters* (Yale University Press, 2009)
Zertal, Idith, *Israel's Holocaust and the Politics of Nationhood* (Cambridge University Press, 2005)
Zinn, Howard, *A People's History of the United States* (Harper Perennial Modern Classics, 2005)

Articles

Abrams, Norman, 'Interpreting the Criminal Code Ordinance, 1936 – The Untapped Well' (1972) 7 *Israel Law Review* 25
Arendt, Hannah, 'The Aftermath of Nazi Rule' (1950) *Commentary* 342, https://web.stanford.edu/dept/DLCL/files/pdf/hannah_aftermath_of_nazi_rule.pdf
Arendt, Hannah, 'Authority in the Twentieth Century' (1956) 18(4) *The Review of Politics* 403
Aron, Raymond, 'The Essence of Totalitarianism According to Hannah Arendt' (1993) 60 *Partisan Review* 366
Australian Broadcasting Corporation, 'Oskar Groening: Bookkeeper of Auschwitz Sentenced to Four Years in Jail' 16 July 2015, www.abc.net.au/news/2015-07-15/bookkeeper-of-auschwitz-sentenced-to-four-years-in-jail/6622862
Australian Broadcast Corporation, 'Holocaust Architect Adolf Eichmann's Final Plea for Mercy Released by Israel' 28 January 2016, www.abc.net.au/news/2016-01-28/holocaust-nazi-war-criminal-adolf-eichmann's-plea-letter-reveale/7119562
Bachmann, Michael, 'Theatre and the Drama of Law: A "Theatrical History" of the Eichmann Trial' (2010) 14 *Law Text Culture* 94
Baehr, Peter, 'Identifying the Unprecedented: Hannah Arendt, Totalitarianism, and the Critique of Sociology' (2002) 67(6) *American Sociological Review* 804
Bazyler, Michael, and Julia Scheppach, 'The Strange and Curious History of the Law Used to Prosecute Adolf Eichmann' (2012) 34 *Loyola of Los Angeles International and Comparative Law Review* 417
Ben-Naftali, Orna and Yogev Tuval, 'Punishing International Crimes Committed by the Persecuted, The Kapo Trials in Israel (1950s–1960s)' (2006) 4 *Journal International Criminal Justice* 128

Benhabib, Seyla, 'Who's On Trial, Eichmann or Arendt?' *New York Times*, 21 September (2014a) http://opinionator.blogs.nytimes.com/2014/09/21/whos-on-trial-eichmann-or-anrendt/

Benhabib, Seyla, 'Richard Wolin on Arendt's "Banality of Evil" Thesis' *Jewish Review of Books*, 14 October (2014b) https://jewishreviewofbooks.com/articles/1313/richard-wolin-on-arendts-banality-of-evil-thesis/

Ben-Gurion, David, 'The Eichmann Case as Seen by Ben-Gurion' *The New York Times*, 18 December 1960, 7

Beste, Ralf, Georg Bönisch, Thomas Darnstaedt, Jan Friedmann, Michael Fröhlingsdorf and Klaus Wiegrefe, 'From Dictatorship to Democracy: The Role Ex-Nazis Played in Early West Germany' *Spiegel Online*, 6 March 2012, http://www.spiegel.de/international/germany/from-dictatorship-to-democracy-the-role-ex-nazis-played-in-early-west-germany-a-810207.html

Bilsky, Leora, 'The Eichmann Trial: Towards a Jurisprudence of Eyewitness Testimony of Atrocities' (2014) 12(1) *Journal of International Criminal Justice* 27

Bix, Brian, 'Radbruch's Formula and Conceptual Analysis' (2011) 56 *American Journal of Jurisprudence* 45

Browning, Christopher, 'How Envy of Jews Lay Behind It' *The New York Review of Books*, 8 January 2015

Brunner, Jose, 'Eichmann's Mind: Psychological, Philosophical and Legal Perspectives' (2000) 1 *Theoretical Inquiries in Law* 429

Burdon, Peter, Gabrielle Appleby, Joe McIntyre, Rebecca La Forgia and Ngaire Naffine, 'Review Essay: Hannah Arendt: Eichmann in Jerusalem: A Report on the Banality of Evil' (2014) 34(2) *Adelaide Law Review* 213

Burdon, Peter, 'Hannah Arendt: On Judgment and Responsibility' (2015) 24(2) *Griffith Law Review* 221

Burger, Jerry, 'Replicating Milgram: Would People Still Obey Today?' (2009) 64(1) *American Psychologist* 1

Butler, Judith, 'I Merely Belong to Them' (2007) 29(9) *London Review of Books* 27–28

Butler, Judith, 'Hannah Arendt's Death Sentences' (2011) 48(3) *Comparative Literature Studies* 280

Caldwell, Peter, 'National Socialism and Constitutional Law: Carl Schmitt, Otto Koell-Reutter and the Debate Over the Nature of the Nazi State, 1933–1937' (1994–1995) 16 *Cardozo Law Review* 399

Carrier, Nicholas, 'The Autonomy and Permeability of Law: The Case of the Canadian Prohibition of Cannabis' (2007) 22(1) *Canadian Journal of Law and Society* 123

Cowell, Alan, 'Tutu Urges Israelis to Pray for and Forgive Nazis' *The New York Times*, 27 December 1989, http://www.nytimes.com/1989/12/27/world/tutu-urges-israelis-to-pray-for-and-forgive-nazis.html

Cowles, Willard, 'Universality of Jurisdictions Over War Crimes' (1945) 33 *California Law Review* 177

Der Spiegel, 'Germany to Prosecute 30 Auschwitz Guards' *Spiegel Online*, 3 September 2013, www.spiegel.de/international/germany/nazi-murder-germany-may-prosecute-30-former-auschwitz-guards-a-920200.html

de Wall, Tamar, 'Personal Responsibility under Totalitarian Regimes' (2012) 4(1) *Amsterdam Law Forum* 131

Dodes, Lance, and Joseph Schachter, 'Mental Health Professionals Warn About Trump' *The New York Times*, 13 February 2017, https://www.nytimes.com/2017/02/13/opinion/mental-health-professionals-warn-about-trump.html?

The Economist, 'What's Gone Wrong With Democracy?' 1 March 2014, http://www.economist.com/news/essays/21596796-democracy-was-most-successful-political-idea-20th-century-why-has-it-run-trouble-and-what-can-be-do

Engel, J Ron, 'A Covenant Model of Global Ethics' (2004) 8(1) *Worldviews: Global Religions, Culture, and Ecology* 29

Eviatar, Daphne, 'The Show Trial: A Larger Justice?' *The New York Times*, 20 July 2002, www.nytimes.com/2002/07/20/books/the-show-trial-a-larger-justice.html?pagewanted=all

Felman, Shoshana, 'Theatres of Justice: Arendt in Jerusalem, the Eichmann Trial, and the Redefinition of Legal Meaning in the Wake of the Holocaust' (2001) 27(2) *Critical Inquiry* 201

Flessas, Tatiana, 'A House Haunted by Justice: Eichmann in Jerusalem' (2005) 9 *Law, Text, Culture* 215

Fradella, Henry and Brenda Vogel, 'An Empirical Analysis of the Relationship Between Law, Morality, and Personal Conduct: Implications for Theory and Policy' (2009) 5(2) *Applied Psychology in Criminal Justice* 203

Frances, Allen, 'An Eminent Psychiatrist Demurs on Trump's Mental State' *The New York Times*, 14 February 2017, https://www.nytimes.com/2017/02/14/opinion/an-eminent- psychiatrist-demurs-on-trumps-mental-state.html?_r=0

Fuller, Lon, 'American Legal Philosophy at Mid-Century' (1954) 6 *Journal of Legal Education* 457

Gordon, Gregory, 'Book Review: The Eichmann Trial' (2012) 26 *Emory International Law Review* 589

Gray, Eliza, 'The Last Nazi Trials' *Time Magazine*, 2016, http://www.time.com/nazi-trials/

Habermas, Jürgen, 'Civil Disobedience: Litmus Test for Democratic Constitutional State' (1985) 30 *Berkeley Journal of Sociology* 95

Hart, HLA, 'Positivism and the Separation of Law and Morals' (1958) 71 *Harvard Law Review* 593

Hershovitz, Scott, 'The End of Jurisprudence' (2015) 124(4) *Yale Law Journal* 1160

Humphreys, Elizabeth, and Tad Tietze, 'Anti-politics: Elephant in the Room' *Left Flank*, 31 October 2013, http://left-flank.org/2013/10/31/anti-politics-elephant-room/

Jackson, Michael W, 'Thinking and Judging' (1987) 7 *Windsor Yearbook of Access to Justice* 80

Jacobson, Eric, 'Why did Hannah Arendt Reject the Partition of Palestine' (2013) 17(4) *Journal for Cultural Research* 358

Jaconelli, Joseph, 'Rights Theories and Public Trial' (1997) 14(2) *Journal of Applied Philosophy* 169

Jewish Telegraphic Agency, 'Eichmann Shows Temper Against Servatius; Court Orders Shorter Answers' 30 June 1961, www.jta.org/1961/06/30/archive/eichmann-shows- temper-against-servatius-court-orders-shorter-answers

Kadri, Sadakat, 'Short Cuts' (2015) 37(12) *London Review of Books* 14

King Jr, Martin Luther, 'Loving Your Enemies' sermon delivered to the Dexter Avenue Baptist Church, Montgomery, Alabama, 25 December 1957, http://www.kingencyclopedia.stanford.edu/encyclopedia/documentsentry/doc_loving_your_enemies/

Kinsley, Michael, 'Donald Trump is Actually a Fascist' *The Washington Post*, 9 December 2016, https://www.washingtonpost.com/opinions/donald-trump-is-actually-a-fascist/2016/12/09/e193a2b6-bd77-11e6-94ac-3d324840106c_story.html?utm_term=.a70f097956b4

Klabbers, Jan, 'Possible Islands of Predictability: The Legal Thought of Hannah Arendt' (2007) 20(1) *Leiden Journal of International Law* 1

Kohen, Ari, 'The Personal and the Political: Forgiveness and Reconciliation in Restorative Justice' (2009) 12(3) *Critical Review of International Social and Political Philosophy* 399

Lai, Ho Hock, 'Liberalism and the Criminal Trial' (2010) 32 *Sydney Law Review* 243

Lane, Charles, 'Why the Way Trump Won Makes Him More Dangerous' *The Washington Post*, 9 November 2016, https://www.washingtonpost.com/opinions/why-the-way-trump-won-makes-him-more-dangerous/2016/11/09/03a5a608-a6a6-11e6-ba59-a7d93165c6d4_story.html?utm_term=.a4a212a8f24c

Lefkowitz, David, 'On a Moral Right to Civil Disobedience' (2007) 117 *Ethics* 202

Lilla, Mark, 'Arendt & Eichmann: The New Truth' (2013) *The New York Review of Books*, www.nybooks.com/articles/2013/11/21/arendt-eichmann-new-truth/

Lis, Jonathan, 'Bill Seeks to Increase Role of Jewish Law in Israel's Legal System' *Haaretz*, 23 February 2016, www.haaretz.com/israel-news/.premium-1.704866

Lisread, Jonathan, 'Netanyahu Tells Knesset: I'm Determined to Pass Jewish Nation-state Bill' *Haaretz*, 26 November 2014, http://www.haaretz.com/israel-news/1.628644

Luban, David, 'Hannah Arendt as a Theorist of International Criminal Law' (2011) 11 *International Criminal Law Review* 621

McKeown, Tessa, 'The Nuremberg Trial: Procedural Due Process at the International Military Tribunal' (2014) 45 *Victoria University of Wellington Law Review* 109

Milgram, Stanley, 'Behavioural Study of Obedience' (1963) 67 *Journal of Abnormal and Social Psychology* 371

Miller, Arthur G, Barry Gillen, Charles Schenker and Shirley Radlove, 'The Prediction and Perception of Obedience to Authority' (1974) 42 *Journal of Personality* 23

Miner, Julius H, 'The Jury Problem' (1946–1947) 37 *Journal Criminal Law and Criminology* 1

Noakes, Jeremy, 'The Development of Nazi Policy Towards the German-Jewish "Mishlinge"' (1989) 34 *Leo Baeck Institute Year Book* 291

Nussbaum, Martha C, 'When Is Forgiveness Right?' *The Indian Express*, 9 October 2012, http://www.indianexpress.com/article/opinion/columns/when-is-forgiveness-right/99/

Nussbaum, Martha C, 'Painful Love: Anger and Forgiveness in Intimate Relationships', ABC Religion and Ethics, 11 August 2016b, www.abc.net.au/religion/articles/2016/08/11/4517922.htm

Paulson, Stanley, 'Lon L. Fuller, Gustav Radbruch, and the "Positivist" Theses' (1994) 13 *Law and Philosophy* 313

Paulson, Stanley, 'Radbruch on Unjust Laws: Competing Earlier and Later Views' (1995) 15 *Oxford Journal of Legal Studies* 489

Paxton, Robert, 'Is Fascism Back?', Project Syndicate, 7 January 2016, https://www.project-syndicate.org/onpoint/is-fascism-back-by-robert-o–paxton-2016-01?barrier=accessreg

Radbruch, Gustav, 'Statutory Lawlessness and Supra-Statutory Law' (2006) 26(1) *Oxford Journal of Legal Studies* 1

Radelet, Michael L, and Tracil Lacock, 'Do Executions Lower Homicide Rates?: The Views of Leading Criminologists' (2009) 99(2) *The Journal of Criminal Law and Criminology* 489

Rattner, Arye, and Gideon Fishman, 'Crime and the Criminal Justice System in Israel: A Sociohistorical Perspective' (1997) 13(1) *Journal of Quantitative Criminology* 1

Ravid, Barak, Jonathan Lis and Jack Khoury, 'Netanyahu Pushing Basic Law Defining Israel as Jewish State' *Haaretz*, 1 May 2014, http://www.haaretz.com/israel-news/1.588478

Ravid, Barak, 'United States Announces $38 Billion Israel Military Aid Package' *Haaretz*, 13 September 2016, http://www.haaretz.com/israel-news/1.741838

Rising, David, 'Trial of SS Medic Who Served at Auschwitz Begins in Germany' *Associated Press*, 12 September 2016, http://www.bigstory.ap.org/article/13f52f6f8a3f496dbdf965b1825551a7/trial-ss-medic-who-served-auschwitz-begins-germany

Robin, Corey, 'Did Hannah Arendt Ever See Eichmann Testify? A Second Reply to Richard Wolin', 2 October 2014, http://coreyrobin.com/2014/10/02/did-hannah- arendt-ever-see-eichmann-testify-a-second-reply-to-richard-wolin/

Robin, Corey, 'The Trials of Hannah Arendt', *The Nation*, 12 May 2015, http://www.thenation.com/article/trials-hannah-arendt/

Ross, Lee, 'Situationist Perspectives on the Obedience Experiments' (1988) 33 *Contemporary Psychology* 101

Seymour, David M, 'From Auschwitz to Jerusalem to Gaza: Ethics For the Want of Law' (2010) 6(2) *Journal of Global Ethics* 205

Shanab, M, and K Yahya, 'A Behavioural Study of Obedience in Children' (1977) 35 *Journal of Personality and Social Psychology* 530

Shaw, Barry, 'Archbishop Tutu, Revisit Israel!' *The Jerusalem Post*, 4 November 2013, www.jpost.com/printarticle.aspx?id=309477

Smith, David, 'South African Death Squad Leader Eugene de Kock to be Freed from Jail' *The Guardian*, 20 January 2015, https://www.theguardian.com/world/2015/jan/30/south-africa-eugene-de-kock-released-prime-evil

Solomon, Daniel, 'The Many Trials of a Nazi War Criminal' *New Republic*, 5 April 2016, https://newrepublic.com/article/132380/many-trials-nazi-war-criminal

Sontheimer, Michael, 'Germany's WWII Occupation of Poland: When We Finish, Nobody is Left Alive' *Spiegel Online*, 27 May 2011, www.spiegel.de/international/europe/germany-s-wwii-occupation-of-poland-when-we-finish-nobody-is-left-alive-a-759095-2.html

Staudenmaier, Peter, 'Hannah Arendt's Analysis of Antisemitism in *The Origins of Totalitarianism: A Critical Appraisal*' (2012) 46(2) *Patterns of Prejudice* 154

Straschnov, Amnon, 'The Judicial System in Israel' (1999) 34(3) *Tulsa Law Journal* 527

Taylor, Greg, 'Retrospective Criminal Punishment Under the German and Australian Constitutions' (2000) 23(2) *University of New South Wales Law Journal* 196

Volk, Christian, 'From Nomos to Lex: Hannah Arendt on Law, Politics, and Order' (2010) 4 *Leiden Journal of International Law* 759

Weitz, Yehiam, 'The Knesset "Nazi and Nazi Collaborators Punishment Law" as Justice Against the Nazis and Their Cohorts and the Relationship of Israeli Society to the Holocaust and Holocaust Survivors in the 1950's' (1996) 82 *Cathedra* 158

Wolf, René, 'Judgement in the Grey Zone: The Third Auschwitz (Kapo) Trial in Frankfurt 1968' (2007) 4(9) *Journal of Genocide Research* 617

Wolin, Richard, 'Thoughtlessness Revisited: A Response to Seyla Benhabib', *Jewish Review of Books*, 30 September 2014, http://jewishreviewofbooks.com/articles/1287/in-still-not-banal-a-response-to-seyla-benhabib/

Yablonka, Hanna, 'The Development of Holocaust Consciousness in Israel: The Nuremberg, Kapos, Kastner, and Eichmann Trials' (2003) 8(3) *Israel Studies* 1

Young-Bruehl, Elisabeth, 'On the Origins of a New Totalitarianism' (2002) 69(2) *Social Research* 267

Young-Bruehl, Elisabeth, 'Philosophy, The Big Ideas' *The Guardian*, 18 August 2011, http://www.theguardian.com/commentisfree/audio/2011/aug/17/big-ideas-podcast-banality- of-evil

Zertal, Idith, 'A State on Trial: Hannah Arendt vs. the State of Israel' (2007) 74(4) *Social Research: An International Quarterly* 1127

Zimbardo, Philip, 'On Obedience to Authority' (1974) 29 *American Psychologist* 566

Zuroff, Efraim, 'Opinion: Why Nazi Hunting is Still a Worthy Pursuit' CNN, 25 September 2012, www.cnn.com/2012/09/24/opinion/zuroff-nazi-hunting/

Conference presentations

Agamben, Giorgio, and Judith Butler, 'Eichmann, Law and Justice' presented at the European Graduate School, 2009, https://www.youtube.com/watch?v=ySu0HYfx2VY

Arendt, Hannah, 'Remarks of Professor Hannah Arendt' presented at the American Society of Christian Ethics: Fourteenth Annual Meeting, Virginia, 21 January 1973b

Bernstein, Jay, 'Lecture' presented at ICI Berlin, Judgment in Extremis, 16 May 2013, www.ici-berlin.org/videos/judgment/part/3/

Butler, Judith, 'Judith Butler. Hannah Arendt, Ethics, and Responsibility' presented at the European Graduate School, 2009, https://www.youtube.com/watch?v=vOwdsO6KkkI

Yavnai, Lisa, 'Vengeance or Justice? Trials of Kapos' presented at Yad Vashem, Holocaust and Justice, 2006, http://www.yadvashem.org/yv/en/holocaust/insights/podcast/nuremberg_yavnai.asp

Movie/Documentary

Conspiracy (Directed by Frank Pierson, HBO Films, 2001)

Eichmann (Robert Young, Entertainment Motion Pictures, 2011)

The Eichmann Show (Directed by Paul Andrew Williams, British Broadcasting Corporation, 2015)

The Final Solution: The Wannsee Conference (Directed by Heinz Schirk, Bayerischer Rundfunk, 1984)

Hannah Arendt (Directed by Margarethe von Trotta, Heimatfilm, 2012)

The Specialist – Portrait of a Modern (Directed by Eyal Sivan, The Criminal Kino International, 1999)

Other

The Avalon Project, 'The International Military Tribunal for Germany Contents of The Nuremberg Trials Collection' (2008) www.avalon.law.yale.edu/subject_menus/imt.asp

Center for Opinion Polls and Survey Studies at An-Najah National University, 'Results of Palestinian Public Opinion Poll No. 53' 13–15 October 2016, https://www.najah.edu/en/community/community-news/2016/10/17/results-of-palestinian-public-opinion-poll-no-53/

The NizkorProject, 'The Trial of Adolf Eichmann: Record of Proceedings in the District Court of Jerusalem' (1991) www.nizkor.org/hweb/people/e/eichmann-adolf/transcripts/

Simon Wiesenthal Center, 'Wiesenthal Center 2015 Annual Report on the Investigation and Prosecution of Nazi War Criminals' www.wiesenthal.com/site/apps/nlnet/content.aspx?c=lsKWLbPJLnF&b=8776547&ct=14583557

Wiesel Commission, 'International Commission on the Holocaust in Romania' (Editura Polirom, 2004) www.inshr-ew.ro/ro/files/Raport%20Final/Final_Report.pdf

United States Department of State, 'Diplomatic Papers, 1942. General; the British Commonwealth; the Far East' (1942) http://images.library.wisc.edu/FRUS/EFacs/1942v01/reference/frus.frus1942v01.i0012.pdf

Index

For Product Safety Concerns and Information please contact our EU representative GPSR@taylorandfrancis.com
Taylor & Francis Verlag GmbH, Kaufingerstraße 24, 80331 München, Germany

www.ingramcontent.com/pod-product-compliance
Ingram Content Group UK Ltd.
Pitfield, Milton Keynes, MK11 3LW, UK
UKHW011017180926
475701UK00004B/803

* 9 7 8 0 3 6 7 2 3 2 2 6 9 *